D1273325

the DUKE *of* KENT

a memoir

Darcy McKeough

with Rod McQueen

Foreword by
Brian Mulroney

ECW PRESS
TORONTO

Published by ECW Press
by arrangement with BPS Books, Toronto.
665 Gerrard Street East
Toronto, Ontario, Canada M4M 1Y2
416-694-3348 / info@ecwpress.com

To the best of his abilities, the author has related
experiences, places, people, and organizations
from his memories of them. In order to protect
the privacy of others, he has, in some instances,
changed the names of certain people and details
of events and places.

Editor: Don Bastian

The publication of *The Duke of Kent* has been
generously supported by the Government of
Canada through the Canada Book Fund.

PRINTED AND BOUND IN CANADA

LIBRARY AND ARCHIVES CANADA
CATALOGUING IN PUBLICATION

McKeough, W. Darcy, 1933–, author
The Duke of Kent : a memoir /
Darcy McKeough with Rod McQueen;
foreword by Brian Mulroney.

ISSUED IN PRINT AND ELECTRONIC FORMATS.
ISBN 978-1-77041-123-4 (hardback)
ALSO ISSUED AS: 978-1-77090-890-1 (EPUB)
978-1-77090-891-8 (PDF)

1. McKeough, W. Darcy, 1933–.
2. Cabinet ministers—Ontario—Biography.
3. Ontario. Legislative Assembly—Biography.
4. Legislators—Ontario—Biography.
5. Ontario—Politics and government—1943–1985.

1. McQueen, Rod, 1944–, author II. Mulroney,
Brian, 1939–, writer of foreword III. Title.

FC3076.1.M36A3 2016   971.3'04092
C2016-900411-2   C2016-900412-0

PRINTING: FRIESENS   5   4   3   2

To my granddaughter
Kate
From Gapa

FOREWORD   VII

A BRIEF FAMILY TREE   IX

CHRONOLOGY   X

ONE | In the Beginning   I

TWO | Cock of the Walk   II

THREE | Loyalty and Luck   21

FOUR | Running for Office   31

FIVE | The Love of My Life   41

SIX | Third Time Lucky   52

SEVEN | Reforms and Regrets   62

EIGHT | The Best Laid Plans   72

NINE | Kingmaker   83

TEN | New World Order   94

ELEVEN | Working with Bureaucrats   104

TWELVE | Honour Upheld   115

THIRTEEN | Back in the Saddle   126

FOURTEEN | The Energy Imperative   137

FIFTEEN | A Minority View   148

SIXTEEN | Balancing the Budget   158

SEVENTEEN | The End of Days   169

EIGHTEEN | The Constitution and Other Reforms   180

NINETEEN | Behind Boardroom Doors   191

TWENTY | Hostile Takeover   202

TWENTY-ONE / The Sugar House   213

TWENTY-TWO / A Life Well Lived   224

APPENDIX | Extract from a Speech by the Hon. W.   235
Darcy McKeough to the Government Relations
Club at the School of Business Administration,
University of Western Ontario, March 5, 1985

ACKNOWLEDGEMENTS   240

AUTHOR'S NOTE ON PERSONAL REFERENCES   241

BIBLIOGRAPHY   243

INDEX OF NAMES   246

Foreword

I first met Darcy McKeough when I ran for leader of the Progressive Conservative Party in 1976. I had phoned Darcy to seek his support, but, rather than just chat on the phone, he invited me for breakfast with his wife, Joyce, and their two boys, Stewart and Jamie.

I liked how he included his family in his political life, just as I did. Maybe it was our shared Irish heritage, our mutual interest in politics, or our joint love of Canada, but whatever the combination, we hit it off immediately.

Joyce was the daughter of Senator Davey Walker, whom I had known and enjoyed since meeting him in the early days of Prime Minister John Diefenbaker's government. Joyce was the apple of his eye, and I quickly came to admire her wisdom and value her thoughtful approach to public policy issues and life in general.

Darcy and Ontario Premier Bill Davis were, in my judgment, two of Canada's most accomplished and impressive leaders, as their transformational initiatives on behalf of Ontario quickly made clear.

What I respected most about Darcy, then treasurer of Ontario, was that you always knew where you stood with him. Moreover, we were both fiscal conservatives, favoured thoughtful social policy when governments could afford it, and believed in greater Canadian ownership of our companies and our resources.

When I was prime minister, my government often turned to Darcy, who was, by then, in the private sector. In 1984, Darcy was the point man between business and government on the Task Force on Program Review as we sought to eliminate program duplication, reduce red tape, and improve efficiency.

During the 1988 election, Darcy was an effective treasurer of the Canadian Alliance for Trade and Opportunities, a business group that promoted free trade with the United States. Along with others, Darcy helped, in a major way, bring about the pact that has so significantly benefitted the economies of both countries.

My government then established the Select Auto Panel with Darcy as Canadian co-chairman. This thirty-member Canadian–American blue-ribbon group acted as a valuable forum for ideas and information on employment, labour skills, technology, and competitiveness in the automotive industry.

Privatization was another key objective, and Darcy was a crucial member of the team as chairman of Canada Investment Development Corp. as we sold off crown corporations ranging from Canadair through Petro Canada to Air Canada, thereby reducing the size of the Government of Canada by almost 100,000 employees.

Darcy was a generous visionary in the vital area of national unity, and I will always appreciate his support of our constitutional efforts, the Meech Lake and Charlottetown Accords.

Whenever his country asked for his help, Darcy always replied, "Ready, aye ready." Canada needs more citizens like Darcy McKeough who can call on their experience in both the public and private sectors, lead others in common cause, and solve the problems of today while building bridges to tomorrow.

I am grateful for his service and honoured to call him a friend.

Right Honourable
Brian Mulroney,
P.C., C.C., LL.D.

A Brief Family Tree

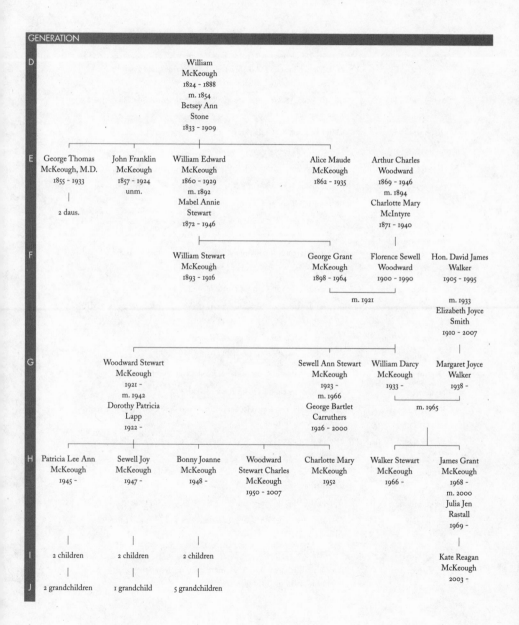

GENERATION

D

William
McKeough
1824 - 1888
m. 1854
Betsey Ann
Stone
1833 - 1909

E

George Thomas
McKeough, M.D.
1855 - 1933

2 daus.

John Franklin
McKeough
1857 - 1924
unm.

William Edward
McKeough
1860 - 1929
m. 1892
Mabel Annie
Stewart
1872 - 1946

Alice Maude
McKeough
1862 - 1935

Arthur Charles
Woodward
1869 - 1946
m. 1894
Charlotte Mary
McIntyre
1871 - 1940

F

William Stewart
McKeough
1893 - 1916

George Grant
McKeough
1898 - 1964

Florence Sewell
Woodward
1900 - 1990

m. 1921

Hon. David James
Walker
1905 - 1995

m. 1933
Elizabeth Joyce
Smith
1910 - 2007

G

Woodward Stewart
McKeough
1921 -
m. 1942
Dorothy Patricia
Lapp
1922 -

Sewell Ann Stewart
McKeough
1923 -
m. 1966
George Bartlet
Carruthers
1926 - 2000

William Darcy
McKeough
1933 -

Margaret Joyce
Walker
1938 -

m. 1965

H

Patricia Lee Ann
McKeough
1945 -

Sewell Joy
McKeough
1947 -

Bonny Joanne
McKeough
1948 -

Woodward
Stewart Charles
McKeough
1950 - 2007

Charlotte Mary
McKeough
1952

Walker Stewart
McKeough
1966 -

James Grant
McKeough
1968 -
m. 2000
Julia Jen
Rastall
1969 -

I

2 children

2 children

2 children

Kate Reagan
McKeough
2003 -

J

2 grandchildren

1 grandchild

5 grandchildren

Chronology

January 31, 1933	Born, Chatham General Hospital
1938–1945	Attended kindergarten, Central Public School, Chatham; grades 1-6, SS #3 Raleigh-Harwich Public School, Cedar Springs; and grades 7 and 8, Central Public School, Chatham
March 31, 1939	Moved from 329 King Street West, Chatham, to Bally McKeough, Raleigh Township (later postal address: Cedar Springs)
1945–1951	Ridley College, St. Catharines
1951–1954	University of Western Ontario, London
1954–1963	McKeough Sons Limited, Chatham
1959	Elected Alderman, City of Chatham, for 1960–1961, 3rd place overall
1961	Re-elected Alderman for 1962–1963, 1st place
September 25, 1963	Ontario election, Mr. Robarts winning 77 of 108 seats; I was elected MPP for Kent-West, winning by 1,739 votes
June 18, 1965	Married Margaret Joyce Walker, Trinity College Chapel, Toronto
May 22, 1966	Walter Stewart McKeough born, Chatham
November 24, 1966	Appointed Minister without Portfolio
October 17, 1967	Ontario election, Mr. Robarts winning 69 of 117 seats; I was elected MPP for Chatham-Kent, winning by 1,291 votes
November 23, 1967	Appointed Minister of Municipal Affairs
July 3, 1968	James Grant McKeough born, Chatham
December 8, 1970	Mr. Robarts announces to Cabinet his decision to retire
January 3, 1971	Announced my candidacy for the leadership
February 12, 1971	William G. Davis elected leader of the Progressive Conservative Party of Ontario; I ran third
March 1, 1971	Davis government sworn; I was appointed Treasurer and Minister of Economics
October 21, 1971	Ontario election, Mr. Davis winning 78 of 117 seats; I was re-elected MPP for Chatham-Kent, winning by 2,208 votes
February 2, 1972	Appointed Minister of Municipal Affairs
April 10, 1972	Treasurer of Ontario, Minister of Economics and Intergovernmental Affairs (TEIGA)
August 31, 1972	Resigned from cabinet
January 15, 1973	Appointed Parliamentary Assistant to the Premier with special responsibility in the field of energy

July 4, 1973	Appointed Minister of Energy
January 14, 1975	Appointed Treasurer of Ontario, Minister of Economics and Intergovernmental Affairs
September 18, 1975	Ontario election, with Mr. Davis reelected, minority 51 of 125 seats; I was reelected MPP for Chatham-Kent, winning by 2,719 votes
June 9, 1977	Ontario election, Mr. Davis reelected, another minority, 58 of 125 seats; I was reelected for Chatham-Kent, winning by 4,287 votes
August 16, 1978	Resigned as Minister and MPP
October 1, 1979	Appointed President & CEO, Union Gas Ltd., later Union Enterprises Ltd.
October 26, 1979	Honorary Doctorate of Laws, University of Western Ontario
May 25, 1980	Honorary Doctorate of Laws, Wilfrid Laurier University
November 16, 1984	Appointed Private Sector Advisor, Nielsen Task Force, ended June 1984
October 22, 1985	Resigned (fired) Union Enterprises
1987–1994	Chairman, Canadian Development Corporation
July 27, 1988	Appointed President & CEO of Redpath Industries
July 28, 1989	Redpath sold to Tate & Lyle; resigned as President, stayed on as Chairman until December 31, 1990
1989–1994	Harbourfront Corporation
1990–1992	Co-chairman, Canada–U.S. Automotive Select Panel
July 24, 1991	Appointed Chairman & President, McKeough Sons Co. Ltd.
October 27, 1993	Appointed Officer, Order of Canada (investiture April 13, 1994)
October 10, 2000	Jamie married Julia Jen Rastall, Vancouver
May 8, 2003	Honorary Doctorate of Divinity, Huron University College
September 24, 2003	Kate Reagan McKeough born, Vancouver
January 1, 2009	McKeough Supply Limited sold
May 1, 2009	Moved my office to Bally McKeough
2015	Edited Rod McQueen's editing of *The Duke of Kent*, in my 76th year at Bally McKeough, 50 wonderful years with Joyce

1

▼

In the Beginning

When I was born in Chatham, Ontario, on January 31, 1933, my father sent a wire to my grandmother announcing a "ten and a half pound boy arrived safely, both well." At that unusually heavy weight I should have been as healthy as a horse, but my going home from hospital was delayed. I suffered from prickly heat, an itchy skin rash usually associated with hot and humid weather. The fact that I came down with this malady during one of the coldest winters on record seemed to predict my future. I would never be one of those who tested which way the wind was blowing and then followed the crowd.

Chatham, founded in the nineteenth century on the Thames River in southwestern Ontario, was later one of the last stops on the Underground Railway and a haven for slaves who fled the southern United States to gain their freedom in Canada. The population of Chatham-Kent, as it is now called, is 108,000, but when I was growing up, the city of Chatham's population was more like 20,000: large enough so you could know a wide range of people but small enough that neighbours and others played a role in raising you. I had the run of the place early and felt the joyful independence that such liberty brings.

Home was 329 Wellington Street, where my parents had lived since 1923. There I joined a brother, Stewart, born in 1921, and a sister, Ann, born in 1923. I was obviously an afterthought in the previously settled family life of my parents, Grant and Sewell McKeough, both of whom were in their early thirties when I was born.

I was christened William Darcy McKeough. William was a family name borne by my grandfather and great-grandfather. But where Darcy came from I never knew. My Uncle Stewart had a university friend by that name. Some in the family think this was the origin, though he spelled it D'Arcy. Maybe I was called Darcy simply because my mother liked it. Since I was ten years younger than my sister, I always felt I had to run harder than my siblings and try to act older in order to catch up. I have been in perpetual motion ever since.

▼

My great-grandfather William McKeough was born in County Tipperary, Ireland. He came to Canada with his father, Thomas, and stepmother, Joanna, around 1833 and settled in Paris, Ontario. Thomas returned to Ireland in 1838, leaving behind his two sons, John, fifteen, and William, fourteen, who were apprenticed to Edward Jackson, a Hamilton stove manufacturer. In 1847, John and William moved one hundred and fifty miles farther west to Chatham, where they established the J. & W. McKeough hardware store on King Street.

John married but had no children. William married Betsey Ann Stone, whose family had come to Canada in 1820 from County Carlow in Ireland. The Stones farmed at Elizabethtown, near Kingston, and in 1840 moved to another farm just outside Highgate in Kent County. Betsey Ann lived in Chatham with her uncle, Thomas Stone, so she could be educated. William and Betsey Ann married, lived near Bushy Park (now called McKeough Park) on Grand Avenue West, and had four children: George Thomas, John Franklin, William Edward (my grandfather), and Alice Maude.

My grandfather, known as Will, worked for a while at J. & W. McKeough but left the family hardware business in 1880 to article with a Toronto law firm. In 1886, he joined the Chatham firm of Robinson, Wilson, Rankin & McKeough. Thus settled, Will married my grandmother, Mabel Annie Stewart, in 1892. Her father, Charles Edward Stewart, had owned newspapers in Brantford, Hamilton, and Ottawa but died when she was only two, leaving her well off but raised by a succession of family members.

Will and Mabel had two sons. The elder, my Uncle Stewart, was in his third year of medicine at the University of Toronto in 1915 when he enlisted in the 18th Canadian Infantry Battalion of the British Expeditionary Force. He was killed on September 15, 1916, at the Battle of the Somme. In 1993, I visited France with my wife, Joyce, and found his name on the Vimy Ridge Memorial among the names of more than 11,000 Canadians who were killed on French soil during the First World War and have no known graves. With its commanding view of the countryside, the monument is surely one of the most magnificent anywhere in the world. Equally breathtaking was the display in 2014 of the nearly 900,000 red ceramic poppies in the moat around the Tower of London to represent British and Commonwealth deaths in the First World War. I walked reverently among those poppies, knowing one of them was for Uncle Stewart.

▼

My father, Grant McKeough, was a big, broad-shouldered man, six feet tall, who weighed at least 250 pounds. He played football for Chatham Collegiate, golfed, loved to fish, and hunted ducks and pheasant every fall. In 1915, he dropped out of school to join the local branch of the Canadian Bank of Commerce as a lowly clerk, filling inkwells and sweeping out the vault.

In 1917, with my grandparents' reluctant consent, he enlisted in the 24th Kent Regiment and went overseas. He was seventeen. He joined the Royal Navy Voluntary Reserve and served in a motor launch with the Dover Patrol, a vital wartime command consisting of cruisers, boats, minesweepers, and aircraft operating in the Dover Straits and southern portion of the North Sea.

Dad served on Motor Launch 282, joining just after the raids on the Belgian harbours of Zeebrugge and Ostend, in the spring of 1918, when the British sank several of their own obsolete vessels in an attempt to block the German navy from hiding in the canals so they could prey on shipping in the English Channel. The *Vindictive*, an elderly 6,400-ton cruiser, was sunk as a blockship during the attack on Ostend. The bow section still remains as a memorial to the battle. Dad brought home three planks from the quarterdeck of the *Vindictive*, from which he made several canes, a cigar box, and a chest. The *Vindictive* chest still stands resolute in my library, adorned with brass hinges and a nameplate made from German shell cases fired at the cruiser. The family motto is "Fortune favours the brave." I've had my share of luck, but I've also found that I can make my luck by taking a risk.

▼

While overseas, father corresponded with the woman who became my mother, Florence Sewell Woodward. On January 3, 1921, they eloped to Windsor, Ontario, and were married that night. My mother had come to Chatham as a babe in arms when her father, Arthur Woodward, bought the *Chatham Evening Banner*. Mother was tall, pretty, and had a quiet but firm presence. One friend called her "Duchess." If mother was not a duchess, she certainly was a lady. A local Anglican rector once said he had 763 people in his flock, 762 of whom he called by their first name, and one he called "Mrs. McKeough," such was her manner and bearing.

After the death of my great-grandfather in 1888, the name and focus of the family firm changed. In 1905, it became McKeough & Trotter Limited, a machine shop that manufactured gasoline engines, small boats, and drainage wheels. My father joined the business in 1919 and, at twenty-six, was thrust into the leadership role as general manager following the deaths of a partner, Sam Trotter, in 1921, and of his own uncle Frank in 1924. Under my father, the firm ceased manufacturing and evolved into a wholesale plumbing and heating business. In 1928, my father bought out the other shareholders and became sole owner of what was, in 1943, renamed McKeough Sons Limited.

My father was an exacting boss. If someone on staff sold some window screening, he always reminded the employee, "Be sure you sell them a box of tacks." I don't know if the profit was higher on tacks than screening, or whether he just wanted to ensure the customer had everything he needed for the job. Whatever it was, Dad was ever watchful. He was also a founder of the local YMCA, chaired Red Cross campaigns, and was seven times chairman of the Victory Loan campaigns.

War, and the tragic outcome of such conflicts, was bred in the bone of my boyhood. I grew up hearing of my uncle's sacrifice at the Somme and my father's camaraderie with the Dover Patrol. He always referred to the First World War as The Big War, but now another terrible war appeared to be on the way. I vividly recall lying on the living room floor, in 1938, with my sister, Ann, listening to news on the radio about Adolf Hitler's annexation of the Sudetenland.

▼

In March 1939, we moved from Wellington Street to Bally McKeough, the house my parents built in a cornfield at Highbanks, a summer community with a dozen cottages on Lake Erie in Raleigh Township, fifteen miles from Chatham. For those of us who are of Irish descent, Bally is a well-known prefix to Irish town names. It comes from the Gaelic word "baile," meaning town or place, so Bally McKeough simply means the place or the home of the McKeoughs.

My parents bought twenty acres of land in an L-shape, including 300 feet of beach frontage on which they built a two-storey home. It was the first building in the area used year-round. Excavation was laborious. A man used a horse-drawn bucket to scrape off a few inches of clay soil at a time, eventually digging out the basement. I regularly accompanied my father to the site as he checked on progress. We sat on the floor of the unfinished structure eating cold bacon sandwiches and gazing through the uprights at the lake 200 yards away, trying to imagine the finished product complete with sofas and ceilings and family laughter.

The ground floor measured 60 by 40 feet and contained a living room, dining room, kitchen, powder room, and library. There was a full basement and bedrooms upstairs. For a while, Dad raised pigs and carried them to market in the back seat of his Plymouth coupe, and one year we had a cow for milk. Most of the years I was growing up, my parents worked on their gardens and grounds, planting the lilacs, cottonwoods, Chinese elms, and maples that still grace the property.

Dad served in the Second Battalion of the Kent Regiment (Reserve) throughout the Second World War. He was also "messing officer" of the Army Cadet Corps for several summers. There were as many as 1,200 fourteen-to-sixteen-year-old boys at camp in the nearby rifle ranges. He complained loudly that the army rations of tea, bread, and jam at five o'clock were not enough for the famished cadets. When his protests fell on deaf ears, he bought additional food with his own money. In 1949, he was named Honorary Lieutenant Colonel of the Kent Regiment, which in 1954 became the Essex-Kent Scottish Regiment.

My father spent many happy hours in his Victory Garden planting, weeding, cultivating, and watering what annually became a nature's bounty. He gave away bushels of vegetable marrows and watermelons to his employees and friends. Most of all, I remember his devotion to his family. He was particularly caring to his mother (known to us as Granny) after she became an invalid. He visited three or four times a week, often taking me along, until she died in 1946. That kind of caring and concern rubs off and is part of what made me who I am today.

Dad was also frugal to a fault. He'd say, "If you can borrow a book from the library, why buy it?" For him, there was nothing better in life than a good day's pay for a good day's work. He always had a project on the go. Once it was erecting a flagpole at Bally McKeough using a length of steel pipe from the shop. My role was to mix the cement in which the pole would be set. For years, my mother's words, "Darcy, get the cement," signified I was expected to help out with chores.

Some of my earliest recollections of my mother involve her feeding the hungry people who begged at our back door on Wellington Street during the Great Depression. I suppose we were an upper middle class family, and though I never felt rich, neither did I lack. Those poor wretches offered me an early lesson in how society should function. People who are fortunate should help those who are not. Government-sponsored social programs are not the only answer; helping one another directly is more natural and often more effective.

Mother was a tireless volunteer in many organizations, but her greatest enthusiasm was for the Canadian National Institute for the Blind (CNIB). The first annual CNIB picnic was held at Bally McKeough in July 1944. In 1948, I met and befriended a blind man in Ridgetown and invited him home to the picnic. "I think that made the day for me," wrote my mother in her diary.[1] Over a period of twenty years she transcribed into Braille almost two hundred books, from *Procedure in the House of Commons* to *The Apprenticeship of Duddy Kravitz*. Her work was so well and widely known that, years later, when I was in government, a blind lawyer, a civil servant, asked me, "Are you any relation to F. S. McKeough?" He had been reading her handiwork.

Without fail, weeknights included, my parents always had drinks before dinner. Dad's was rye and water. "No soda, Darcy," he'd say. "That will upset your tummy." The surest way to incur his wrath was by not refilling the ice trays. He liked a constant supply on hand.

In a place like Chatham, you made your own fun. Most Saturday nights my parents played poker with friends, starting about seven o'clock and ending around eleven with supper. The cards were secondary to the socializing. Several people took turns playing the piano for a singalong, while Dad played the ukulele — in his own

---

1 The F. Sewell McKeough diary, July 8, 1948.

way. Piano players had to adjust to *his* tune as my father also sang, although not well. Dad disdained a pick, using instead an empty Buckingham cigarette package. At the end of the evening the floor at his feet would be littered with shredded cardboard.

▼

After graduating from Chatham Collegiate in 1939, my brother, Stewart, enlisted in the Kent Regiment. He went overseas in 1942 to join the 12th Manitoba Dragoons in France. On August 20, 1944, by then a lieutenant, he was ordered to discover by what route the Germans were escaping from the Falaise pocket southeast of Trun. He and his troop sergeant worked their way across difficult country to a position on Hill 117. From there he could see large columns of enemy infantry and transport moving northeast between his position and Chambois. They engaged the enemy until their ammunition was gone. Stewart was mentioned in despatches and later awarded by France the *Croix de Guerre avec étoile d'argent*. After the war, rather than go to university, he joined the family business. Stewart married Dorothy Lapp in 1942 and, in 1947, moved with her to Four Winds, a house they built next to my parents' property, just east of Bally McKeough.

My sister, Ann, attended school in Chatham and Toronto, then in 1942 she also joined the family business, focusing on helping Dad. In 1953, she left to do office work in Toronto, then moved to Mont Gabriel in Quebec and finally, in 1960, to Florida, to work in an office near our parents' winter home on Casey Key, south of Sarasota.

An excellent golfer with a handicap of six, Ann won numerous club and amateur tournaments in Chatham and Florida. She married George Carruthers, and in 1969 they built the Court House on the Bally McKeough property. In 2000, Stewart and Dorothy's daughter, Charlotte, bought a house to the west of us, so there are now four family houses in the Bally McKeough compound.

▼

As a child, I was a bit of a rebel. I ran away from Central School once when I was in kindergarten. I didn't get far. I hid behind a tree on Cross Street, just a block or so from the school, a red-brick Victorian structure with a turret, bell tower, and separate entrances for girls and boys. From there, I could see my anxious mother drive by looking for me. Miss Belle Angus, the principal, had called her. My mother soon found me and marched me back to class, an early lesson that, if you break the rules, you get caught.

About the same age, I started to swear. Mother tried washing my mouth out with soap and confining me to my room, but nothing worked. Finally, she packed a little bag, shooed me out the front door, and told me to stay away until I stopped swearing. Five minutes later, I was back. Mother expressed surprise at my speedy return. "I didn't know where the hell to go," I said. I can still swear a blue streak.

Beginning in grade two, I attended SS#3 Raleigh-Harwich Public School, a two-room school, walking or biking a little over a mile each way. I was a model student and gained self-confidence by winning prizes in public speaking contests. I read the boys' historical adventure novels of G. A. Henty, as well as the many volumes by C. S. Forester in the seafaring Horatio Hornblower series.

Before we moved to Bally McKeough, I spent my summers at our cottage on Erie Beach, where cottagers take their rowboats out along the shore, fishing for perch to fry for supper. Farther out on Lake Erie occasionally you can see a passing low-slung Great Lakes freighter carrying its cargo of grain or iron ore. Like most Canadians who grew up listening to the nearby U.S. radio stations, I was steeped in matters American all the way from music to who was in the White House. Having this window on the wider world made me feel connected yet independent; neighbourly but not too tightly tied to a foreign power.

I wasn't a handsome child. I had bands on my teeth and was over-weight until I suffered a terrible bout of the flu. "He has regained the weight he lost in September but I would be surprised if he is ever a 'fat' boy again," my mother wrote in her diary in December 1945. In grade eight, I was included in a special program for promising students. The principal, Colonel Ivan Nurse, took a dozen of us brighter kids out of class for three or four hours a week. The teacher in charge, Jane Watson, led the group on a series of field trips to the library, a city council meeting, and several factories. She also gave us tough mathematical quizzes, all meant to challenge us beyond the regular curriculum.

▼

I not only grew up at Bally McKeough, but in 1966, after I was married, my father was dead, and my mother had moved to a smaller house in Chatham, I bought the property, with my wife, Joyce. As a result, I've lived there for all of my life since I was six years old. Joyce and I have expanded and remodelled the house, planted a walnut woodlot, and created a trout pond. In so doing, we created a small "hill" with the soil dug out to create the pond because Joyce — who grew up in Toronto — wanted some respite from the topography of the region: mile after mile of land so flat it could have been created with a rolling pin. We also spent five years building a seven-tier terrace with railway ties as a retaining wall to halt erosion caused by the lake thirty-five feet below the property. The terraces are planted with rows of forsythia, spirea, grapevines, daffodils, Russian sage, and cornflowers.

At one point in the 1990s, when we doing extensive remodelling, I met a local man who said, "I hear you're putting on an addition. Is Mrs. McKeough in the family way?" Given that we were in our sixties, it was a great compliment to both of us.

Somewhere along the way, I became known as the Duke of Kent, a title given to me by Elmer Sopha, the Liberal MPP from Sudbury from 1959 to 1971. The first published reference I've been able to find was in the *Toronto Star* of November 23, 1967. Sopha's nomenclature was likely meant to mock me, suggesting I had lordly ways, but I came to like the name. After all, I know my roots, am proud of where I come from, and have a desire to help others that is becoming rare in an era in which the relentless search for materialism often substitutes for what really matters.

2
▾
Cock of the Walk

After the Second World War, my parents began to spend their winters in Florida. I'd like to think their decision for me to go to boarding school was 100 per cent for educational purposes, but I've always suspected it had something to do with their annual desire to escape the cold weather. Whatever the reason, in September 1945 I started grade nine at Ridley College, an independent school in St. Catharines, Ontario. A note in my mother's diary set the tone for my time there. "We had our first letter on Monday 24th and Darcy is happy as a lark and getting settled beautifully. I hold high hopes for his years at Ridley and do not think I will be disappointed in him."

Ridley was named after Nicholas Ridley, a Bishop of London burned at the stake in 1555. Hugh Latimer, who died along with Ridley, famously said, "Be of good comfort, and play the man, Master Ridley! We shall this day light such a candle, by God's grace, in England, as I trust shall never be put out." The school motto echoes their sacrifice: *Terar dum prosim*, "May I be consumed in service." I like to think the motto is also my own.

Many boys flounder when they leave home for a boarding school. I flourished from the beginning, made friends quickly, and liked every aspect of the school, especially chapel. If I have been a faithful churchgoer since, that's where it began. We attended Anglican services twice a day, morning and evening, six days a week. The chapel was completed in 1923. I loved its Gothic architecture, Ontario stone structure, British Columbia cedar ceiling, oak pews, and the morning sun streaming through the stained glass east window depicting Christ as a teacher. The names of sixty-one Old Boys killed during the First World War are listed on a wall. I remember the official opening, in 1950, of the Great Hall, with its lofty interior and beautiful cloister running across the front, built as a memorial to the eighty-one Ridleians who died in the Second World War.

From 1921 to 1949, the Upper School headmaster was Dr. H. V. Griffith. He had attended the University of Toronto and coached their football team to the Grey Cup. He taught French and coached Ridley Football to numerous Little Big Four Championships, an Ontario conference consisting of Ridley, Upper Canada College in Toronto, St. Andrew's College in Aurora, and Trinity College School in Port Hope.

Dr. John Russell Hamilton succeeded Dr. Griffith. As an educator and an excellent teacher of physics and chemistry, it was Hammy — as he was called by the boys — who changed Ridley's culture from "jock" to "scholar." He set up weekly discussion groups on current affairs and created a Students' Council in 1950. He was also tough and had a fiery temper. No master could deliver "six on each" — six whacks with a strap to each hand — to greater effect.

Most of the masters had nicknames. J. C. "Herf" Ashburner taught algebra, had a glass eye, and walked with a cane. He would try to get someone's attention by calling out, "You, boy!" It was hard to know whom he meant with the glass eye lifelessly aimed straight ahead, his wagging cane pointed one way and his working eye the other. Helen Boyd, known as Betty Boop, was the housekeeper and dietitian. R. S. "Twink" Cobourn ran the bookstore and the rifle range.

Tom "Pro" Coburn was the groundskeeper and made ice for the hockey rink. If you asked, "Will there be ice today, Pro?" you always got the same gruff answer, given in his thick Yorkshire accent. "What do you want me to do, piss on it?" I once asked him who was the best cricketer he ever coached. His answer was Ross "Sandy" Somerville, the first Canadian schoolboy to score a double century, the second highest ever made in Canada – 219 not out against Hamilton in 1919. Added Coburn, "But the stupid bugger quit cricket and took up golf." Indeed, he did, and was the first Canadian to win the U.S. Amateur Championship.

I was no jock. I was six foot one inch and weighed over 200 pounds, but I was a bit flabby. I swam and played football, soccer, and cricket — it was required. I enjoyed the collegiality, but other than making the second team in football, I did not excel. My father, who had been a good athlete, pushed that side of me, but it wasn't there to be pushed. I made captain in cadets and thoroughly enjoyed inspections while visiting Ridley in the years when our sons Stewart and Jamie attended. The school is now co-ed, with six hundred and fifty young men and women – about twice as many students as when I was there.

I joined the Dramatic Society. Among my star turns was the anarchist Nitro Gliserinski in Ian Hay Beith's *The Crimson Cocoanut*. Because this was an all-male school, I also played various female characters, including my signature role as the formidable Lady Bracknell in Oscar Wilde's *The Importance of Being Earnest*. Also in the cast, as Cecily Cardew, was Bob Johnstone, who went on to be a high-ranking public servant and Consul General of Canada in New York. On a good day, I can still summon some of my lines for anyone who will listen. The stage was good training for politics, because you adopt a persona that's not your own and try to be larger than life.

Words and their delivery mattered to me, and I found several ways to hone my talent. As president of the Speakers' Club for three years, I won first prize, a gold watch, for my prepared talk entitled "Free Enterprise — Passport to Prosperity." I was invited to give the same speech to the St. Catharines Rotary Club, and won second prize in the Lincoln County Oratorical Contest, a $100 scholarship to any university. My mother saw where my talents would lead. "My pride and happiness knows no bounds over these successes and I think it is a good indication that he may go far in this direction in later life," she wrote in her diary.[2] Because the club functioned like a debating society, I also became skilled at making extemporaneous remarks. Unlike giving a set speech, you have very little time to prepare and must rely on your instincts. With practice, you get better until you can talk about anything at the drop of a hat.

I revelled in the written word as well. *ACTA Ridleiana*, the school magazine, published three times year, contained articles about sports, prizes, plays, Old Boy news, opinion pieces, and essays. In the two-volume official history of Ridley, Kim Beattie writes, "Ridley's top orator of these years, W. D. McKeough, was also an excellent writer. He authored a piece for *ACTA*, which he would use for speech material: *Canada and World Peace*. He demanded full support for the UN and the Atlantic Pact."[3]

My name first appeared on the ACTA staff list in the 1948 Christmas edition; by Michaelmas Term in 1949, I was editor-in-chief, a title that hadn't previously existed because a master had always been in charge. Beginning with that issue, the names of the magazine staff — with mine right at the top — were listed on the masthead above those of the Ridley prefects and house seniors who had formerly held that prized upper placement. Obviously, I did not hesitate to advance my standing! Among the three dozen members on the *ACTA Ridleiana* staff was Robin Korthals, later the president of the Toronto-Dominion Bank. Another, Peter Gzowski, who was a year behind me, would become a nationally revered CBC broadcaster.

Despite what I believed were improvements to *ACTA*, the student body was not in favour of change. Wrote Beattie: "There was a general desire to leave the journal much as it was in appearance and content. This caused the editor to comment tartly: 'Our opinion is that while at Ridley the boys are dyed-in-the-wool radicals, but when they leave Ridley they promptly become sure-fire conservatives.'"[4]

As editor, I was not afraid to state my views. For example, I complained that some of Ridley's Little Big Four teams had not done

---

2 April 30, 1949.
3 Beattie, Kim, *Ridley: The Story of a School* (St. Catharines, Ontario: Ridley College, 1963), p. 801.
4 Beattie, p. 803.

well against their rivals because, in my view, they were "not trying." When Dr. Hamilton, the headmaster, read it, he was furious. He called me into his office, berated me mercilessly, and sent a blistering report to the Board of Governors.

I must have been forgiven. In my graduating year, I won the Headmaster's Prize for Zealous Achievement. But, like my father before me, I was no scholar. I had a few firsts in English and History, but my marks were mostly seconds and thirds. In what should have been my graduating year, I had no firsts, a second in math, and failed both Latin and French.

Even so, my overall marks were sufficient to graduate, but I returned for a sixth year because I felt that, at seventeen, I was too young to go on to university. It was the best decision I could have made. I had previously been a House Duty Boy, but in my final year of high school, 1950–51, I was a Prefect, then Head of the Prefect Body, a leadership role that taught me how to work with people and achieve great goals.

In that same year, I became close to Dr. Hamilton. I lived in Gooderham House, which adjoined the headmaster's house. His son, Dick, often appeared at my door about 9 p.m. with an invitation to play bridge with him and his parents. Dr. Hamilton had an acute mathematical mind, so he knew the whereabouts of every card, but he was very patient with Dick and me as rank beginners.

In 1961, ten years after I graduated, Dr. J. R. "Hammy" Hamilton collapsed from a stroke while in chapel and died. His intended remarks, entitled "Ridley, A Canadian School," remain the best description I've ever read of the purpose of education. "Most important is the awakening and broadening of your minds — in the development of initiative, determination, ambition, self-control, self-denial, as well as the willingness to accept difficult tasks and to master tough assignments," he wrote. "Lessons in the necessity for punctuality, obedience, doing one's duty, observing law and order, respecting other people and their property as well as their rights are included here."

Dr. Hamilton wove current events into his speech. That April, Soviet cosmonaut Yuri Gagarin was the first human in space. In May,

U.S. President John F. Kennedy announced the ambitious goal of sending a man safely to the moon and back by the end of the decade. Dr. Hamilton wrote: "A future worth contemplating will not solely be achieved by flights to the moon, nor will it be found in space. It will be achieved, if it is to be achieved at all, only in our individual hearts." This man, who took me to task more than once, was one of the prime influences in my own approach to life as I lived it later in government and business as well as in all my dealings with people.

▼

Although my family was well off, I always had a summer job. At twelve, I worked in the stockrooms of the family business for $2 a week. One year I was in the tobacco fields, cutting leaves and hoisting them into the barn for drying. Another summer I helped Ed "Laddie" Miller build a house at Erie Beach.

There were no political clubs while I was at Ridley, but I admired politicians and was thrilled to be in their company, even for a moment. In 1950, my parents and I visited friends in North Carolina and stopped in Washington, D.C. on the way home. We stayed at The Mayflower and happened to be in the hotel lobby when a hero of mine, Senator Robert Taft, arrived to make a speech. I can still feel my heart racing to be only ten feet from him. Taft, eldest son of President William Howard Taft, had fought against both President Franklin Delano Roosevelt's New Deal and the growing strength of organized labour. I admired his principles and pluck in the face of powerful forces.

In 1951, my parents and I drove to Ottawa, where we visited George Drew, Leader of Her Majesty's Loyal Opposition and a fraternity brother of my uncle who had been killed during the war. My parents and Drew had been friends for years. Drew was premier of Ontario from 1943 to 1948, then became leader of the federal Progressive Conservative Party through two elections against the Liberals under Louis St. Laurent, losing both times. In 1956, he resigned as leader and was replaced by John Diefenbaker. In my mind, Drew was dignified, intelligent, and gracious.

My parents often talked about policy issues and politicians, so I was familiar with elected officials and issues of the day. I saw men like Taft and Drew as larger than life, able to command attention and mobilize people with their words and deeds. However, there wasn't a particular occasion or individual that drew me to politics.

In speeches, I have told the story that, when I was a child, my parents were curious what my profession would be. My father put a Bible, a bottle, and a deck of cards on the table. The idea was if I picked up the Bible I'd go into the Church; if the bottle, I'd become a drunkard; and if I took the cards, a gambler. When I grabbed all three, Mother shrieked, "My God, he's going to be a politician!" My sister, Ann, distinctly remembers me as a youngster speaking from pretend podiums and showing a keen interest in televised election results. Opportunities come to those who are ready. I guess I was always ready.

▼

But before any such grand plan of life could begin, I needed more education. I applied to Trinity College at the University of Toronto but was turned down because I had failed French. I then applied to the University of Western Ontario and was accepted. London was just an hour from Chatham, so I knew people who had attended and gone on to do well in their lives.

I enrolled in the four-year Honours Business program. Graduates were expected to become executives at such companies as Procter & Gamble or Imperial Oil. There was too little emphasis on those who might join a family firm like ours or start their own business. My impression is that, today, the Ivey School, as it is now called, is much more attuned to entrepreneurship.

I did well in the business program and was able to apply in later life some of what I learned about accounting, debits, credits, and financial analysis. I struggled with the required arts courses, with the exception of economics, taught by Dr. Mark Inman. One of the more memorable lectures, delivered the day after King George VI died, in 1952, was a brilliant analysis of Britain's constitutional monarchy and its value and worth for Canada.

Outside class, my interests were similar to those I had pursued at Ridley. I worked on the yearbook, *Occidentalia*, as well as the student newspaper, the *Gazette*. As a member of The Player's Guild, I even got a few notices. When I played Hebble Tyson, the mayor in Christopher Fry's romantic comedy *The Lady's Not for Burning*, the review by F. Beatrice Taylor in the *London Free Press* said, "Darcy McKeough was a pompously comic mayor." The reviewer's only complaint was, "Could he not have had a little more circumstance about his robes?" I guess we couldn't afford sufficiently grand costumes for this medieval play. Also in the cast were Fraser Boa, who became a Jungian analyst, writer, and filmmaker, and Jerry Grafstein, later a senator. I always enjoyed being surrounded people with talent in whatever field they excelled. The better they were, the better I was.

One of my wiser decisions was joining the University Naval Training Division (UNTD). First, I spent the summers making excellent money, $178.50 a month, which is the equivalent to about $1,500 today. Second, we were in the middle of the Korean War. Young men in the United States were being drafted. Canada did not have compulsory military service, but I felt, as did others, that it was a good idea to get some military experience in case the need arose. I could have joined similar programs in the Army or Air Force, but in my case the choice was easy: Dad had been in the Royal Navy, and it was, after all, known as "the senior service."

I spent three enjoyable years in UNTD. During the school term, about forty of us trained one night a week at HMCS *Prevost*, the London-based naval reserve unit. We received a half-day's pay and were welcome afterwards in the wardroom for a nightcap. In the summer of 1952, we took the train to Royal Roads, the military college in Victoria, to spend ten weeks at sea aboard the destroyer HMCS *Sioux*, sailing as far south as Long Beach, California. Also memorable that summer, before I headed west, was having to take our fourteen-year-old black cocker spaniel, Soot, to the vet to be put down. After I left him with the staff, I went outside, sat in the car, and wept.

The second summer we were at sea again, this time on HMCS *Antigonish*, a frigate with bunks rather than hammocks. Again we went to Long Beach where, on shore leave, I saw comic actor Phil Silvers perform in *Top Banana*, a role for which he won a Tony. I stayed on in the naval reserve after I graduated, and in 1955 we cruised up the Thames River to Chatham in *PTC 779*, one of the many 112-foot-long Fairmiles built in Canadian shipyards during the Second World War. Carrying twenty-millimetre guns, as well as eighteen officers and men, the patrol boats had fought German submarines. After the war, *PTC 779* was based in Port Stanley on Lake Erie for use by the reserves. The visit was the first by a naval ship to Chatham since sometime before 1818.

While I was in UNTD, Stewart stopped smoking and gave me my first pipes. Cigarettes at Navy prices cost only eleven cents a pack, so you could hardly refuse. I have since given up cigarettes, but I still smoke my pipe. Like Bill Clinton, I never inhaled. Unlike him, I never smoked pot. In politics and business, the pipe is a useful prop because it makes you look thoughtful. Moreover, it can be a delaying tactic. If you don't know what you want to say, you can suck on your pipe or go through the time-consuming process of loading the bowl, tamping down the Edgeworth tobacco, pulling out your lighter or wooden matches, and finally, firing up. The person waiting for an answer is distracted by all this activity and doesn't realize you're playing for time. As premier, Bill Davis perfected this performance.

During the winter of 1954, I was made a Sub-Lieutenant, taught the new reserves at HMCS Prevost, and was chosen best cadet or "cock of the walk," a wonderful title that has spread from its naval meaning as "winner" into wider public usage as someone who is fashionable or a leader. Of all the awards I've ever won, "cock of the walk" certainly has the best ring.

My academic career, however, continued to be haphazard at best. I had an A in Geography and a solid B average in Business, failed first-year French three times, and repeated several courses at summer school. I decided not to proceed with the fourth year of the Honours Business program and instead applied to graduate with a three-year B.A. My transcripts went before the Academic Standing Committee, where Helen M. B. Allison — Western's first female registrar — came up with the idea of obtaining a certificate for my military studies. That gave me an additional half course, enough to fulfill the requirements for my Bachelor of Arts degree. While there's the B.A. and the B.A. with honours, I've always regarded my B.A. as C.A.S.C. — "Courtesy Academic Standing Committee." In September 1954, I joined McKeough Sons as managing director. With Stewart already in harness, the corporate name was finally accurate. I would spend the next nine years at the family firm, honouring the past and formulating my future.

3

▾

Loyalty and Luck

My first task, as office manager and the new boy, was to keep quiet and learn the business. Over time I established a system for collection letters, cash flow projections, and monthly profit-and-loss statements. I also launched profit sharing and an employee pension plan. In 1959, Luster Corp., a Wallaceburg manufacturer, went bankrupt owing us $3,396. Creditors were offered shares in the company. I asked another creditor, Abe Lampel, a Sarnia scrap dealer, for his opinion. "No way," he said. "I'd rather be an unsecured creditor than an unhappy shareholder!" We persevered and collected about 65 cents for every dollar owed, pretty good under the circumstances and an important lesson learned.

A major part of my role during the winter was three or four times a week sending a report to my father in Florida on sales, bad debts, and the number that interested him most, cash on hand. I often began with a joke, usually off-colour. "Do you know why the Doukhobor women disrobed in front of Diefenbaker? Because he's a big prick." I received a stream of queries back from Dad, such as, "What was that cheque for?" or directives to "get after so-and-so" on the past-due report. Dad had a portfolio of stocks, bonds, and real estate, and I reported on everything from dividends to overdue rent.

In those days, we had thirty-five employees including nine women working in the office plus two or three men handling purchasing and pricing. By 2008, the firm had eighty employees with only seven in the office. Computers, copiers, and all the other modern amenities ended drudgework and improved productivity.

For my first ten years back in Chatham, I lived at Bally McKeough when my parents were at home, then the rest of the year in a large one-bedroom apartment above the office on 30 Dover Street. During the day, that part of the town was fine, but after dark things could get dicey. One night, I heard strange noises I thought were coming from the tobacco factory next door. But I could see from my window that the building was all in darkness. I opened my door, got to the top of the stairs, and realized the disturbance was being caused by intruders in the office. I tiptoed back to the apartment and called the police.

"Stay where you are!" they said.

"Don't you bloody well worry!"

In fact, I couldn't remain impassive. I heard the police at the front door, unable to get in. I ran down the stairs and opened it just as the burglars fled through a rear window.

"Stop or I'll shoot," yelled one of the officers. When they didn't stop, he fired, but the shot missed.

I sent the police around to the Thames Street door, where the intruders were apprehended. For years, there was a bullet hole in the office wall.

When Dad was not in Florida, he would come into the office in the morning, have lunch at the Kent Club, go home for a nap, and spend the rest of the afternoon in his beloved garden. Stewart ran the business, taking in about $1 million a year in sales in 1954, when I joined, rising to $1.3 million when I left in 1967. The company could have grown at a faster pace, but Dad held Stewart back. The only significant expansions Dad allowed were a new warehouse in 1961 for our line of steel products and a new stockroom in 1963. As far as Dad was concerned, he had built the business, so no risks would be taken.

As a result, within three years of joining I felt underused and insufficiently challenged. I looked for a different job, but not too seriously. There is a certain pride in being in the family business, and in a community like Chatham it's expected you'll work there even if you'd rather be somewhere else.

Seeking activities, I began to expend my pent-up energies outside the office. I served on the boards of the CNIB and the Chatham Community YMCA. I got involved with the local Chamber of Commerce, the Community Chest, and Christ Church, where I went on the Board of Management and became Rector's Warden, from which position I attended General Synod on three occasions in the 1960s. On the church's hundredth anniversary in 1961, I chaired a building program, which added to the chancel as well as a new sacristy, nursery, and classrooms. The changes meant the church achieved a true cruciform layout, which, to this day, makes me proud.

I also joined the Chatham Little Theatre. Among other roles, I played Sir John Fletcher in Terence Rattigan's comedy *Love in Idleness*, our entry in the 1959 Western Ontario Drama Festival held at Stratford's Avon Theatre. According to a review in the *Windsor Star*, "In the third act Mr. McKeough sat down on a chair on the set and it collapsed when one of the legs gave. The audience got its biggest laugh of the evening as he ad-libbed his way out of the situation." The review quoted the adjudicator as saying, "Darcy McKeough as the Cabinet Minister possessed an easy naturalness and charm of manner." [5] I won best supporting actor in the festival even though my role was actually the leading actor.

▾

For additional fun, there was always Detroit, a little over an hour away. We rooted for the baseball Tigers and the hockey Red Wings. Even though the Toronto Blue Jays arrived in 1977, the majority of people in the Chatham area still follow the Tigers. There were

---

5 *Windsor Star*, February 13, 1959.

also concerts and performances by the Metropolitan Opera at the Masonic Temple. And of course there was shopping. You'd wear scruffy shoes, buy a new pair at Hudson's department store, toss away the old ones, and wear your purchase back home across the border, quietly saying "nothing to declare."

Such pilgrimages had occurred for generations. My grandfather's diary contains entries from the 1920s about going to shows at the Cass Theatre on Lafayette Boulevard in the entertainment district. I went to Detroit with my mother to see *Mr. Roberts* and once with Peter Gzowski, then working at the *Chatham News*, to see *Most Happy Fella*. Many of the great actors came to Detroit, so I saw Laurence Olivier in *Becket*, John Gielgud in *The School for Scandal*, and Carol Channing in *Hello, Dolly!* before that show went to Broadway.

But Detroit was changing. In 1968, when Joyce was expecting Jamie, the two of us had dinner at the luxurious Hotel Pontchartrain, then took a taxi to the Masonic Temple for an evening of opera. When we came out, there were no taxis to take us back to our car. As we started to walk, we were pelted with beer bottles and ran the rest of the way. That once-great city has spiralled downward ever since and is now bankrupt.

I also travelled to New York in 1963, with friends Bob and Mary Heath, to stay with Max and Pam Thayer for a weekend. We were headed by cab to the Imperial Theatre on 45th Street when all traffic halted. The driver said President Kennedy must be in town because Jackie had been spotted shopping earlier that week. We walked the last two blocks and joined those milling about waiting to see the young couple. We had tickets to *Oliver!*, right across the street from the play the Kennedys were seeing, *Beyond the Fringe*. When they arrived, Bob and I clapped and cheered like delegates at a Democratic Party convention. As a resident New Yorker, Pam Thayer was far more accustomed to seeing celebrities and was horrified at our exuberance, but I didn't care. The only other time I'd been in New York, as a boy with my father, we had seen President Harry Truman. I was two for two on seeing sitting presidents while in the Big Apple.

My earliest direct exposure to partisan politics came during the 1945 Ontario election when I was twelve. Auntie Maude Stone, our next-door neighbour in the summer, was the daughter of the Liberal MPP for the riding of East Kent. She sprained her ankle on election day and could hardly walk, but said she could drive to vote, so her grandsons and I got her into the car and off we went. She was normally a Chatham resident, but the polling station at Cedar Springs was closer. Although she was not on that voters' list, she thought she could be "sworn" there and then cast her ballot.

The returning officer likely knew exactly who she was, but said she had to be identified by someone who was on their voters' list. A neighbour, "Coonie" Lyons, came along, and Auntie Maude asked him to tell the officials who she was. Coonie was a bit daft. He used to "shoot" birds on Highbanks Lane with his golf club. He may have been just playing a joke, but for whatever reason, he said he had never seen her before. Fortunately someone else arrived who vouched for Auntie Maude and she voted. I realized then how seriously everyone took politics.

I first learned about the organizational end in the 1948 provincial election. An uncle of mine, Jim Baxter, whose Toronto firm McKim did the Tory advertising, visited my family just before election day. He said the Progressive Conservative Party would win overall, but the leader, Colonel Drew, would lose his seat in the Toronto riding of High Park. Drew's opponent, CCF prohibitionist William Temple, had rallied the local temperance vote after Drew loosened the Ontario liquor laws to allow cocktail lounges. Both of his predictions turned out to be right. I was amazed Uncle Jim could predict outcomes.

My first federal election was March 31, 1958. John Diefenbaker was the populist federal PC leader; Harold Danforth was our local candidate. I was helping in Danforth's campaign office in the William Pitt Hotel opposite the fire hall. On election day, there was a panicked call about 4 p.m. from a poll in Chatham's east end saying they needed more "liquid refreshment." Jack Langford, the campaign manager, didn't want to send anything. His wife, Audrey, was more practical. She pointed out there were bottles sitting in the closet, said they were the cheapest rye whisky available, and concluded, "Let's get rid of them."

They looked at me, so I took my cue, loaded a dozen mickeys into my raincoat pockets, and went clanking on my way. As I stowed the bottles in the trunk of my car, I could hear the fire hall door across the street rattling up behind me to reveal three or four firemen convulsed in laughter at my mission. I delivered the encouragement and Danforth won the riding – but not that poll. Prime Minister Diefenbaker, who had led a minority government after defeating the Liberals in 1957 under Louis St. Laurent, swept to a commanding majority of 208 seats with almost 54 per cent of the popular vote. The Liberals, under their new leader, Lester Pearson, won only 48 seats.

▼

Politics was part of the warp and woof of the McKeough family. My great-grandfather William and my grandfather William Edward had both been mayors of Chatham. My great-uncle George and my father had been on the Board of Education. My brother, Stewart, was an alderman on Chatham City Council for eight years, from 1951 to 1958.

When I ran for alderman in 1959 for the term of 1960–1961, I was the sixth family member to seek public office. For me, politics was as much a family business as plumbing and heating were. My father encouraged me to run and gave me time off work. When I was campaigning, people said, "You're Dr. George McKeough's son." I carefully explained that Dr. George was my great uncle and that my grandfather Will had twice been elected mayor.

Inevitably, they ignored my elaborations about the family tree and said Dr. McKeough had brought them into this world or had saved their life or the life of a loved one. I soon realized it was better to let people say and believe what they wanted, even if it meant a slight departure from the facts. So, when they got my lineage wrong,

I just nodded and agreed rather than disappoint them. I had crossed the Rubicon and become a politician.

Campaigning was hectic and hard work, but I loved it. I visited service clubs, factory gates, King Street shops and restaurants, bingo, hockey games, supermarkets, and church bazaars. Anywhere two people gathered, I was the third, handing out my card, asking them to put up a poster, looking for votes. One factory worker shook my proffered hand and said, "Well, I might as well vote for you, you son of a bitch, as any of the other sons of bitches." Mark him down as a yes.

Stewart had taken two runs at council before he was elected. I won a seat on my first try. Campaigning reduced my weight to 179 pounds, the first time I'd been below 180 for several years. Another couple of weeks and I'd have wasted away. In 1961, I ran again and this time headed the polls, so my responsibilities increased. I was named a city appointee on the Lower Thames Valley Conservation Authority as well as chairman of the finance committee that prepared the budget and set the mill rate for approval by the whole council. I enjoyed city council: the ability to work with others, the pleasure of seeing an idea become reality, the thrill of entering a room to applause.

▼

My horizons expanded when I was chosen as one of the ten voting delegates from West Kent to attend the 1961 convention that replaced Leslie Frost, known as Old Man Ontario, as leader of the provincial Progressive Conservative Party. There were another ten delegates representing East Kent, so all six leadership candidates came to Chatham to woo the twenty of us as a group.

Among the candidates was an MPP from London, John Robarts. The education system was expanding rapidly for the postwar baby boomers. Every time a new school opened, Robarts, as minister of education, cut a ribbon. He had come that summer to open a one-room schoolhouse at Erie Beach. A friend, Doug Barlow, was on the Erie Beach council. He and his wife, June, had invited Robarts to their house for a drink and asked me to join them. Robarts had an easy laugh, his eyes glittered with delight, and when he spoke his gravelly voice exuded gravitas. I liked and admired him immediately.

Robarts had studied business administration at Western, served as an officer in the navy during the Second World War, graduated from Osgoode Hall law school, and held two cabinet posts in the Frost government. He was our next-door neighbour from London and would see that southwestern Ontario was well treated, so we delegates decided to vote for him as a block.

At one point during the leadership convention held that October in Toronto's Varsity Arena, I stood talking to the Right Reverend William Townshend, Suffragan Bishop of Huron and a Robarts supporter. Someone approached Townshend and said several delegates from Grey County were wavering in their commitment to Robarts. "Give me their names," he said and strode off to do some arm-twisting. So much for the separation of church and state.

Voting was much simpler in those days. Boxes were passed along the rows for delegates to deposit paper ballots. Counting was slow, so voting went on longer than expected. Some delegates from Lambton County had to get home to do their chores and gave their ballots to Lorne Henderson who put all thirteen of them into one box during the last ballot. Everybody knew Lorne. He had been a reeve, warden, and tax assessor in Lambton, so there was no questioning his honesty. Still, such activity gave new meaning to the words "absentee ballots."

Robarts won on that sixth and final ballot. The reason he ran for leader was simple. "I'd rather govern than be governed," he once said. "I'd rather stir the pot than be stirred." I wanted to follow his lead. I had my eye set on something beyond city council.

▼

By the time of the next federal election in 1962, the shine was off John Diefenbaker right across the country. Although Diefenbaker came to Chatham to campaign for Harold Danforth, Danforth lost his seat and Dief ended up with a minority government. In 1963, when another election quickly came along, the Tories in Chatham were pretty dispirited. I was so fed up with Dief, I was inclined to sit that one out.

After the election was called for April 8, 1963, William Hamilton, Postmaster General in the Diefenbaker government, arrived in Chatham to get things rolling because we hadn't even nominated a candidate. When I told Hamilton about my disenchantment, he said he had heard my name bandied about as a possible provincial candidate. Was I interested? I allowed as how I might be. Hamilton then said something I've never forgotten. "You are either a Tory or you're not," he said. "You'd better sort it out and make up your mind. Loyalty is the name of the game in politics. Loyalty to the leader and the party. The whole system is built on loyalty."

I got the message. If I didn't help the federal party, I could kiss any hope for the provincial nomination goodbye. And so I went to work. Harold Danforth was nominated again for the federal seat. We ran a campaign against Pearson's plan for a new Canadian flag and won by 202 votes. Our riding and Lambton-Kent — where M. T. "Mac" McCutcheon squeaked in by 24 votes — were the only two ridings in Ontario where a Liberal was thrown out and a Tory won. The Liberals, under Pearson, brought an end to the Diefenbaker years in office and formed a minority government.

Dief remained a formidable politician. He visited Chatham in December 1963 and gave a speech to a crowd of 450 at the Thames Theatre. I had never heard him perform so well. He spoke quietly, almost chatting to the audience, rather than ranting and raving. Whatever his faults, Diefenbaker was the best speaker in the country in his day, and few have been better since.

▼

Some people claim they go into politics because they want to make a difference. Others are there simply because of ego. While both of those reasons played a part in my decision to get involved in politics at the provincial level, there was a third significant one: I liked the people I met who were already in politics and wanted to work with them. Yes, I had goals I wanted to achieve, ideals to espouse, and wrongs I wanted to right. And yes, I had a high enough opinion of myself to think people might vote for me. But the bottom line for me was the people you worked with, the way you needed to be at the top of your game — remembering people's names and their families, helping those less fortunate, making a mark by doing more meaningful work than cash flow charts and office management.

If the situation in Ottawa had been more stable and Diefenbaker hadn't been on the way out, I might have considered federal politics, but Ontario seemed a more likely place because my party was in power, and I could do some good. It also seemed to me the provincial government was all about real people and their problems rather than post offices, diplomacy, and monetary policy. Moreover, Queen's Park, the seat of the Government of Ontario, was closer — only a three-hour drive to Toronto rather than a day-long train trip to Ottawa.

I'd like everyone who reads this book to think any success I've had in politics was due to hard work, native intelligence, political acumen, a great marriage, and even good looks. But none of those mattered as much as good timing. George Parry, a farmer from Dover Township, had been MPP for West Kent since 1945. He decided not to run again in 1963, thereby creating an opening. Had he taken that step before the previous election, I would have been too much of an unknown to have been nominated. And who knows what would have happened if I had decided to wait for the next opportunity after 1963.

I was also the beneficiary of someone else's public mistake. One of the West Kent delegates at the leadership convention that chose Robarts broke ranks. Although we had decided to support Robarts as a block, the night before balloting this delegate imbibed too much at a reception for another candidate, Dr. Matthew Dymond. The next day he was prominent in Dr. Dymond's demonstration. Until then, that delegate would have been a front-runner to replace Parry, but that blunder scuppered his chances. In politics, luck trumps all else.

4

▼

Running for Office

The first person to ask me if I would be interested in running for the Progressive Conservative Party in West Kent was George Parry, the retiring MPP. The second was Hugh Latimer, the party's paid organizer. I couldn't have had two better supporters. As the next election grew closer, I met with John Robarts in his Queen's Park office in April 1963. Robarts had grown in stature since winning the party leadership and had a new, even more statesmanlike manner about him. Although he did not diminish the amount of hard work that would be involved, he encouraged me and made it clear there was room at the top for a man like me.

I admired Robarts as someone who had sagacity and a genuine interest in public service. Not for nothing was he called the Chairman of the Board. Robarts knew Ontario was not just a province in the centre of the country but was also central to the national economy. "I'm a management man," Robarts said. "This is the era of the management man . . . I'm a complete product of the times."[6]

The riding of West Kent was no safe seat. Since 1875, the Liberals and the Conservatives had each won five times. Nor was the Liberal

6 Cited in Joseph Schull's *Ontario Since 1967* (Toronto: McClelland & Stewart, 1978), p. 379.

candidate any pushover. He was Garnet "Cookie" Newkirk, six times elected mayor of Chatham. The local paper called me a city boy who couldn't represent rural voters. "Darcy doesn't know a bull from a cow,"[7] wrote *Chatham News* columnist Reg Myers. Ruby Sheldon, a friend, arrived at a party that night carrying a small china cow with the newspaper clipping tied around its neck. On its horns was a sign, "Darcy, this is a cow."

On August 16, John Robarts called an election for September 25, his first as leader. August 24 was set for the nomination meeting in Kent West. I decided to run. My opponents were Dick Whittington, the director of the Children's Aid Society, and Tom Swanton, a farmer. With only two weeks available, I couldn't meet all one thousand delegates personally so support from the retiring MPP was crucial. George Parry was too diplomatic to pick a favourite, but he did let on that his brother Frank, his wife Myrtle, his son Rob, Rob's wife Verna, etc., etc. were all supporting McKeough.

At the meeting, held on a hot and sultry August evening at Chatham's Capital Theatre, I had some fun with my supposed lack of rural knowledge. "I make no pretense at having a farm background. I do know and recognize and appreciate the needs of our rural people, just as I know the needs of city people," I said. "Beyond that, I can learn. I assure you of this — I know a cow when I see one. The difference between bull and a Liberal platform is somewhat harder to distinguish."

To define what kind of a conservative I was, I quoted Edmund Burke, the eighteenth-century British parliamentarian who believed political institutions and society must change over time. Like him, I said, I believed in "the vision to create and the courage to retain."

I told the crowd I was no tax-and-spend politician. "I have no quarrel with those who say we need more and better welfare legislation. It is vital and desirable, but I must tell you, in all frankness, that I am in the ranks of those who, first and foremost, consider the cost. Before we can implement further programs of social legislation, we

---

7 *Chatham News*, July 5, 1963.

must find the resources to finance such programs. I am a politician of the school which promises to do all that it can to let *you* spend your dollars, rather than one who tells you how well *he* can spend your dollars." During my fifteen years in office, I never deviated from those core beliefs. Too many politicians try to have it both ways and end up with neither beliefs nor backbone.

Speeches by three candidates ran late that night, plus there was a lengthy stem-winder from Minister of Agriculture William Stewart. The theatre grew hotter, and everyone was restless and sweltering. When the outcome was finally announced, I had won on the first ballot. Though the numbers were not revealed, and the ballots were destroyed, I was unofficially told I had received 496 of the 976 cast, just over 50 per cent. Two weeks later, I learned I was actually just a few votes short of a majority. Those in charge decided the night had gone on long enough. They added sufficient McKeough ballots to put me over the top. Sometimes, common sense prevails and democracy needs a little help.

▼

Kent West riding was sizeable. It included the cities of Chatham and Wallaceburg, the town of Tilbury, the villages of Wheatley and Erie Beach, as well as five townships. In order to heal any wounds caused by my nomination, I involved my opponents. Dick Whittington was named official agent and Tom Swanton county chairman. Rather than hand out pamphlets for publicity, we gave away matches. They were less likely to end up as discarded litter. We made an exception with nursing homes, to which we delivered chocolate bars wrapped in McKeough literature.

Robarts visited the riding twice to bolster my cause, accompanied by his long-time pal and confidant Ernie Jackson and his driver Jack Smith. Today, there would be an entourage of aides, an advance team, and a security detail. Every riding received an initial $5,000 for expenses, but, because it looked like I might win, Jackson sent a second $5,000. Another $10,000 was raised locally, with the list of donors kept from me so I would never feel beholden. I was, however, given twenty names so I could write thank-you notes, although I was assured they were not necessarily the largest donors, just ones who would be glad to hear my appreciation.

On election day, I toured polls to greet voters and check on the turnout. At my last stop at Ouvrey, the polling place looked like a morgue. I took the Tory scrutineer aside and asked if he shouldn't be trying harder to get out our vote. No, he said, forty-five people had voted, he knew there were six more to come, and we'd end up winning the poll 28 to 23. He said if he started to chase after other Tories, so would the Grits. His strategy was not to stir things up.

For the most part, all you can do on election day is wait. As it turned out, the wait was over quickly. A few minutes after the polls closed, Mayor Newkirk conceded, and I was the new MPP for West Kent, winning by 1,739 votes. Later that night I saw the scrutineer I'd spoken to in Ouvrey and asked him about the final results in his poll. "We won 27 to 24," he said, "and I know who the son of a bitch is!"

Across the province, the Progressive Conservatives won a seventh consecutive term in office — stretching back twenty years to 1943 — while increasing the number of seats from seventy-one to seventy-seven. I was one of thirty-two new members in the PC caucus. Liberal leader John Wintermeyer lost his own seat and resigned as leader.

I wanted to thank twenty key volunteers with a bottle of Crown Royal each. The local liquor store didn't normally carry that many of the premium rye whisky. When I went in to place a special order, I quickly realized how far my star had risen. The manager, who had never so much as looked my way in the past, let alone said hello, almost vaulted over the counter to offer his congratulations and shake my hand. In those days, roles such as his were provincial appointments. He was a Grit, given the job before George Parry was elected, and Parry had never disturbed him. I guess he was hoping I wouldn't disturb him, either. Nor did I. As the newly elected MPP for West Kent, I had more important matters on my mind.

The Ontario Legislative Building, opened in 1893, is a magnificent structure built of dark pink sandstone marked by rounded archways and domed towers in the Richardsonian Romanesque style. Set on verdant Queen's Park, the legislature is surrounded by statues of famous figures from history including Queen Victoria, John Sandfield Macdonald, George Brown, and William Lyon Mackenzie. The legislative chamber on the second floor has a leather seat for each MPP, detailed wood carvings, steeply raked galleries, a coffered ceiling with a maple leaf motif, and a giant clock to remind us time was a-wasting. I never grew tired of being in that grand space.

I was sworn in on October 24, 1963, as a Member of Provincial Parliament, MPP for short. Ontario is the only province to use the designation of "parliament" just as they do in Ottawa. We sat for all of two days that fall. The next session did not start until January 15, 1964, and then ran until May 8 with three weeks off for Easter. In total, we sat fewer than four months that year. In each of the next three years, 1965 to 1967, sessions lasted five months, so the workload wasn't nearly as onerous as it is today.

For most out-of-town MPPs, the usual place to stay was the Royal York Hotel. John Robarts, who led a merry after-hours life, didn't want to be seen by the likes of Mrs. Leslie Frost and her Methodist lady friends, who inevitably would be sitting in the lobby when he arrived after partying all night. Robarts stayed instead at the Westbury Hotel on Yonge Street. I had no intention of similar behaviour, but most visitors from Chatham stayed at the Royal York, so that was sufficient reason for me to find accommodation elsewhere.

I ended up at the Benvenuto Place Apartments, off Avenue Road. Now a condo containing the world-famous Scaramouche Restaurant, the building then consisted of rental units. When I was looking, all they had was a room next to the entrance. It did not, they apologized, have a bathtub, just a shower. That was fine with me; I hadn't had a bath since I was a baby. I always took showers.

It did have a fridge with a freezer compartment for ice — always important — and a small stove. After a day at the legislature, I'd hole up in my place, have a drink, and open up a can of stew. No bachelor ever had it better.

I shared an office at the legislature with fifteen other members. Inside the entrance was a cloakroom with drawers to store a few items. Phones were available in the caucus lounge, and there was a secretarial pool if you wanted to dictate a letter, but that was the extent of support. In 1966, as they moved public servants to other buildings, more space became available, and I shared an office with George Kerr, Len Reilly, and Bud Price. In Chatham, I worked from McKeough Sons while continuing my business duties. It wasn't until 1975 that MPPs were given a constituency office with an assistant.

The first time I spoke in the House was on February 5, 1964, with a "planted" question to the minister of agriculture. Next was an off-the-cuff five-minute speech during debate on a bill about water shortages. I shook like a leaf, I was so nervous. I was relieved when it was over, then angry the next day after scouring all the newspapers and not finding a word about my contribution.

My work as an MPP ran the gamut from delivering speeches to solving a milk-delivery problem at the seniors' home. One of my victories involved getting a liquor licence for the Halfway House in Dover. The hotel had six rooms that were fully rented only during duck hunting season. The law said a hotel needed ten rooms to be able to sell beer. On behalf of the owner, I called on Walter Robb, chairman of the Liquor Licence Board. "If they build four more useless rooms, McKeough Sons would probably supply the plumbing, but to build unnecessary rooms would be completely wrong," I told Robb. "They should have a licence despite the shortage of rooms." A few weeks later, the licence was granted. My reputation in caucus soared. It was the first time the arbitrary rule had been lifted. The owners of the Halfway House became great friends and supporters, but even so, I never carried Dover in any election.

Walter Robb had a checkered history. It was he who solved the problem with "vote buying" back in the day when such activities took place. How do you know if the $2 you gave a voter meant he actually voted for your candidate? When Robb was campaign manager for James Allan (a former mayor of Dunnville and MPP for Haldimand-Norfolk), he suggested a scheme whereby the twenty-two voters who had each been paid $2 would go to the polling station, indicate they were deaf and dumb, and ask to have the returning officer mark their ballot. The returning officer, who was a Tory, then cast all twenty-two votes for Allan, who won the poll.

By the time I was an MPP, alcohol was a more likely aid than cash. My riding had numerous unionized firms including International Harvester, Libby's, Eaton Springs, Ontario Steel, and North American Plastics. While some union members voted NDP, I had my share of supporters. A union leader, Stan Green, was a friend who would turn to me in time of need. On one occasion there was a vote on a check-off that would have benefitted the NDP coffers. Stan called to say the "pro" side would be supplying free beer as part of their campaign and could I help out with money for beer to fuel the opposing side? I agreed. That was typical of deals that took place well off the official electoral map.

I got home to Chatham nearly every weekend. There were six trains a day. As an MPP I had a free pass; $2 bought an upgrade to the club car with a swivel chair, hassock, and a table for your drink. (It was bring your own booze until 1967, when our enlightened government finally allowed liquor to be served in club cars.) There usually were people aboard you knew, and there was always great food: roast beef with Yorkshire pudding on Canadian National and chicken potpie on Canadian Pacific. I met constituents on Fridays and Saturday mornings — but did my damnedest to keep Saturday nights and Sundays free. My number was always in the phone book, but my family sometimes took a message on Sundays if the matter wasn't urgent.

In terms of my legislative work, I was appointed to several committees including chairman of Public Accounts. Among my long-term achievements was obtaining provincial money for dikes and diversions to prevent flooding in Dresden and Wallaceburg. I also brought together several municipalities to turn Highway 40 into the beautiful St. Clair Parkway.

More controversial than such local successes was Bill 99, An Act to Amend the Police Act, introduced by Attorney General Fred Cass in March 1964. Cass told cabinet the legislation contained minor amendments. In fact, Bill 99 was an all-out attack on organized crime. One provision permitted an individual to be held indefinitely for questioning without any access to a lawyer and without charges being laid. Bill 99 became known as "the police state bill." The legislation was denounced by the Opposition and numerous newspaper editorials. Even some members of the Tory caucus, including Alan Eagleson and Allan Lawrence, spoke out against the bill's infringement on individual rights.

The day after Bill 99 was introduced, I flew to Florida to watch a Canadian–American Golf Tournament, which my sister, Ann, won. While in Florida, I visited my father — wintering there as usual — for the last time. We spent a wonderful evening together in an oyster bar, talking about my exploits as a newly elected MPP. Two months later, on May 18, 1964, he died in his sleep. I was glad to have had that last joyful occasion with him. To honour his memory, the family had tennis courts and a rink built in McKeough Park, which in turn had been donated by my great-uncle.

When a parent dies, you hear many stories for the first time. At his funeral, a fellow veteran reminisced about the time he and his fellow soldiers stood on the Dunkirk docks late one dismal rainy evening in late 1918 as French refugees returned from England. They shuffled forward in the twilight with their few possessions, clearly anxious as to what they would find when they got to their former homes. My father, viewing this, began to sing "La Marseillaise." The effect was electric. As the refugees joined in the French anthem, their pace quickened and their heads lifted as if suddenly they knew everything was going to be all right.

▼

When I returned from Florida, Robarts noticed my tan and sent a wry note wondering why I looked so good. I replied in an equally jocular manner saying, in effect, "You get into trouble when I'm away." Outrage against Bill 99 grew until April, when Robarts finally ordered the offending sections removed. Cass resigned as attorney general and was replaced by Arthur Wishart. Robarts appointed Ontario Chief Justice J. C. McRuer to conduct a Royal Commission into civil rights. His recommendations led to better protection for individuals.

I had one run-in with Wishart. I recommended Cy Perkins, a Chatham lawyer, as magistrate for Kent. Perkins had represented Rev. Russell Horsburgh, a United Church minister in Chatham, who had been convicted on morals charges. (The conviction was later overturned.) A former partner of Perkins urged Wishart not to appoint Perkins, so no announcement was forthcoming. I pleaded Perkins's case to Robarts. He was appointed and did an excellent job, just as I knew he would.

While Bill 99 attracted front-page coverage and indignant editorials, on most subjects journalists were docile. The local paper would print any press release I issued without changing a word. The Queen's Park Press Gallery didn't have a liquor licence, but it did have a well-stocked blind pig for its thirty members. Drinks were sold to the journalists at all hours, and if an MPP or cabinet minister wanted to join in, we were always welcome. Any conversations we had with the media on such occasions were off the record.

Such ready access to booze caused trouble for some reporters. Jack Pethick, Queen's Park correspondent for the *London Free Press,* started his workday at 11 a.m. with a shot of rye in his coffee. There were evenings when a gallery member from another publication filled in for Jack and filed a story on his behalf because he was under the weather. Despite his problems, Jack was always a good friend. He would phone and say, "Darcy, we haven't had anything from you for a while. Tell me what I can write."

▼

Normally, all those representing the government sit to the right of the speaker, facing the Opposition on the other side, separated by an aisle of the traditional two sword lengths. But, with such a large majority, there wasn't enough room for all of us to sit together. The Liberals and NDP enjoyed the customary prestige of front-row seats on their side, so I was one of six government members relegated to sit behind the Opposition. This rump group was made up of George Peck, Gaston Demers, Lou Hodgson, Tom Wells, Alan Eagleson, and me.

The unusual placement turned out to be a bully pulpit. Because we were literally breathing down Opposition necks, we could heckle them mercilessly. We acquired such a reputation, we were given not just one but two names: the Chicago Gang and the Hallelujah Chorus. "Besides enthusiasm, the Gangsters had the advantage of outflanking the Opposition," wrote John Dafoe in the *Globe and Mail*. "When particularly acerbic Opposition speakers, like Vernon Singer and Elmer Sopha of the Liberals, or Kenneth Bryden and Donald Macdonald of the New Democratic Party, rose to denounce the Government, the Tory members could descend on them from behind with a barrage of shouts, taunts and comments — occasionally witty, but usually just loud."[8] Sopha enjoyed calling me "the boy soprano from Kent West."

Beyond the catcalls, there was honour in our roles. Shortly after I arrived at Queen's Park, Ernie Jackson invited several new backbenchers including Wells, Eagleson, Bob Welch, and me for dinner at La Scala to meet some of the party contributors. La Scala, on Bay Street, was one of the premier restaurants in Toronto. I dined there so regularly in the years to follow that it became known as "the cafeteria." But that night was my first time hobnobbing with big shots in such fine surroundings. When I arrived, I admitted to Jackson I was nervous. "Don't be," he said. "You've done something these guys have never done despite their success in business. You've been elected!"

---

8 *Globe and Mail*, March 4, 1967.

5

▼

The Love of My Life

For all my early success, nothing was more important to my career and my happiness than meeting and marrying Margaret Joyce Walker. I dated a few women at Western, none of them seriously. In Toronto, I saw a bit of Eve Hargraft, a law student originally from Chatham. I was interested in her, but my ardour went unreturned. Eve did, however, have a friend from Trinity College at the University of Toronto she wanted me to meet. We three had lunch in January 1964 at The Captain's Table in the Lord Simcoe Hotel, then at the northeast corner of King Street and University Avenue. Joyce and I hit it off immediately.

Four years younger than I, Joyce was all things bright and beautiful. She had grown up in Toronto, attended Whitney School, Branksome Hall, and Trinity, was working at advertising agency Ronalds-Reynolds, and was the daughter of Elizabeth Joyce "Bunty" Smith and the Honourable David Walker. First elected to the House of Commons in 1957, Walker had been minister of public works in the Diefenbaker government. Defeated in 1962 in Rosedale by Donald Macdonald, his Liberal opponent, in 1963 Walker was appointed to the Senate, where he sat until he retired in 1989.

Joyce and I enjoyed the same things — theatre and the symphony — and soon discovered a favourite restaurant, L'Aiglon in Yorkville. I also learned she had been presented at the court of Queen Elizabeth II and Prince Philip in 1957. Joyce's most vivid recollection of her coming out was a close-up look at "the devastating eyes of the Prince."[9]

I planned to propose on April 13, 1965. I visited my safety deposit box in Chatham, took out the diamond ring Granny McKeough had left me, and arranged dinner with Joyce in Toronto that night. When I arrived in the city, I realized I had left the ring on my apartment bureau. I made a frantic phone call to my secretary, Pat LaMarsh, who retrieved the ring and entrusted it to a porter on the afternoon train to Toronto. I met him at Union Station, produced the errant piece of jewellery at dinner, and popped the question. Joyce said yes.

In those days, the permission of your future father-in-law was de rigueur, so I had lunch with Senator Walker at the Albany Club, the Tory bastion in Toronto. He gave us his blessing and told his friends, "Darcy's all right. He's a Tory and an Anglican." On June 18, 1965, Joyce and I were married in a white-tie-and-tails ceremony in Trinity College Chapel. We honeymooned at the Coral Beach Club in Bermuda, where we have returned many times since. My mother was delighted her thirty-two-year-old son was finally married. She reminded me that her friend, Jean Baxter, had always said, "Don't worry, sooner or later the wrong girl will come along."

▼

Senator Walker not only welcomed me into his family but also put up with me when our views differed. After Lester Pearson and the Liberal Party were elected federally in 1963, Diefenbaker's grip on his party leadership weakened. By 1966, many PCs were in revolt, led by advertising executive Dalton Camp, who was seeking re-election as party president on a platform of writing a leadership

---

9 Walker, David, *Fun Along the Way: Memoirs of David Walker* (Toronto: Robertson Press, 1989), p. 108.

review mechanism into the party's constitution. Running against Camp was Arthur Maloney, a Toronto lawyer and a Diefenbaker diehard. The vote, to be held at the party's general meeting at the Château Laurier Hotel in Ottawa in November 1966, was seen as a pronouncement on Diefenbaker's leadership.

Fellow MPP Robert Welch and I took the overnight train to Ottawa to vote for Camp, the leadership review, and the ouster of Diefenbaker. Walker, a staunch Diefenbaker supporter, knew why we were there but let us shave and shower in his hotel room anyway. Asking us to keep quiet about our mission, he invited us for lunch in the parliamentary restaurant. Another of Walker's guests that day was Colonel Pierre Sevigny, a former associate minister of defence in the Diefenbaker cabinet. Sevigny had been publicly disgraced when it was revealed he had slept with Gerda Munsinger, an East German prostitute with ties to the Soviet Union. When a Royal Canadian Mounted Police investigation uncovered the dalliance, Sevigny resigned from cabinet and was defeated when he ran for re-election in the 1963 election.

As a result, there were many in Ottawa who treated Sevigny as a pariah. Not my father-in-law. Sevigny had served in the Second World War, lost a leg, and been decorated for valour. Walker saw Sevigny as a war hero and a committed Canadian, no matter his personal peccadillos. Our table was at the farthest end of the restaurant. As we passed by other parliamentarians, Walker stopped, said hello, and then made them stand up to shake Sevigny's hand: the finest example of loyalty, political or otherwise, I have ever seen.

Camp was re-elected and won the leadership review, and the federal party held a convention the following year. I had met former Manitoba premier Duff Roblin, a candidate, through Ernie Jackson. Roblin asked me to give his nominating speech. "Here is a man who can win," I told the delegates. "Mr. Roblin understands the country in the diversity of its needs and its people in the diversity of their heritage and aspirations." Roblin wrote in his memoirs, *Speaking for*

Myself, "Darcy McKeough, a rising young Ontario cabinet minister, did me proud."[10]

The Walker family was divided. My father-in-law supported Diefenbaker, who ran to replace himself, did poorly, and dropped out. Joyce's brother David worked for his uncle-in-law, Donald Fleming, a minister of finance in the Diefenbaker government, who lasted three ballots. I supported Roblin right through to the final ballot when he lost to Nova Scotia premier Robert Stanfield. Roblin and I remained in touch. I attended his ninetieth birthday dinner in 2008. Senator Michael Meighen and I were the only two among the twenty invitees who were not from Manitoba. When Roblin died at ninety-two in 2010, I went to his funeral at All Saints' Anglican Church across the street from the Manitoba Legislative Building. He was a fine man who believed in Canada every bit as much as his beloved Manitoba.

▼

In the fall of 1966, the press speculated about changes in the cabinet of John Robarts. My name was included, but I dismissed the idea as far-fetched. New MPPs were not promoted that quickly. Robarts had been an MPP for eight years before joining the cabinet. I had been around for only three. The prime minister, however, wanted rejuvenation.

When Robarts told Ernie Jackson and London developer Don Matthews over drinks that he planned to appoint me to the cabinet, Jackson was vehemently against the idea. When Jackson left to go to the men's, Robarts said to Matthews, "He has no right to talk to me about Darcy. The reason he's saying he doesn't want Darcy in the cabinet is that Darcy doesn't do what Ernie wants him to do. Maybe that's why I like Darcy." In November 1966, Robarts dropped two ministers and brought in five new faces: René Brunelle, Bert Lawrence, Bob Welch, Tom Wells, and me.

---

10   Roblin, Duff, *Speaking for Myself: Politics and Other Pursuits* (Winnipeg: Great Plains Publications, 1999), p. 179.

At thirty-three, I was the youngest minister. Said the *Globe and Mail*, recalling my days with the Chicago Gang, "One of the youngest and most powerful set of lungs in the Legislature has moved over to the cabinet benches as a Minister without Portfolio. During the first few days of the session, he was silent, apparently awed by the power and dignity of his new seatmates. He soon returned to his old form, however, and now berates the opposition as loudly from the right of the House as he did from the left."[11]

I was sworn in as a minister at 10:30 a.m. on November 24, attended a brief cabinet meeting, had lunch in the cabinet dining room, then saw the deputy minister of public works about an office. None was available. Minister of Tourism and Information James Auld lent Tom Wells and I his office in the main Legislative Building. We had a full-time secretary and later our own office, as well as access to the pool of drivers and cars.

I marvelled at how little of my own money I spent. While I was on government business, meals and drinks magically appeared, paid for by staff or others. I paid for my own haircuts, but that was about it. Because I was a minister, my annual MPP's salary of $8,000 was supplemented by an additional $2,500 a year plus a non-taxable representation allowance of $1,000. Later I told my deputy, William Palmer, the only reason he would be fired was for failing to mix my martini properly. At Christmas he gave me a silver oilcan so the ingredients could be dispensed precisely.

Robarts also gave Christmas gifts. He summoned each minister individually to his office. When my turn came, he thanked me for my contribution and handed me an envelope with "Darcy" written on the outside. In the hallway I peeked and found five crisp $100 bills. One year I sat beside Charlie MacNaughton after we had all made our visits. Whispered MacNaughton, "How much?" On the pad in front of me I wrote "5." "Ditto," he said. To a young guy like me, $500 at Christmas was a wonderful gift. In the Davis era, such cash from party funds was no longer appropriate. Instead there'd

---

11 *Globe and Mail*, March 4, 1967.

be an Inuit print or an editorial cartoon done by the *Toronto Sun*'s Andy Donato. Such gifts were fine, but I have to admit they were not appreciated as much as the cash was in those early days.

▾

I tried not to let anything go to my head. Events usually conspired to keep me humble. At one meeting, someone looked at my name, concluded he knew how to pronounce it, and introduced me to the assembled as Darkie McKuff. I was assigned to Treasury Board (now called Management Board), a role that was the best education a new minister could possibly have. Treasury Board was examining departmental spending requests for the 1967–1968 fiscal year in preparation for the spring 1967 budget. We went through each department's proposal on a line-by-line basis, so I was able to scrutinize every nook and cranny of government. At one point, for example, the deputy minister of highways made a pitch for twenty-two new positions to maintain and install benches in roadside parks. James Allan, who had stepped down as treasurer and was, like me, a minister without portfolio, attended all meetings. Asked Allan, "If only ten positions were granted, how many lives would be lost?" Ten positions it was.

Patronage was an intrinsic part of the process. During the estimates for the Ontario Northland Railway, Wilf Spooner, the minister of municipal affairs, asked about the firm handling the liability insurance, "Who are Cronyn, Pocock?" Some of the rest of us knew that was where Robarts's friend Ernie Jackson was a partner. Said Treasurer Charlie MacNaughton, who chaired the meeting, "Moving right along."

As a new minister, my days were full. When the legislature was in session, we sat Monday to Thursday afternoons. Treasury Board met every Wednesday at 9:30, followed by a caucus meeting before the House at 2:30. Cabinet met on Thursdays at 10:00 a.m. and was often followed by another, shorter caucus meeting at 1:30. I was given a variety of tasks, such as speaking to riding associations and service clubs, as well as representing the province at Centennial Year events.

I also began travelling with the movers and shakers. In July 1967,

I flew with Robarts to Windsor, for the funeral of Richard Graybiel, general manager of the *Windsor Star*. Also in attendance at the service was Roy Thomson, Lord Thomson of Fleet, who built an international media powerhouse from a single newspaper in Timmins, Ontario. Paul Martin Sr., who represented the Windsor-area riding of Essex East federally, told us that when he remarked that Thomson had come a long way from London, England, for such an occasion, Thomson rubbed his hands and said, "I never want to miss an opportunity for an acquisition."

Robarts also had a story to tell. Beland Honderich, publisher of the *Toronto Star*, had seized the occasion to urge Robarts to run for the leadership of the federal Progressive Conservative Party. Robarts had no interest in the role, but he went on to say that Honderich's comments surely meant the *Star* — long-time Liberal backers — would support us in the next provincial election. Robarts assumed too much. When he called an election for October 17, 1967, the *Star* stayed firmly in the Liberal camp.

Just prior to that election, the name of my riding had changed from Kent West to Chatham-Kent. Slightly smaller, it still included Chatham, Wallaceburg, Dover, and Chatham Township. Bally McKeough was no longer in the riding, but no one seemed to mind. The McKeoughs had been around too long for me to be a called a carpetbagger. I spent some time speaking in support of other candidates in London, Toronto, Brockville, and Scarborough, and still won my seat with a majority of 1,291 votes, down slightly from 1,739 in 1963.

In an expanded legislature with nine new seats for a total of 117, we lost eight seats in the election but remained in power with sixty-nine seats, defeating the Liberals, led by Robert Nixon, and the NDP under Donald C. Macdonald. As usual, I lost weight while campaigning — twenty-one pounds this time — but nonetheless, I prefer the Canadian system in which cabinet ministers have to fight for their jobs, unlike the U.S., where the president picks a cabinet from many walks of unelected life. In Canada, as a cabinet minister, you are also an elected member, beholden to the people, and you'd better not forget it.

Still, that did not make me a mouthpiece for my electorate. I was guided by Edmund Burke in his oft-quoted speech about parliament, delivered in 1774 to the electors of Bristol: "Parliament is a deliberative assembly of one nation, with one interest, that of the whole; where, not local purposes, not local prejudices, ought to guide, but the general good, resulting from the general reason of the whole. You choose a member indeed; but when you have chosen him, he is not a member of Bristol, but he is a member of parliament."

While I worked for what I thought was right, I loyally adhered to the decisions arrived at by the prime minister, cabinet, and caucus, even if I did not agree. On such occasions, I always had an opportunity to make my case, and if the consensus went the other way, so be it.

Nor was I ever under the thumb of any interest group, be they sugar beet farmers or corporate tycoons. I would, however, temper my views to take account of other regions of the province. That quest for consensus is one of the great strengths of any political party. No one had all the answers, certainly not I. I always went into a cabinet or caucus meeting armed with a point of view that was based on a set of principles but tried to keep an open mind to the beliefs of others.

▼

The cabinet room, the inner sanctum of government, was on the second floor at the east end of the Legislative Building. On the walls were several large paintings of early Ontario scenes, all ten provincial flags, and imposing portraits of former prime ministers. The red carpet and leather-covered cabinet table, surrounded by a dozen chairs lining the walls for senior officials and aides, were all safely set for quiet and secrecy behind a double set of doors.

The prime minister's suite adjoined the cabinet room, and there was also a series of five offices, which included that of the secretary of the cabinet. Although all five offices had doors opening onto the main hallway, they also had interconnecting doors leading to the government caucus lounge adjacent to the legislature. Robarts and his successor, Bill Davis, always used this inner route between their office and the House, thereby avoiding the media.

Among the members of the Robarts cabinet, Charlie McNaughton and Stan Randall had strong opinions on most subjects and weren't afraid to express them. John White, who like Robarts was from London and enjoyed a bit of fun at night, showed a wide range of emotions, from good humour to grand arrogance. As minister of agriculture, Bill Stewart was sound, but he never strayed too far from his rural roots and perspective. Les Rowntree could be stuffy, even self-righteous at times, but generally held a balanced view.

When Minister of Education Bill Davis proposed something, he usually did so with the full backing of Robarts, himself a former education minister. Today, health is the biggest expenditure — eating up 41 per cent of the provincial budget — but in that era it was education, where the amount of money spent was equal to the total of all the other ministries combined. Over a period of two-and-a-half years, Davis opened a new school every day, so he was always on the road raising his profile. As a result, he attended cabinet sporadically and, when he did, usually arrived late. René Brunelle was wise, articulate, and an excellent spokesman for northern Ontario and francophones. Before we were married, Joyce rented a third-floor apartment from his sister in a house where Brunelle stayed when he was in Toronto. We always said, "Joyce slept on top of René."

In some cases, cabinet decisions were made on slight evidence. One such issue concerned S&H Green Stamps, given to shoppers as a reward for their patronage. Collect enough stamps and you could choose a gift from a catalogue. Begun in the U.S. in the 1930s, by the 1960s various versions of the stamps were offered by Canadian retailers. NDP leader Donald Macdonald feared stamps were luring low-income families into spending beyond their means.

Robarts often came to cabinet late, thereby avoiding debate on routine items. At one meeting, Chairman of Cabinet Les Rowntree explained to him we'd been talking about Green Stamps and couldn't reach a decision. "I'll tell you what we're going to do," said Robarts.

"We're going to do nothing." There was a stunned silence until someone finally asked, "Why?" "Norah likes Green Stamps." End of discussion. His wife had spoken. The NDP leader could rant and rave all he liked.

There was probably more cabinet debate on how and where alcohol could be sold and served than any other topic. Booze had been a touchy issue ever since 1948, when Premier Drew lost his seat to Bill Temple and the temperance vote. The province was divided into the "wets" and the "drys," and our voters tended to include the "drys," so we didn't want to upset them. Moreover, MPP Syl Apps, who had played for the Toronto Maple Leafs, was a teetotaler and a constant advocate in caucus and later in cabinet against creating more outlets where alcohol could be consumed. The rules dealing with alcohol were so persnickety that, at one cabinet meeting, we actually debated the amount of liquor allowed in chocolate-covered candies. I can't recall the size of the proposed increase, but it was sufficient to cause Charlie MacNaughton to blurt, "Well, that will knock the rats off the rafters."

▼

As for security protection at Queen's Park — there was none. At one point, Quebec Premier Jean Lesage visited Robarts and said he was interested in learning more about the provincial budget-making process. Said Robarts, "Well, I'll show you." He led Lesage out of his office, through the east door of the legislature, over the manicured lawn, and across the road to the Frost Building, just the two of them. Flabbergasted, Lesage said he would never dare venture outside the National Assembly in Quebec City without an armed escort.

Queen's Park became more cautious after the October 1970 kidnapping of British envoy James Cross, the murder of Quebec Labour Minister Pierre Laporte, and the invocation by Ottawa of the War Measures Act. Even then, I wasn't too concerned for myself, but I did agree that the Ontario Provincial Police could increase their vigilance on my family at Bally McKeough, which, after all, was at the end of long, dark lane.

Initially, an officer followed Joyce on shopping trips, which Joyce didn't like one bit. I suggested the OPP cease such tailing and instead drive by the house once or twice a night. The police agreed and said that, if there was any trouble, Joyce should overturn a chair on the front porch as a signal. I said that if an intruder were holding Mrs. McKeough at gunpoint, she hardly would be able to excuse herself to go outside and tip over some wicker furniture. So another signal was arranged: if the front-door powder room light was on, everything was all right. The one and only time there was an issue I got a call saying, "The light's out. Is there a problem?" I told them everything was fine. I checked and the light was on. It turned out the police had been peering at the residence of my brother Stewart next door.

6

▼

Third Time Lucky

Just as luck had played a role when I won the nomination for Kent West in 1963 and when Robarts went looking in 1966 for a backbencher from southwestern Ontario as minister without portfolio, I was third time lucky after the 1967 election. Two ministers had been defeated: Minister of Mines George Wardrope and Minister of Municipal Affairs Wilf Spooner. When Robarts offered me the position of minister of municipal affairs, he admitted it was "a tough, miserable, hot seat." I asked for the weekend to think about it. Even now, almost fifty years later, I am amazed at my cheek in not agreeing to his offer immediately. Was it arrogance or insolence, hubris or hesitation? Perhaps I was simply worried about whether I was up to the job. By Monday I had dealt with my various dilemmas. I let Robarts know I would accept the role. It could have been minister of mines!

Some members of the media were dubious about my capacity to take on the job. "It is to be hoped that there reposes in Mr. McKeough the kind of drive and original thinking that the job calls for. The new minister will have his work cut out to demonstrate these talents, for he has left little proof of them in the record," sniffed the *Globe and*

Mail.[12] The *Windsor Star* was more upbeat, buoyed by my time on Treasury Board. "Word has seeped out that he has been one of the most effective members of this inner cabinet, which examines and approves government spending. It is said that he has had a businesslike attitude and has been very much to the point. Also, he has shown himself to be a convincing leader and well able to handle himself on his feet. He has demonstrated an aptitude for cutting through red tape and verbiage and getting to the heart of things. You feel he will be able to put his department in good shape."[13]

▼

I have no idea how many municipalities there were when Governor John Graves Simcoe began a system of municipal government in 1792 in what was then Upper Canada. But as minister of municipal affairs, I was responsible for 964 different municipalities all the way from Metropolitan Toronto to the tiniest police village. My department had a staff of 334 and a budget of $250 million.

My first step was to deal with the former deputy minister, Lorne Cumming, who occupied the office next to mine and was making life difficult for his successor, William Palmer. With some trepidation I went to Robarts and said I'd like to move Cumming but was worried because he was held in such high regard. Said Robarts, "You're the minister." I took the point. Robarts had put me in to the job to do it, not run to him with every problem. I told Cumming I needed his office for my executive assistant, then moved him across the street and out of the action. Bill Palmer turned out to be an excellent advisor and a close friend.

You need such relationships with senior people. They need to be committed, knowledgeable, and enjoy good chemistry with the minister. Even a mediocre minister can look better with good staff work. I was fortunate over the years to have staff who were among the

---

12   *Globe and Mail*, November 24, 1967, p. 6.
13   *Windsor Star*, November 24, 1967.

best at Queen's Park: Neil Dunne at Municipal Affairs, Jean Hunter at Treasury, followed by Kendal Woodhouse, Paul Little, and Tom MacMillan.

Other ministers hired assistants who were political, but I looked for a broader skill set. Political savvy was important, of course, because we wanted to be re-elected. But I also needed help with my administrative duties as minister. That required intelligence, analytical skills, and a good rapport with the department.

Peter Deane, a civil servant who worked in Treasury, had such expert knowledge of my riding that he left in 1976 to become the executive director of the Kent District Health Council. He was replaced by Kim Phillip, who stayed until I left politics in 1978. The two of them solved hundreds of problems for constituents. I was also blessed with two excellent secretaries: Edna Eaton and May Sullivan, who succeeded Edna on her retirement. Both were conscientious, long-time civil servants who knew their way around Queen's Park.

Such people helped me succeed, particularly when was I was green. "The man who made the most strides on the government side," wrote Eric Dowd in the *Telegram*, in his wrap-up story at the close of the 1968 session, "was Darcy McKeough, who piloted through his first estimates as Municipal Affairs Minister with coolness and confidence."[14]

After the House rose in the evening, I often hitched a ride to my Toronto apartment with Allan Grossman, the first Jew in a Tory cabinet in Canada. Before picking us up, Grossman's driver stopped at the Royal York Hotel for a copy of the bulldog edition of the *Globe and Mail*, which was available around 9 p.m. I pored over the pages in search of reports of that day's political events as if reading the first reviews after a Broadway opening. We claimed to pay little attention to the media, but, of course, the media mattered, influencing as they did everything from our personal feelings to our political futures.

During my early years at Queen's Park, the business of the House expanded substantially. When I started in 1963, the session lasted four

14 *Telegram*, July 24, 1968.

months. By 1969, it lasted nearly eight months. In addition to the daily sittings, we were in the legislature two nights a week, often with votes on various matters, so it was all hands on deck. Throughout my time, there was always a well-stocked bar in my office. Most days, I'd invite someone to join me around 5 p.m. for a drink. Mine was always a martini, very dry: Beefeater gin with just a drop of vermouth, stirred, not shaken. In preparation for such gatherings, I had a quick shave and changed into a clean shirt. My guests for these sessions on politics and policy included colleagues from cabinet or caucus, Bay Street business people, civil servants, association executives, and lobbyists. They were excellent discussions at which I could think out loud, try on ideas, and listen to other points of view. Every once in a while, an official letter from the office of the Attorney-General would arrive noting that we were serving alcohol without a licence, but we took no notice and no action ever followed.

After drinks, it was on to dinner at the Albany Club on King Street, or closer by at Malloney's, or La Scala, where owner John Greico always seemed to be able to find a table for me. In my personal time, I was equally active at no-nonsense activities such as hard-charging games of tennis or building a new retaining wall for the garden.

I was a high-energy workhorse who needed the constant stimulation of others in order to hear new ideas and test the validity of my own thinking. As a result, I was constantly "on" and "up" and regularly worked eighteen-hour days, week after week, year after year. I liked to open every speech with a joke, like the one about the young man buying condoms in the drugstore for the first time who is told there will be tax. "Tacks? I thought they stayed on by themselves."

▼

My responsibility and interest in municipal affairs endured for most of my years in cabinet except for two interruptions. The first came on March 1, 1971, when I was named treasurer, minister of economics, and chairman of the Treasury Board, at which time Dalton Bales succeeded me as minister of municipal affairs. In April 1972, after a reorganization flowing from the recommendations by the Committee on Government Productivity, my department was renamed the Treasury of Ontario and Ministry of Economics and Intergovernmental Affairs (TEIGA). In addition to the federal dossier, my expanded role also included municipal affairs. The ministry was also responsible for economic research, statistics, and regional development. The second interruption came when I resigned on August 31, 1972 (for reasons I'll go into in chapter eleven). John White succeeded me until I was reappointed to the TEIGA role on January 14, 1975, and I continued there until August 16, 1978, when I left government.

To properly tell about my time in Municipal Affairs, I have to begin with some history. During previous decades, the province had taken over more and more of what had been municipal matters. Many towns and cities had mistakenly invested in railways, gotten into financial trouble, and had to be bailed out. Financial hardship during the Great Depression of the 1930s brought more supervisory control by the province through such entities as the Ontario Municipal Board, which was placed in charge of municipal borrowing.

In the 1960s, there were two thorough reviews of provincial–municipal relations. The Select Committee to Enquire into the Municipal Act, known as the Beckett report after Chairman Hollis Beckett, recommended strengthening county governments. The Ontario Committee on Taxation, known as the Smith Committee after Chairman Lancelot Smith, recommended reform of government aid and taxation, as well as the establishment of regional government. Smith urged the creation of about thirty regional governments throughout the province, a process that would consolidate more than nine hundred local municipalities as well as get rid of special bodies such as library boards and parks commissions. At the same time, the provincial government would take over the responsibility of assessment for property and business taxes based on market value assessment (MVA). MVA was a proposal that would dog me all my days at Queen's Park and was among the least successful of my adventures, but more on that later.

The first major structural change to Ontario municipalities since 1849 took place in 1953. Thirteen local municipalities were amalgamated to create Metropolitan Toronto. The council was made up of all the mayors and chaired by Frederick Gardiner, the former reeve of Forest Hill Village, who was cajoled by Leslie Frost into taking the job. He served for eight years and became known affectionately as Big Daddy.

In a November 1968 speech, Robarts set out his plan for regional government: "We must ensure that the people of Ontario have an opportunity to participate in local units of government, which are large enough to be meaningful, and which will have a resource base sufficient to their responsibilities. We have the opportunity to avoid the troubles of the cities to our south. We have the opportunity to provide for the people of Ontario horizons of such breadth that a person will feel an obligation to his community beyond his obligation to his family. Indeed, we must provide a framework within which he will be eager to participate in the further strengthening of local government."[15]

In my more detailed remarks a few days later, I told how we sought to create strong, new economic bases that offered economies of scale for access to and delivery of services. At the same time, we aimed to create new, natural regions with a core urban centre, suburban ring, and a rural fringe overseen by either one- or two-tier governments, depending on local circumstances.

Regional government had four aims. The first was to make local government stronger. The second was to have the municipalities take over police, arterial roads, sewage plants, welfare, and hospitals—all formerly the purview of the province. Third was fiscal equalization, to be created by pooling property assessment in regions so demand and need for services could be more readily met. Fourth was the return, as much as possible, of decision-making power to locally elected officials.

---

15 Ontario Legislature, November 28, 1968.

Each regional government would have industrial activities for jobs plus a population in the range of 150,000 to 200,000. The combination would provide a sufficient tax base to pay for government services as well as an appropriate and efficient size to deliver those services economically. In so doing, we intended to bring more prosperity to slower-growth areas of the province as well as a fairer delivery of services.

In a speech to the Ontario Association of Rural Municipalities I declared that a "municipal structure created for a horse-and-buggy society is hopelessly inadequate for this age of space travel."[16] Local dialogue during the formation of these new governments was crucial, I told the House, but local governments would not be able to block regional development: "One of the cardinal principles we are following during implementation is the meaningful involvement of the local communities. Our desire for local participation is such that we will, in some cases, endure delays in the establishing process in order to give local opinion time to form and express itself. While this will not become an excuse for inaction, it does mean that we should not begin the process by setting inflexible target dates, which will inhibit or could even prevent the local participation we all want."[17]

▼

Federal–provincial relations in Canada is a confused thicket of divided responsibilities. But in the case of municipalities, the law and the tradition are clear: municipalities are "the creatures of the province," a phrase I never liked and never used. In fact, I avoided it like the plague because, to me, it sounded demeaning. But had they not been "creatures," Metro Toronto would never have been created. In January 1966, the thirteen municipalities were compressed into a city and five boroughs, again by provincial legislation.

A letter about me from Gardiner to Frost captured the promise

---

16 *Municipal World*, March 1969, p. 65.
17 Ontario Legislature, December 2, 1968.

and the peril of my goals. "There is quite a generation gap between your and my generation and his and I think perhaps there is a reluctance in the younger generation to listen to what are intended to be words of humble advice from some of us who have been through the mill," wrote Gardiner. "He has had this theory about Regional Government in the back of his head for quite a time but the difficulty which he did not realize is that to establish Regional Government it must be done on an evolutionary basis over an extended length of time, not in a revolutionary manner."[18]

I was not fomenting revolution so much as devolution. I believed strengthening local government required bringing cities and counties together as one unit to deal with their mutual interests and mutual conflicts. Charles MacNaughton and I travelled the province, delivering speeches at sixteen locations over a three-month period, explaining our plans to bring decision-making closer to the people.

Robarts had named the meetings Municipalities of Tomorrow, but staff called it the M and M Tour for MacNaughton and McKeough. Included in those plans were: reform of aid to local government (which also included education), reform of local taxation, and the reform of local government structure. In my view, it was all of a piece: reforming aid and taxation would not work without changing the overall structure. Sometimes it felt like a grind. In a letter to my mother on November 26, 1968, I wrote, "I was supposed to fly to Sault Ste. Marie, but thank heavens there were no flights, the weather was too bad so I could not go. That is my definition of happiness — a cancelled meeting."

In fact, the process was so evolutionary, it was sometimes too slow for my liking. I met with and listened to every group that asked for a meeting, many of them open to the public. In recent years, all governments have become more transparent. I was an early advocate that the public should always know what's going on.

One municipal conference was televised from the Ontario Science Centre just before the new venue opened in 1970. "A

---

18 Letter, September 26, 1969.

successful meeting that brought no practical results although on the provincial side there was a refreshing frankness," said the *Chatham News*. "The municipal representatives left the meetings with their heads noticeably higher. There was much talk that they were no longer 'creatures' but rather 'partners' of the province."[19]

During the period 1968 to 1973, we restructured nine governments, each very different from the other: Moosonee, Ottawa-Carleton, Thunder Bay, Niagara, Muskoka, York, Sudbury, Timmins, and Waterloo. I also paved the way for five more from 1972 to 1975: Hamilton-Wentworth, Durham, Peel, Halton, and Haldimand-Norfolk. Because they replaced the old ways with new efficiencies, all were locally controversial.

Throughout the process, I was reassured by my belief there were serious discrepancies in the system in bad need of fixing. In my own neck of the woods, for example, Erie Beach, population 264, had one vote on county council. Wallaceburg, population of 10,714, had four votes. The proportions were way out of whack. Municipal consolidation was one way to bring about better balance and less government at the same time. But there were many people in elected roles who feared losing their positions. No matter how minor such functionaries may have been in the scheme of things, those jobs meant everything to them.

Moreover, we clashed with other departments of government. There's a natural tendency in all bureaucracies to build up power and refuse to cede hard-won gains. As a result, there were lots of egos to feed, and we had to move carefully every step of the way rather than follow a rigorous one-size-fits-all strategy. We regularly modified our plans to accommodate local concerns.

For example, Moosonee, near James Bay, was isolated, but Robarts knew it well because he loved to fish in the nearby lakes. There was no road access to the community of 1,500, so we travelled from Toronto on an Ontario Northland Railway private car, a way of life long gone, alas. On my first visit, many of the stores were

---

19 *Chatham News*, April 30, 1970.

boarded up, they'd been broken into so often. We appointed a five-member Moosonee Area Development Board — all were local residents, including two Cree — to inaugurate self-government. The province also provided funds for a sewer system, indoor plumbing, schools for children, and job training for adults. Moosonee became a full-fledged town in 2001.

None of this was an easy sell. Often there was opposition, particularly from rural areas, where petitions were gathered with hundreds of signatures. As a result, I worked my ass off. Promoting regional government meant thousands of miles travelled by land and air.

There was no staff at the Chatham airport with its grass runway where I was regularly dropped off late at night. There would be a note on the chalkboard saying, "Leave the lights on the runway, Darcy is coming in tonight." Then there was a second line, adding, "Darcy, please turn the lights off when the plane has taken off."

7

▼

Reforms and Regrets

Ottawa-Carleton was the first to acquire regional government because, outside Toronto, it was Ontario's fastest-growing area. Growth was spilling into Nepean and Gloucester with no comprehensive plan for roads, water, or sewers. In 1969, we brought together a diverse federation: Ottawa, Eastview (later Vanier), eleven townships, and three villages, representing 1,100 square miles with 400,000 people. Under the first chairman, Denis Coolican, regional government was responsible for assessment, arterial roads, sewage and drainage, welfare services, and capital financing.

Ten years later, improvements were obvious. Among them were improved public transit that relieved Ottawa's downtown of thousands of cars and the welcome sight of people swimming again at Mooney's Bay because of successful pollution-abatement programs. "The welfare department was haphazard and was spread all over the region in a half-a-dozen places," said former Ottawa alderman Ken Workman. "After the region took over, the general population received much better service."[20]

There was one holdout against restructuring. Rockcliffe Park, a

---

20 *Ottawa Citizen*, July 3, 1989, p. C3.

leafy enclave of about 2,500 residents, including federal cabinet ministers and high-ranking civil servants, wanted to remain apart. The redoubtable Beryl Plumptre, former president of the Consumers Association of Canada, lined up powerful backers, including Prime Minister Lester Pearson's wife, Maryon, and Minister of Finance John Turner's wife, Geills. In turn, they had the support of the Regional Council and the Ottawa Council.

I backed off and left Rockcliffe as a separate municipality. It remained an outlier until its special status was ended by the Mike Harris government in 2001, when all municipalities in the Ottawa-Carleton Region were amalgamated into a single-tier City of Ottawa.

In the case of uniting the cities of Port Arthur and Fort William, I goofed. When we asked school children for possible new names, the three finalists were Thunder Bay, Lakehead, and The Lakehead. We should have had just one version of Lakehead because the votes favouring those two names totalled 23,678, but, because they were split, Thunder Bay won with just under 15,821.

At the official celebration, feelings ran so high, I had police protection. Eventually concurrence prevailed. "I think that most people have accepted amalgamation and will concede that it has been a good thing," said CKPR open line show host Rick Smith in 1974. "I had Mr. McKeough on the show recently and he was received very well. Four years ago he was a hated man here."[21]

Timmins was equally problematic. We were creating a new city that included more than two-dozen townships, none of which wanted to lose any powers. I met with 300 citizens on June 12, 1972, guarded by eighteen uniformed and plainclothes officers in the hall who were backed up with three cruisers outside. "It would have been easier to sell bilingualism to the dowagers sipping tea in Victoria's time-resistant Empress Hotel," wrote Del Bell in the *London Free Press*. "They claimed there would be more moose than people in the massively expanded boundaries of the city. It was thumbs-down time in the coliseum. But McKeough weathered the storm almost

---

21 *Weekend Magazine*, September 21, 1974.

effortlessly. Which is not to say he made a lot of friends and influenced people, but if he left them still fuming, they also walked out of that auditorium admiring his guts."[22]

The new City of Timmins was created on January 1, 1973. It incorporated the Town of Timmins, the organized Townships of Whitney, Tisdale, and Mountjoy, as well as thirty-one geographically unorganized townships in order to bring in the taxes from the Kidd Creek Mine for the benefit of the town and townships where the voters lived. With a population of 42,000 over 1,000 square miles, Timmins was one of the largest cities in North America.

At the other end of the province, regional government for Niagara meant combining twenty-six municipalities across two counties. We also created one police force to replace the Ontario Provincial Police, one of the rare occasions when the province devolved a function. "I know there have been plenty of critics, plenty of people who said it wouldn't work. But it did work, no matter what anyone said," Bob Bell, a member of the first Niagara council, told the *St. Catharines Standard* in 2009. "People forget, or maybe they just don't want to admit it, but some of our municipalities were not in very good [financial] shape back then. The Region is taking care of most of the key services now, and I think doing a pretty good job of it."[23]

▾

Perhaps it's productive to compare what we did in Ontario with what happened in such U.S. cities as Detroit with a population of a half million people, 90 per cent of whom were black and poor. To create a regional government similar to that of Ontario, the mostly white suburban enclaves of Detroit needed to vote in favour, but this was never going to happen. Frances Frisken's book *The Public Metropolis: The Political Dynamics of Urban Expansion in the Toronto Region 1924–2003*, compares the "home rule" regime in the United

---

22 *London Free Press*, August 26, 1978.
23 *St. Catharines Standard*, December 28, 2009.

States, where unity was impossible, with Ontario, where we were able to use our authority to make sweeping changes in the structure and function of local government. Frisken concluded that the provision of services in Ontario had improved as a result.

Admittedly, there were occasions when politics came into it. Cobalt's mines, where silver had been discovered in 1912, were depleted by the 1960s, and the local economy was depressed. Hugh Sutherland owned much of the city; many inhabitants were squatters. I met with Sutherland and said the problem was his to fix. Then Colonel Harry Price, the Tory bagman, called on me and asked if I knew about Sutherland's problem. I, the brash young minister, replied too quickly, "I know all about it."

Colonel Price was not diverted. "That's fine, Mr. Minister, but you may *not* know that Hugh Sutherland has supported our party for many years. You may *not* know that he was always someone we could go back to if we were short, and once we went back to him a third time." We bought the town site from Sutherland for a small sum, created a subdivision plan, and sold off the houses and lots, which is what we should have done in the first place.

A major blunder occurred in Haldimand-Norfolk, where there were two large developments: Ontario Hydro's Nanticoke generating station and Stelco's new steel plant. In addition, Dofasco had bought land for a new operation. My initial view was that we should be cautious, but my successor, John White, went off half cocked and paid $30 million for 4,500 hectares to create a new municipality called Townsend. White purchased a further 4,900 hectares in South Cayuga on the grounds it was better to have two small communities than one behemoth. Dofasco never did proceed, and most of the workers in the area commuted from elsewhere. Today, Townsend has paved streets, a municipal building, an enormous water tower — and damn few homes.

▼

By the time I began my second stint as treasurer in 1975, regional government had stalled. There were other priorities and a lack of will on the part of cabinet and caucus to continue with restructuring. From 964 municipalities in 1967, there were 836 in 1978. Not much happened after I left politics that year until a big spurt during the Mike Harris era. By 2010, there were 444.

There were three steps I could have taken but didn't. After consolidation of the school boards, Davis came back to Cabinet for more money to smooth the changes in local mill rates. As treasurer, I could have greased the restructuring wheels but chose not to.

Second, Municipal Affairs maintained, as an article of faith, one mill rate for all — no pluses or minuses for services provided or not provided. In fairness, the rising use of the computer has made setting different rates much easier. Had computers been available in those earlier years, the results would have been fairer. Area rating, as it is known today, is now commonplace.

Third, we guaranteed jobs for everyone after restructuring, which resulted in flabbiness and overstaffing. In the private sector, when two enterprises merge, there are staff reductions. Having jobs for everyone set the wrong tone. Yes, I should have pushed harder, but I'm pleased my key original objectives — reducing the province's control, supervision, interference, and bureaucracy — were achieved.

▼

As a minister, I had little impact on Metro Toronto, but Lord knows I spent a lot of time on the subject. When I first became minister of municipal affairs, in 1967, I accepted the view of Robarts and the cabinet that Metropolitan Toronto should remain as it was, with the City of Toronto and five boroughs (York, East York, North York, Etobicoke, and Scarborough) operating under a Metropolitan Council.

Premier Davis handed the issue back to Robarts in 1974 by appointing him head of a Royal Commission on Metro Toronto. After Robarts delivered his report in 1977, I drafted legislation to bring about some of his 126 recommendations, but there was little enthusiasm from Davis, the cabinet, or the Toronto Tory caucus. After David Peterson became premier in 1985, his Liberal Government implemented most of the recommendations. In 1995, the Mike Harris government eliminated local municipalities in favour of one Toronto council, a policy that led to political disaster. The Progressive Conservative Party ended up with no MPPs in Toronto after the 2003 election.

In my view, the number of Toronto councillors should be cut in half and party politics should be introduced. That would mean election of the mayor by the largest caucus, mirroring the federal and provincial patterns. Greater provincial involvement in some aspects is needed for what is now the Greater Toronto Area (GTA) with Hamilton-Wentworth, Halton, Peel, York, and Durham. Metrolinx, which offers regional transportation for the GTA and Hamilton, is a good start. Such overarching goals should be expanded to include arterial roads, water and sewage lines, sewage treatment, and electrical distribution. Everything else can be left to local municipalities.

▼

One of the biggest bugaboos during my time as treasurer was property tax, the second biggest tax collected in Ontario after income tax. The province wrote the rules; the municipalities set mill rates and collected the money. But each municipality used a different valuation system, and, as a result, market value assessments (MVA) were far too low. Some valuations were set in the 1940s and remained unchanged. Provincial transfers, grants, and subsidies to municipalities and school boards are based on "need" — usually meaning how much they are above or below a provincial norm. So the foundation, the local assessment base, has to be reliable and uniform. Otherwise, some municipalities get too much grant money while others receive too little.

In 1969, Ontario decided to assume responsibility for the administration of property assessment. A bill passed in 1971 set a timetable for reassessing all property at current market value in 1974 for the 1975 municipal tax year. In October 1973, the minister of revenue announced that MVA would be delayed because the escalation of property values made it impossible to establish current market value for about two-thirds of the properties.

Meanwhile, property taxes weren't even keeping up with inflation. From 1970 to 1975, the consumer price index rose 44 per cent while property taxes increased only 17 per cent. In 1978, I tried again. I asked officials to come up with a plan that would pay particular attention to Toronto, where the increases would be the largest. There seemed to be no solution that didn't cost the province money. Moreover, the premier and my colleagues were not supportive.

My other great regret is that MPPs, including me, spent far too much time on funnelling government grants into their ridings. As James Allan, a former minister of highways, used to say, "What the voter appreciates is better roads and bridges — don't forget that." Looking through my files, I am embarrassed to see how often I sought what were relatively modest amounts of money from various ministries for projects such as museums or summer recreation in my own riding and then took the credit.

Some grant programs were just plain crazy. The half-mile access road to Bally McKeough and a dozen other homes off Highbanks Road used to be about twenty-five feet wide. It was a pleasant, tree-lined, gravel road where drivers slowed down politely to let an oncoming vehicle pass. A neighbour, who didn't like the dust, complained to a friend who happened to be the township consulting engineer. Rather than having the gravel sprayed twice a year, we ended up with a paved roadway sixty-six feet wide as mandated by the Department of Highways. I call it the Spadina Expressway. To create this monstrosity, trees were felled, and two or three acres of top agricultural land were taken out of production. All because township council could apply for a grant for half the required money from the Department of Highways, where numerous engineers sat around just waiting to design these subsidized projects. Mike Harris finally ended this foolish system in the 1990s.

While some jobs may have been eliminated when those grants ended, there remain too many overpaid civil servants. I include in those numbers provincial and municipal police forces. It's ludicrous that someone with a high-school education can earn more than $100,000 a year as a police officer, go on paid leave even when charged with a serious offence, and take early retirement with a fully indexed pension. If I were a nurse, I'd be angry that others paid by the public purse had such special status. God help me if any police officer reads this book and catches me speeding, but it needs to be said. The costs for police and firefighters are completely out of control.

Provincial civil servants can also be too powerful and ultimately get their own way. The classic example of the supremacy of the Department of Highways and the Ministry of Transportation is still with us. In 1966, Robarts proposed that Highway 401, eventually to run from the Quebec border to Windsor, and at the time still under construction, be named the Macdonald-Cartier Freeway to honour two fathers of Confederation. Officials believed in numbering not naming, despite the fact that for almost thirty years we'd had the unnumbered Queen Elizabeth Way. Robarts compromised: it would be called both the Macdonald-Cartier Freeway *and* Highway 401. Large blue signs reading "Macdonald-Cartier Freeway" were erected at intersections but they are all long gone. For a time, there were smaller signs saying MCF, but those signs have also disappeared. In the end, the bureaucracy won, despite the wishes of the prime minister of Ontario.

▼

Lest any reader think I was just some kind of a rigid bean counter worried about battles with the bureaucracy, here's part of a memo I wrote to Bill Davis on May 10, 1976, about Ontario's strengths and where our government could make a difference on culture in particular and the quality of life in general:

> I think we should probably be coming out in favour of Massey Hall, and without waiting to be asked indicate that the Province is going to put money into it. Name the amount. You should be talking about the standard of excellence, which we are trying to achieve in this

country and in this province. Perhaps we can't do it all at once, but you would like to see some day the Toronto Symphony in a hall and as an orchestra recognized among the top half dozen of the world, that the Canadian Opera Company should ultimately perhaps be in its own facilities and we should be seeking the level of excellence equivalent to, say, La Scala in Milan, and that the National Ballet has the potential and will have our support to achieving a level of excellence equal to that of the Royal Ballet. In other words, I think some inspiration is probably needed, backed up by some cash, small as it may be.

Let's, however, stop giving away $1,500 so that the yo-yo contest winner can go to Fiji to represent Ontario. Again, let's talk about a standard of excellence, be it an Art Gallery, the Museum, the Science Centre, Ontario Place, a baseball team, the London Art Gallery, the Hamilton-Burlington Beach strip, the C.N. Exhibition; a whole host of things. How do we achieve all of this? Well, I think, again, we start talking about standards of excellence — e.g. the Auto Pact, in research and development, in science policy, making no bones of the fact that we are going to put our emphasis on the things that we do well and we are going to try and do them best; not disregarding other things, but run with the winners rather than trying to shore up all the losers. That's a tough practical message and it's also needed. I would think that we should be starting to think, about now, of ways of reinforcing that in a Budget.

Since then, some of my ideas have come to fruition in the form of a beautiful new Four Seasons Centre for opera and ballet, designed by Jack Diamond, as well as additions to the Royal Ontario Museum and the Art Gallery of Ontario by renowned architects Daniel Libeskind and Frank Gehry.

For all the enemies I made fighting waste and promoting thoughtful spending, I wish I had been bolder. I console myself, however, with how history has judged my accomplishments. After citing John Robarts as a statesman who brought about most of the remarkable events of the era, Nigel Richardson, an environmental policy planner, praised me, saying, "McKeough's commitment, drive, intellect, and political skill as the minister responsible for overseeing most of the events that have been mentioned place him unequivocally as the dominant figure, indeed the very symbol, of the times."[24]

24 Richardson, Nigel, Guest Editor's Foreword, *Plan Canada*, December 24, 1984.

8

▼

The Best Laid Plans

Of all my responsibilities as minister of municipal affairs and treasurer, planning was both the most fundamental and the most frustrating. On the one hand, we were preparing for the future; on the other hand, problems abounded whether the focus was on local planning or provincial planning. A major issue was the length of the processes involved. Both the official municipal plans and the subdivision plans required ministerial approval before they came into effect. Moreover, zoning bylaws were supposed to conform to the official plan.

Such rules and regulations meant all municipalities had to send drafts of each and every proposal to municipal affairs. The ministry then circulated those drafts to other government departments and agencies to ensure they conformed to specific provincial policies such as protection of agricultural land, adequacy of waste water treatment, and so on. This would involve endless meetings and negotiations among multiple government officials as well as representatives of the local municipality.

To make matters even more complicated, a locally appointed planning board offered advice before a local council could act. In turn, council hired staff to help planning boards, but the boards were often unaware this meant they had "political masters" — and that could be a problem. As if all that weren't convoluted enough, any developer whose proposal was denied by a local council could appeal to the Ontario Municipal Board (OMB). When such hearings were held, municipal affairs would send comments.

All too often, the belief, in rural areas and smaller urban municipalities, was that any development was good and should be approved. But few of those smaller municipalities had planning staff. The result often was a hell of a lot of friction between councils and planning boards, where they did exist, and between both of those bodies and municipal affairs — not to mention private sector developers, concerned neighbours, other interested citizens, and well-meaning activists. Too many of those disputes ended up at the OMB with the result that badly needed development, particularly rental housing, was delayed.

Even all these years later, I remain of two minds about whether the OMB should be abolished or retained. My bias toward giving power to local government favours abolishing the OMB. After all, Ontario is the only jurisdiction in the world with such an undemocratic oversight body able to reverse municipal decisions. As a result of those powers, the OMB can undermine municipal authority. At the same time, members of municipal councils are often quite happy their decisions can be appealed to the OMB because it gets them off the hook. They can tell voters the final decision is out of their hands. But homeowners and developers have rights, too. For all its warts, the OMB does provide a forum for arbitration, so retaining it makes sense, too.

Eddie Goodman acted for several of the large developers, and he often arranged meetings for me with his clients and others. I was able to hear the views and advice of business leaders like Eph Diamond, Brian Magee, John Bousfield, Murray Webber, and Jim McAllum. They always gave me their frank opinions, even though this often did not serve their own best interests. Still, I wondered if my staff was happy that I was seeking such outside counsel, given their firm belief that only they knew best. I began routinely inviting staff to those meetings because involving them meant they learned about the real world. We benefitted from that advice, and better public policy was the result.

Despite my urgings, some municipalities outright refused to plan or just didn't quite get around to doing anything proactive about how their communities should grow. In 1968, I introduced an amendment to what was then Section 27 of The Planning Act. The amendment created quite a storm because basically I was getting tough with those laggard municipalities. The Opposition in the legislature thought the minister's decision on local planning should be open to appeal, but I hung tough and the amendment passed. The next day, John Robarts sent me a note saying, "Darcy: You did well yesterday. No doubt some of the holier-than-thou ivory-tower editorial writers will flex their minuscule mental muscles but we cannot permit every decision of a minister to be appealable."

Once we began to create regional governments, these larger entities hired well-qualified staffers who were able to carry out better planning and development. I applauded as municipalities began to permit mixed development in their midst with retail, office, and residential elements all coming together as the formerly rigid boundaries on their thinking disappeared. In urban areas in particular, higher density is more economical and makes better use of limited space.

▼

As for regional planning and development, I should make an admission. During my time in office I was a fan, sometimes with reservations, but usually a fan. In the process of writing these memoirs, I have reread my statements, speeches, press clippings, and the many letters and briefs I received on the topic at the time. The outcome of my research is that, when it comes to what I thought about regional planning, I now put myself somewhere on the scale between jaded and downright skeptical. To put it another way, maybe I was carried away by my own rhetoric on the topic.

I was first introduced to regional development when I travelled to St. John's, Newfoundland, in September 1969 to speak to the Community Planning Association of Canada. I arrived the day before the event and took time for a plane tour of some of the isolated outports being closed and consolidated with other communities. Herculean efforts were being made to create communities of a sufficient size so they could have a fish-processing plant to create jobs and replace the old-fashioned methods of drying the catch on the rocks. It may have been a great idea on paper, but in reality it drastically altered a way of life that had existed for several hundred years. Politically, it likely contributed to the ultimate defeat of Premier Joey Smallwood's government.

Beginning in the 1950s, Ontario went through a similar process, albeit less life changing, by creating economic regions. Greater Toronto was one such region, Essex-Kent and Lambton was another. In those days, local municipalities had only a modest role in economic planning. That changed with the first stage of Design for Development, announced in 1966. As part of that process, Regional Development Councils were created that were not highly regarded by the municipalities because they were seen as intruding into what were municipal concerns and responsibilities. That was certainly my view when I was a Chatham alderman: the Regional Development Council was something to be tolerated or ignored.

By March 1971, when I became treasurer, and early in 1972, when I again became responsible for municipal affairs, a second Design for Development had been announced and the stage was set for bringing the two parts together with a clear statement on the role of the province and the role of local government.

Among our fervent hopes was a "go east" growth model. The federal government had decided the expansion of Malton airport (now Pearson) would no longer be possible, and a new location was needed. They favoured a site near Orangeville, north of Toronto, but because Ontario wanted to encourage development east of Toronto, Pickering was designated. Ottawa concurred and expropriated 18,000 acres of land. The province looked at expropriating another 8,000 acres. I told Robarts we should instead assemble 25,000 acres to create a new city called Cedarwood, aiming for a population of 150,000 to 200,000. He agreed. Pickering became a contentious issue at the time of the 1972 federal election when the Trudeau government was reduced to a minority. The airport was never built.

In my view, that was a big mistake. Pickering could have served freight traffic, private planes, and charter flights. I continued to push for Pickering, but Minister of Housing Bob Welch, who inherited the responsibility for Cedarwood, did not follow through. He was a good minister but too much of a politician; he found it easiest to do nothing.

We were, however, able to act in other areas over which we had planning control. We moved the head office of the Ontario Health Insurance Plan (OHIP) with its 900 jobs to Kingston as well as the head office and 750 jobs in the Ministry of Revenue to Oshawa. Other eastern Ontario initiatives included the Urban Transportation Development Corporation's $50-million test track near Kingston and building the LCBO's $40-million warehouse in Whitby instead of expanding in Toronto.

Successive governments took similar steps to spur regional development. Natural resources went to Peterborough; transportation to St. Catharines; Ontario Provincial Police to Orillia; northern development, mines and forestry to Sudbury; and agriculture, food and rural affairs to Guelph.

To the west, the Parkway Belt Plan was a very successful venture leading to urban development in the Lakeshore corridor between Oshawa and Hamilton. When I was treasurer, the province acquired about 70 per cent of the 30,000 acres required; the rest came later. Today, that's the site of Highway 407, a toll road and utility corridor that has improved traffic flows and spurred industrial and residential development.

An equally positive planning decision involved the Niagara Escarpment. John Robarts came up with the idea in 1969 to preserve the forested ridge that runs from Niagara to Tobermory, saying, "These are our crown jewels." The Niagara Escarpment Commission (NEC) was established by legislation in 1973. Purchasing land was easy, getting easements over private land for the Bruce Trail was often difficult, and there were innumerable tussles with individuals, developers, and municipalities — particularly in Grey and Bruce, where some of the residents did not like having their acreage regulated by a provincial commission.

Despite all the tribulations, the province purchased land for what became the Bruce Trail: 1,000 kilometres of main trails and side trails. The Escarpment today is an environmentally secure treasure with recreational facilities encompassing almost 200,000 hectares and has been designated a UNESCO World Biosphere Reserve.

In 2005, the NEC became the cornerstone of the province's larger Greenbelt Plan. In 2005 and 2009, the Province returned lands to the NEC that had previously been transferred to the Parkway Belt West Plan, because the NEC was seen as the more appropriate vehicle to protect escarpment lands where such lands were not required for future roads and urban infrastructure.

Severances, urban sprawl, and related development pressures still remain as challenges to the protection of the Niagara Escarpment. Agriculture, forest management, recreation, and residential uses are permitted in the NEC and form the majority of the land uses found today on the Escarpment. The noisiest tussles are with gravel pit operators. The gravel is needed, and municipalities are often sympathetic because they create jobs, but affected residents protest the increased truck traffic carrying aggregate. While it is not an easy situation, the Niagara Escarpment Commission, for the most part, has been an outstanding success and is a monument to the vision of John Robarts.

▼

There were some good ideas that did not proceed. The province owned the Lake Ontario bottom; great quantities of cheap fill were being created from the demolition of buildings. That's how Ontario Place came into being. In 1968, Minister of Trade and Development Stanley Randall proposed moving the island airport to the Leslie

Street spit, building a bridge, and creating Harbour City, a Venice-like community for up to 60,000 people. Urban planner Jane Jacobs said Harbour City was "probably the most important advance in planning for cities that has been made this century."[25] But Randall did not run in the 1971 election, and the project died.

I lost a few other battles. In the case of the Toronto Islands, we had an opportunity to create a park for everyone by ending the ability of a chosen few to live an idyllic cottage life mere minutes from downtown Toronto. In 1975, the province agreed it was Metro Toronto's decision, a stance I supported. After I left politics, Larry Grossman talked Bill Davis into renewing the leases on all the dwellings. In the 1981 election, Grossman lost the island poll — served him right!

However, other excellent development projects came to fruition. As a result, Toronto has become an international success story. Within a generation, it underwent a personality change from a dull, overgrown provincial town to a lively metropolis that is Canada's premier city.

Toronto has also benefitted from annual cultural events including Luminato, Nuit Blanche, the Toronto Jazz Festival, and the Toronto International Film Festival. Brookfield Place with its six-storey Allen Lambert Galleria and the preserved nineteenth-century limestone facade of the Merchants' Bank are excellent examples of old and new in harmony. I was proud to play a role in that renaissance.

▼

In politics, there is never a shortage of grand plans. But perhaps the end to my participation in those grand plans began in 1976. In a letter to my mother on April 10, 1976, I said: "Thursday, spoke at a breakfast meeting in Dennis Timbrell's riding about the budget, and then meetings, and another press lock-up and at 2 o'clock in the house we tabled a whole series of planning documents, a rather skeptical reaction to them from the press and the opposition but

25 Cormier, Brendan, *Canadian Architect*, March 1, 2011.

at least they are done and we had been working on them for three months and I am delighted."

That was an understatement. There had been arguments about whether to "release" or "not release" the documents. I was becoming less and less enchanted with provincial planning, and I wanted to get it out of the way and behind me. However, I had indicated in a February 16 memo to my deputy, Rendall Dick, "There should be something in the budget about the provincial planning strategy, depending on what happens, and, secondly, on restructuring. Just a brief progress report." I must have swallowed hard when I wrote those words about provincial planning.

But there was "something" in the April 6 budget. "Mr. Speaker," I began, "Ontario must continue to pursue a dynamic strategy for economic growth in the future which includes improvement in the quality of life and careful preservation of our natural resources. Also, all of Ontario must participate in our development to the fullest extent possible. Later this session, we will be tabling a set of documents which advance an economic and social planning framework for the province as a whole, as well as selected areas."[26] Two days later, the statement and the eleven reports were tabled, but the "grand strategy" was no more.

In the end, the problem was that the planners failed to give sufficient thought to implementation and costs — both in terms of dollars and politics. To my mind, the plans were simply too grand to work. Much, however, was learned, and, in my opinion, there were two positive results. First, planning by the new regional governments and municipalities became much better. They picked up the ball the province dropped. Second, at the provincial level there was more coordinated thinking that resulted in positive action by the civil servants and, ultimately, their masters.

Whether these two achievements justify all of the work and palaver involved is debatable. My ultimate disillusionment with provincial planning springs from the enormity of what was proposed

---

26 Budget, April 6, 1976, p. 21.

— compared with what was achieved — as well as my general inclination that, when it came to government intervention, less was better than more. In a speech to Lambda Alpha International on May 16, 2001, I looked at what was happening to planning at the local level, bearing in mind all the background I knew.

> Core Toronto, in my view, continues to prosper. My morning walk, two weeks ago, took me along Front to Bathurst and back via Queen's Quay. The amount of new construction — condos and apartments — is incredible — and most of it good looking. Milt Farrow accomplished a great deal in getting building going in Harbourfront, and it looks nearly completed. A ballet opera house will be built, and in the right location — downtown — helping to create the kind of night-time excitement that there is in a jammed London's west end or Times Square in New York. Finally — my friend David Crombie was probably right about forty-five feet. Unfortunately it was accompanied by an excess of planning rigidity by city hall planners. Thankfully, realism seems to be taking over, and they now encourage the mixing of residential with commercial. We may even get neighbourhood pubs. The planners, I am forced to admit, have done a good job of "saving" the BCE Place Yonge Street facade for example. It was expensive, I assume, for the owner, but the results make downtown Toronto a far more interesting place.

▼

In 2001, Dalton McGuinty's government moved to protect the Oak Ridge Moraine, in effect an implementation of our similar approach with the Niagara Escarpment. In 2004, McGuinty's government produced a discussion paper "Places to Grow — Better Choices, Brighter Future" that led to two key pieces of legislation: the Proposed Places to Grow Act and The Greenbelt Act that eventually created a 1.8-million-acre greenbelt where farms, small communities, lakes, and forests will be protected from development. The area involved stretches from the Niagara River to Rice Lake and north to Lake Simcoe and includes the previously protected Niagara Escarpment. There was the predictable reaction from farmers who had counted on selling for big bucks, from builders who owned land they hoped to rezone for development, and from town and village councils. It was reminiscent of the initial response when we proposed the Niagara Escarpment legislation.

It would appear to me that, by and large, the government of Kathleen Wynne is continuing with that policy and that the Oakridge Moraine and the Greenbelt may be as successful and worthwhile as the Niagara Escarpment legislation has proven to be.

Although I dislike sweeping plans as much as ever, I have some ideas I think would be helpful if followed:

1. Rely more on market forces to dictate where growth will occur, rather than broad-brush provincial plans.

2. Recognize that some cities are probably not going to grow — Chatham is one example — but the good news is that some of finest agricultural land in Canada is being preserved.

3. Make sure investment in education continues to increase. Ontario residents are generally well educated, but we need better investment, not just in terms of dollars, but also in recognizing the merits of universities and community colleges. The best prescription for growing a city is a university, or a satellite of one, such as is the case in Brantford and Cambridge.

4. Continue to preserve, and perhaps expand, the greenbelts.

5. Try to keep up with the demand for provincial infrastructure including highways, high-speed rail, trunk water, and sewer lines, and make certain — perhaps by encouraging the private sector — that we have adequate, secure electrical power.

6. Be ready to use provincial dollars to assist growth, particularly in northern Ontario, keeping in sight the ups and

downs of the resource cycle. Equally important, ensure that any dollars spent are well analysed in advance and will bring a long-term benefit. (Minaki Lodge would be an example of where this was not the case. I was part of that debacle.)

7. Start planning for the inevitable pressure for cottage development in the vast area north of Lake Huron and Georgian Bay with its thousands of lakes.

8. The Greater Toronto Area — *not* the rest of the province — needs large and continuing provincial investment in transit: subways, Go Transit, light-rail — whatever is most appropriate and will lead to a higher (and less expensive) density.

I propose all this while keeping in mind the cautionary words of eighteenth-century Scots poet Robbie Burns: "The best laid schemes o' mice an' men gang aft agley."

9

Kingmaker

During a caucus retreat held in August 1969 at Windermere House on Muskoka's Lake Rosseau, I was trying to sleep. The night was still, and most windows were open, so I heard every word of an argument between John Robarts and Charlie MacNaughton. Robarts insisted he should step down as leader; MacNaughton was equally adamant he should stay.

I had mixed views. I wanted the top job but knew I needed more time to establish myself. But I also was aware the party needed change. Robarts was losing interest. He looked paunchy and heavy-lidded and would doze in cabinet. At one point, when I asked Robarts's Chief of Staff Keith Reynolds to bestir him for an answer on some question, Reynolds replied, "The ship of state is not being steered."

Yet, even in a time of apparent drift, in 1969 Robarts established the Committee on Government Productivity (COGP) to improve efficiency and effectiveness. The group, chaired by John Cronyn, senior vice-president of John Labatt Ltd., included five business leaders and five senior civil servants. Starting in 1970, the COGP brought about the reorganization of cabinet, as well as better coordination among government programs.

The NDP was going through its own regeneration. Donald C. Macdonald had been elected leader of the predecessor CCF Party in 1953. In 1970, Stephen Lewis, a sitting MPP, challenged Macdonald for the leadership. Macdonald did not run in the convention held that October, where Lewis bested Walter Pittman. The NDP were gaining in strength across Canada, forming governments in Manitoba in 1969, Saskatchewan in 1971, and British Columbia in 1972.

In the case of the Liberals, Robert Nixon's father, Harry, held the riding of Brant from 1919 to 1961 and was briefly premier in 1943, the last Liberal leader before the Tory dynasty began. Robert inherited Brant and had been party leader since 1967. Nixon had a mean streak, preferred the cut-and-thrust of debate to dialogues about policy, and could be a titch lazy. "Sometimes," he once confessed, "I just want to go back to the farm and roll up the driveway behind me."[27]

On December 8, 1970, John Robarts announced his retirement as prime minister. That declaration and the February 10–12 leadership convention in Toronto the following year set in motion one of the major events of my life. Even though I had not yet decided to run, the first news I received was disappointing. My mentor, Charlie MacNaughton, told me he would be supporting Bill Davis, thereby reducing likely backing for me in southwestern Ontario, my natural base. I had a similarly discouraging visit from Eddie Goodman, a Toronto lawyer and indefatigable political organizer, who also said he would be helping Davis.

Next, Pat Boyer, a Toronto lawyer who later was a federal MP, asked if I would join him in backing Bob Welch. I had been hoping Welch might support me and was surprised how quickly alliances were forming. One night, Bill Davis asked for my support. Still undecided as to whether I would run, I avoided answering, which in politics is answer enough.

Four days before Christmas, Davis announced his candidacy. He was not only the first to declare but also the immediate front-runner.

---

27 White, Randall, *Ontario 1610–1985: A Political and Economic History* (Toronto: Dundurn, 1985), p. 202.

Over Christmas, I consulted widely with former Chicago Gang member Alan Eagleson; Ed Mahoney and Joe Martin, two men I'd met through Duff Roblin; Brian Turnbull from the Kitchener-Waterloo area; Brian Magee, who I hoped would help raise money; Chatham friends Bill Myers and Bill Watson; Richard Walker, who was a Windsor lawyer and president of the Windsor District PCs; and James Allan. All were supportive to varying degrees. "It's not like an election," Allan said, "just delegates, all Tories; you'll have a great time."

I soon discovered most of the cabinet ministers not intending to run were swinging to Davis. But I kept thinking that, if history was any guide, the job might not come open again anytime soon. Robarts was in office for ten years, Frost for twelve. I invited about twenty people to a 3 p.m. meeting on Sunday, January 3, 1971, at my ministerial offices at Bay and College Streets in Toronto, for one last sounding. Among the participants were some I'd already talked to such as Bill Watson, Dick Walker, Ed Mahoney, and Joe Martin. Also in attendance were real estate broker Joe Barnicke, Doug Bassett of Inland Publishing, and Phil Lind of Rogers Cable TV.

After everybody urged me to run, an impatient Bassett shouted, "Let's go." Somebody asked, "When?" "Tonight," said Bassett in the same loud voice. So, tonight it was. Mahoney, who ran Public Relations Services Ltd. (PRSL), drafted a statement, and we alerted the media about a press conference at 8 p.m.

My platform had three planks: well-planned economic and physical growth, Canadian control of our economy, and stronger local government. I positioned myself as an anti-government candidate, the one who trusted the people rather than the politicians. "I believe that we have to struggle against the human tendency to centralize power, whether it is centralized in Ottawa or in Toronto," I told the journalists. "In a complex society, some of this is inevitable. But we can limit it by giving local government the resources and the authority to do at that level the things that can be done best, most quickly, most economically, and to the greatest benefit of the local residents."[28]

---

28 *Ottawa Journal*, January 4, 1971, p. 1.

I wasn't running for next time, or to assure myself of a cabinet position in someone else's government. I believed I could win. Three more cabinet colleagues announced that week: Bert Lawrence, Allan Lawrence, and Bob Welch. My campaign got a boost when the Ontario Jaycees named me Man of the Year, the only politician out of five given the title.

I named Richard Walker as my campaign manager with Phil Lind and Joe Martin in charge of the convention organization. Then I began visiting every part of the province, meeting delegates and alternates. Larry DeKoning, a friend from Chatham, came along for some of the adventures, including an anxious plane ride when the landing gear wouldn't retract after takeoff. On other occasions, Ted Clifford, a former farm reporter now at PRSL, or Keith Rattray, who was with Rogers Cable in Brantford, accompanied me. Ted McEwan took a leave from the Department of Municipal Affairs to be a driver. Stewart abandoned the family business to travel, as did his wife, Dorothy. Joyce, our boys, and my mother appeared locally in the Chatham area.

The party organized seven all-candidates meetings around the province for delegates and alternates. My aim was to address a different policy issue at each. In Ottawa, I focused on foreign ownership, saying, "Where foreign investors manufacture goods in Canada, we are entitled to require that Canadian plants be of a size which can compete in foreign markets. Where foreign nations wish access to our natural resources, such as our energy resources, we have a right to require free access for our manufactured goods into their markets. The more we can enlarge our industries, the more we can increase processing in Canada. The more we can increase our exports, the greater the percentage of our capital requirements can be generated in Canada."[29]

In Ottawa, I spoke about national unity and drew this description from Jonathan Manthorpe of the *Globe and Mail*: "Darcy McKeough looked the audience straight in its collective eye and willed them to

---

29 Speech, January 4, 1971.

believe that beneath that 'young fogey' exterior there lurked the soul of a Walter Gordon economic nationalist who was also a good Tory. McKeough's speech was better prepared than Welch's, but his delivery was not as good. His saw-edged voice was pitched a little too high for comfort, but he made up for it by the firmness of his delivery, his size, which was something over six feet, and a face which was distinctive and was not too handsome to be a political liability."[30]

There were bumps in the road. At a delegate meeting in Ottawa, I was introduced as D'Arcy McGee, the father of Confederation who was assassinated in 1868. "I hope you don't wish that fate on me," I said, "because I don't intend to end up as unpleasantly as D'Arcy McGee."[31]

With the convention less than a week away, the *Globe* endorsed Bill Davis but said positive things about me. "Mr. McKeough has demonstrated competence, but also courage. He has undertaken the very necessary — and almost equally unpopular — task of introducing regional government in Ontario. The myriads of small municipalities and local governments have to go if people throughout the province are to enjoy twentieth-century services and if the cost of them is to be equitably distributed. There isn't a member of the Legislature of any party that doesn't admit that the job has to be done; and it is Mr. McKeough who is doing it, and collecting the lumps for doing it."[32]

Davis was supported by most of the cabinet and a majority of the sixty-eight-member caucus, but Allan Lawrence showed surprising strength as the anti-establishment maverick. I also expected to be well positioned on the first ballot, so delegates who sought a compromise candidate had somewhere to turn. A *Toronto Star* poll of riding presidents published a week before the voting placed me second behind Davis. Even Louise Heubner, the official witch of Los Angeles, who was in Toronto making a film, had good things to

30 Manthorpe, Jonathan, *The Power and the Tories: Ontario Politics – 1943 to the Present* (Toronto: Macmillan, 1974), p. 102.
31 *Ottawa Journal*, January 30, 1971, p. 4.
32 *Globe and Mail*, February 6, 1971.

say about me after looking at the birth dates of all the candidates. "A very powerful chart," she said. "Something has been building up for him for quite some time."[33]

▼

As the convention grew closer, there was a final flurry of eighteen-hour days focused on the Royal York Hotel, where many of the delegates from the 117 ridings were staying. I visited hospitality suites, delivered speeches, bolstered workers, and glad-handed delegates in hallways, always with a pocketful of "McQ" buttons looking for a willing lapel.

Thirty young women in minidresses known as Darcy's Dolls handed out pamphlets, and we had dynamic graphics in red, white, and blue designed by Jim Hayhurst and Ken Burgeajan of Hayhurst Advertising. We had two songs, one of which was a takeoff of the popular *Ontari-ari-ari-o* ditty featured at Expo 67 in Montreal: "Give him a place to stand/and a place to grow/McKeough's the man/for Ontario."

The second song included these verses:

> To a farmer, it's an even break;
> To the worker, it's a fairer shake;
> To the voter, it's the road to take
> That's what confidence is!
>
> Confidence is Darcy McKeough;
> Confidence is what he gives to you;
> Confidence is knowing what to do
> Confidence is Darcy McKeough!

There was a farewell dinner for John Robarts on the Wednesday night, attended by 2,000 of the party faithful. Following those

---

33 *Ottawa Journal*, February 5, 1971, p. 4.

festivities the McKeough campaign held a party in the Ballroom at the Royal York with free drinks and music by Rob McConnell and The Boss Brass. Usually, for such an event, the many doors to the Ballroom would be wide open to allow ready access. Not that night. Only one door was, and that's where I stood to shake hands and look every one of the thousand attendees in the eye. We watched our expenses carefully. One of Paul Curley's roles was to close the free bar once we had hit our budgeted amount.

Our overall effort drew praise. "McKeough's campaign is different than Davis — it's young professionals from the communications, management and publications field with many flow charts," said the *Telegram*.[34] There were also some hijinks. Whenever any of my people saw Bert Lawrence, they said, "Hello, Al," and they said "Hello, Bert," to Al, just to drive them both crazy. I'm told one of my workers, who was in the trucking business, moved an Allan Lawrence trailer in the middle of the night from a parking lot opposite Maple Leaf Gardens to a shopping centre in North Toronto.

Official proceedings began at Maple Leaf Gardens on Thursday night with the nomination of all candidates. The two speakers who put my name forward were my only cabinet supporter, Energy and Resources Minister George Kerr, and Toronto Alderman David Rotenberg, who ironically ended up not being able to vote for me. As he is Jewish, he left before sunset Friday to celebrate the Sabbath with his family.

The theme of my speech, written by Ed Mahoney and his PRSL colleague Gwyn Williams, was about how governments couldn't solve everything on their own. "Government should create the incentives or, failing that, the penalties, that will persuade every individual, every corporation, every public body, to join in the common enterprise. If they don't, all the material success of the last few years will be meaningless."

I tried also to position myself as the centrist candidate with a poke at Allan Lawrence. "I will unite, not divide. I want the leadership.

---

34 *Telegram*, February 12, 1971.

But I do not want it so badly that I would weaken, undermine, or destroy this party. I'm not for the establishment; I'm not for the dissenters. I'm for the people."

The lines that attracted the most applause described how I would carry forward the Robarts tradition. "We have heard some blustering talk in this leadership campaign about tough negotiations with Ottawa, about demanding a fuller accounting of federal assistance going to other parts of the country. I, too, will stand up for Ontario — but I will not pawn the Robarts mantle of statesmanship and reconciliation for a bigger fistful from the federal till." The *Telegram* called my words "his best speech yet by far."[35]

▼

On voting day, we were in our seats by 1:30 p.m. We wouldn't get to bed until 3:30 the following morning. At the vote for Ontario's eighteenth premier Friday afternoon, machines replaced paper ballots. Some of the machines failed to work properly, so they were scrapped and replaced by paper ballots. The "new" first ballot didn't begin until 7:40 p.m. Meanwhile, although the machine count wasn't supposed to mean anything, the results circulated. The results, finally announced about 10 p.m., with the cancelled vote in brackets, were: Davis 548 (502), Allan Lawrence 431 (379), McKeough 273 (251), Robert Welch 270 (239), Bert Lawrence 128 (152). I probably came into the convention slightly behind Welch, but my speech, a good floor demonstration, and a well-organized team put me those few votes ahead.

The candidate with the least support, University of Ottawa student Robert Pharand, was eliminated. But Bert Lawrence also dropped out. With only three votes separating Bob Welch and me, we needed to make sure Welch was the next candidate to go. Much later, I learned that Phil Lind went to Eddie Goodman and asked if eight or ten Davis delegates would vote for me on the next ballot.

---

35 *The Telegram*, February 12, 1971.

The implicit understanding was that, when I went off the ballot, I would back Davis. Whether those Davis votes came my way or not I'll never know. But my support on the second ballot did rise by fifteen while Welch picked up only one.

Davis increased his first-place standing to 595 with Allan Lawrence gaining ground at 498. But I'd successfully made it to the third ballot. Welch had to withdraw. It was my understanding that Bob and I had agreed that whoever was knocked off first would support the other. I met him in the corridor, which was crowded with media. But now there was no deal. It was not the first time, nor would it be the last, that Bob Welch dithered and did nothing. With no announcement from Welch, his supporters decided for themselves. I would have needed nearly two-thirds of his delegates to leapfrog over Allan Lawrence and end up on the final ballot with Bill Davis. But without Welch's public backing, I had no momentum.

I was angry and bitter. I left the convention floor and went to the director's lounge for a stiff drink away from the hubbub. As I sat alone, morosely watching the proceedings on television, I saw an interview with Joyce, who was bubbling with optimism. Chagrined, I left the lounge, pasted a smile on my face, and rejoined my wife and my workers.

With the Welch delegates released, I gained 58 votes to 346, Davis rose by 74 to 669, and Allan Lawrence went up by 108 to 606, elevating him to within catching distance of Davis. As the low man on the totem pole, I had to drop off the next ballot so Davis and Lawrence could go head-to-head. A horde of reporters clustered in front of our seats in the stands, with outthrust microphones to catch any words we uttered. Said Joyce: "The wolves are gathering."

I had previously made no commitment to either Davis or Lawrence, but my decision was easy. I couldn't support Allan Lawrence. He was smart and funny, but I thought his ideas were simplistic. I had probably made up my mind in favour of Davis four years earlier. In November 1967, Joyce and I had just returned to Bally McKeough at 11:30 p.m. after an evening with friends when Davis arrived unannounced at our door. He and I were meeting the Kent

County Educational Consultative Committee the next morning at 9 a.m. and he had decided to come early so we could get to know each other better. Davis doesn't drink, but I had a couple of what he said his mother, a leader in the Woman's Christian Temperance Union, called "antibiotics." We talked openly about our parents, how our backgrounds were different and yet similar, and we learned a lot about each other by the time he left at 4 a.m. As a result of that bonding, I felt much better about the man now on the verge of assuming the mantle of John Robarts.

Still, I did not look up to Davis in the same way I did to Robarts, who was sixteen years my senior. Davis and I were only four years apart. He was almost shy; I never got to know him well. We were not dinner or drinking pals. Davis was a much better husband and father than I. He had few dinners at La Scala.

Once I had told my advisors I would back Davis, someone said I should wait until he walked over to see me. "No," I said, "the losers go to the winners." I worked my way through the crowded floor to Davis, raised his arm in victory, and led a rousing version of "For He's a Jolly Good Fellow." Clare Westcott, an aide to Davis and father of nine children, blurted his delight by saying, "I'm going to name my next four children Darcy."

When the results of the fourth and final ballot were announced at 2 a.m. Saturday morning, William Grenville Davis had defeated Allan Lawrence by 44 votes, 812 to 768. Of my 346 delegates, a few must have left the convention, because the total votes won by Davis and Lawrence on the final ballot increased by only 305. Of that number, 162 went to Lawrence, 143 to Davis. Despite the fact that more of my delegates went to Lawrence than Davis, I had provided the margin of victory for the latter. In the parlance of the convention floor, I was the kingmaker.

I don't know for whom John Robarts voted on the other ballots, but he was with me on the first. As godfather to our second-born son, Jamie, Robarts made that clear during the proceedings when he told Joyce, "I want you to know I voted for my godson's father." I carry those words in my heart to this day. After the convention, when I sent my thank-you letters, I left his to the last because I knew it would be the most difficult to write. I thanked him for his support at the convention and for taking a chance when he first made me part of his cabinet. "I doubt whether I will ever have a greater privilege and honour and enjoy something so much in my lifetime."[36] Those words still ring true today. Looking back over my time in Ontario politics, the 1971 leadership was a high point. While I may have failed in my ultimate goal, I fought a good fight, and grew in the regard of my party.

36 Letter, April 28, 1971.

10

▼

New World Order

When John Robarts stood with all the candidates on stage in that early morning in February 1971, he told the cheering throng, "I've achieved my objective. I'm a has-been." Of course, at fifty-four, he was nothing of the sort. Robarts went on to serve with distinction as a director of a number of companies including Canadian Imperial Bank of Commerce, Power Corporation, Bell Canada, Metropolitan Life Insurance Company, and Abitibi Paper Company Ltd.

In 1977, Prime Minister Pierre Trudeau asked Robarts and former federal cabinet minister Jean-Luc Pépin to co-chair the Task Force on Canadian Unity. They travelled the county listening to Canadians and produced an excellent report calling for "unity through pluralism." Trudeau simply dismissed their recommendations out of hand. Such harsh disregard not only was rude, it was also wrong. Had Ottawa embraced the report's recommendations, Canadians might have avoided the frustrating and divisive constitutional debates that dominated the 1980s.

For all his public triumphs, however, Robarts's personal life was a private tragedy. All the time he was in office, Norah refused to leave their home in London and move to Toronto, so their marriage deteriorated. In 1973, at the Bombay Bicycle Club, a favourite Robarts haunt on Toronto's Jarvis Street, he met Katherine Sickafuse, a divorced nurse from Rome, New York, who was working as an inspector of nursing homes in Ontario. At twenty-eight, she was half his age. In 1976, Robarts divorced his wife and married Sickafuse. The following year, his son Timothy committed suicide at twenty-one. Robarts was devastated, and that heartbreak began his own downward slide. In 1981, Robarts suffered a series of debilitating strokes, and he committed suicide in 1982 at sixty-five.

Thankfully, his legacy endures. During his time at the top, he built Highway 401; expanded public housing; launched GO Transit commuter service; created the legal aid system and Ontario Housing Corporation; opened four universities: Windsor, York, Trent, and Laurentian; and built Ontario Place and the Ontario Science Centre.

▼

John Robarts was not only my leader and my mentor but also my friend. He was my kind of man, and I think it's fair to say he felt the same about me. Robarts was what they called in those days "a man's man." He once concluded a speech in Chatham by saying, "I'm off to my friend John Bradley's to shoot ducks tomorrow." As for how he felt about Lester Pearson, his judgment was equally direct. "I don't trust him, and more to the point, when you go to his house he only offers one drink before dinner."

On one occasion, Robarts went fishing on a remote lake in northern Ontario. He was cut off from the world in general and Queen's Park in particular. A Lands and Forests plane flew over his campsite daily to provide radio contact with his office. On one of those trips, the plane flashed a message about a crisis requiring the prime minister's attention. When he learned I was on the case, he said, "Not to worry, Darcy can handle it," and returned to his fishing.

We didn't always agree. Although the adoption of a new Canadian flag in 1965 came out of bitter debate and caused deep divisions in the House of Commons, Robarts proposed having an Ontario flag. I worried we not only would be seen to be in conflict with the new flag, but also would reopen the wounds of the debate. His answer to me was as instructive as it was conclusive. "We don't have a flag," he said. "We should have a flag. And besides, Darcy, it's damn good politics."

Maybe it's because he was my first leader and mentor, but thinking back to the cabinet table it's always John Robarts I see in command. His style was to discuss the policy merits of any matter before dealing with the political considerations. Davis was more inclined to reverse the order. To be sure, Davis spent almost half of his time as premier leading a minority government, so he had to tread carefully to retain support in the House. As well, economic times were tougher in the Davis years, and that frustrated me. I simply wasn't the politician Davis was.

In the House, Robarts was a commanding presence. Davis also performed well, but not with the same gravitas. "Bland works," Davis once told the legislature. John Robarts never had a bland moment in his life. "Robarts was Chairman of the Board; Bill Davis was Head of the Family," wrote Sally Barnes, Davis's long-time press officer, in her book, *Bill: A Collection of Words and Pictures*."[37]

Although Davis was as important a force in my life as Robarts, and each man was the right leader for his time, I revered Robarts more. He was both a hero and a father figure to me. When he offered me my first cabinet post, it was because he saw strengths in me I didn't see in myself. I am forever grateful to him for his confidence in my abilities and for setting my sails in the fascinating and far-reaching life I led in politics and the years beyond.

▼

My role as kingmaker of Bill Davis at the 1971 convention was not universally celebrated. I received plenty of letters castigating me for my action. In reply to each irate writer, I sought to find a peaceful resolution, for example: "My supporters, of course, could, would, and

---

37 Barnes, Sally, ed., *Bill: A Collection of Words and Pictures* (Toronto: Deneau, 1985), p. 7.

did do whatever they wanted. On the other hand, I have been born and brought up to believe in standing up for what I believe is the right thing to do. I have no intention of changing my position at this stage in my life. Both of us obviously are under a bit of a strain these days. No doubt, we will meet before too long and perhaps can pursue the subject then." I also wrote individual thank-you letters to my key supporters, but included one line that was the same to all: "Losing is not the ending."

There were scores of key workers who made a difference, but among the closest and best were Richard Walker, who rode herd on everyone, including me; Jack Livesey and John Thompson, who planned and ultimately ran the convention; Bill Whiteacre and his wife, Liz, who, among other things, corrected my wardrobe; Ed Mahoney, who, along with others, wrote first-class speeches; Joe Martin, who offered policy and political advice; Doug Bassett for his never-failing enthusiasm; and Phil Lind for his ideas, both practical and creative.

After the bone-wearying six-week campaign, Joyce and I fled to Nassau for four days of rest and recuperation. I must admit I shed a few tears amid the palms thinking about what might have been. I would rather have won, but I was right to run even though I lost. I had done well and positioned myself as a key player in the party.

We flew back to Toronto on February 17 for John Robarts's last cabinet meeting and a black-tie dinner at Carman's Club, a popular Toronto steakhouse. Some aspects of life quickly got back to normal. Bill Watson of Chatham, a staunch supporter in my campaign, phoned my brother Stewart to ask for a better price on a bathtub he was buying. I had my suits taken in; I'd lost the usual twenty pounds on the hustings.

Fundraising played a crucial role. I was never given all the details, and I was never told the names of major donors; this way there was no possibility I'd feel I had to reward their support. But I do know we raised roughly $125,000, thanks to Bill Watson, but spent only $100,000, thanks to Bill Campbell, who oversaw expenses.

When Bill Kelly, the party's top bagman, heard we had a surplus, he demanded we turn any excess money over to the provincial party office. Watson refused and instead gave $5,000 to the Chatham-Kent PC Association, which had never before had any money between elections. In the past, when I sent flowers to a funeral or wedding of a constituent, I paid for such tributes out of my own pocket. The rest of the surplus, about $20,000, was returned to donors on a proportionate basis, an unheard-of step in the world of politics. In later years, whenever I ran into Eph Diamond, a co-founder of the real estate development firm Cadillac Fairview, he always said I was the only politician who had ever paid a dividend.

More important than the money, I received a warm welcome from delegates wherever I went and a fair hearing for whatever I said. I learned a great deal about our party, our province, and why the combination of the two makes us so great. I was also left with the firm conviction that no political group anywhere in this country could match the Progressive Conservative Party of Ontario for the quality of supporters and their determination, as well as their ability to make the party grow, develop, and renew itself.

▾

Much has been said over the years about how, as premier, Bill Davis embraced the key Allan Lawrence campaign organizers and made them his own. He welcomed Lawrence people like Norman Atkins, Dalton Camp, Ross DeGeer, and others who went on to create the backroom Davis powerhouse that came to be called the Big Blue Machine. But let the record show, I also contributed a few key people, such as Phil Lind, John Thompson, and Paul Curley. In fact, I may have spawned the whole idea. I wrote a memo to Bill Davis on February 22, saying, "In Al's camp, in particular, and to some extent in mine, there were a number of bright people who we should not lose track of. I think it would be a great idea if you pulled a Stanfield [after winning the federal leadership in 1967] and perhaps invited four or five from each of the groups in. Let them pull your campaign and the other campaigns apart and out of that I think you and the party will get some damn good ideas for our next mission to the people."[38]

I didn't expend much energy trying to figure out why I'd lost and why Bill Davis had won. We had to get on a campaign footing for the upcoming election. But in writing these memoirs, I've been able to consider the leadership campaign from a vantage point more than forty years later. Only with the passage of time and whatever wisdom the years have given me is it possible to see the past clearly.

Both Davis and I were relatively young. This was a shared advantage, as was the fact that neither of us was from Toronto. Bill was from Brampton; I was from Chatham. We both knew Toronto, but neither of us was *of* Toronto. Davis had the additional benefit of having been a cabinet minister for eight years, while I had held my post for only three. As minister of education, he was a popular figure. He had money to spend on the new schools so desperately needed as the wave of baby boomers born beginning in 1946 came through elementary and high schools in increasing numbers. Davis was always at the official openings. He averaged a hundred thousand miles of travel a year, and each journey consolidated his hold on the public.

Claire Hoy put it this way in his Davis biography: "If a community needed a new school, Davis was there. If it needed a college, a university, a gymnasium, or an addition to an existing school, he was just a phone call and a press release away. By the late 1960s he controlled almost seventy cents of every provincial tax dollar spent. No wonder he was so popular."[39] Hoy also quoted me in the same book, saying that Davis was rarely around Queen's Park. "His attendance at cabinet was a laughing stock. He would wander in two hours after the meeting had started, if he showed at all. He always got there when he had something to put through, and Robarts, being the former [education] minister, was on the same wavelength. Bill never had much of a problem doing what he was trying to do."[40]

To the delegates, Bill Davis must have seemed like a safe choice

---

38 Memo to William Davis, February 22, 1971.
39 Hoy, Claire, *Bill Davis: A Biography* (Toronto: Methuen, 1985), p. 55.
40 Ibid., p. 26.

compared with me. I had been described by the media as forthright, honest, blunt, and sometimes arrogant. I would be the first to admit to all of these assessments. New schools were an easier "sell" than my plans. Restructuring municipalities and bringing in regional government eliminated relationships and roles of long standing, so I had left a lot of scars.

Of all the candidates, Allan Lawrence was by far the best organized. Our team was clearly number two, with Bill Davis's more establishment organization in third place. As an individual, Davis was conciliatory: he listened and agreed but never promised something he knew he could not deliver. He was initially a boring speaker, but must have discovered, at some point, how much he liked hearing applause. That's when he began developing the style I came to call his Johnny Carson delivery, an auctioneer-paced patter of speaking with apparently unpunctuated sentences mixed together with humorous references to people in the room, random thoughts that came to mind, and numerous plugs for his home town of Brampton.

Davis ended up with the backing of half the cabinet as well as most of the caucus. I had but one minister and a handful of caucus colleagues. Charlie MacNaughton's decision to support Davis hurt me a lot. Charlie and I remained the closest of friends, and he fully supported me when I later became treasurer, his former position. We never discussed his decision. There was nothing to say. Even after all these years, however, it's difficult to look back on my loss with equanimity. I wanted the job and knew I could have done well at it.

▼

Bill Davis joined an unbroken line of successful Conservative leaders beginning with Colonel Drew, through T. L. Kennedy, Leslie Frost, and John Robarts. In a break from the past, Davis renounced the title of prime minister and called himself premier instead. As the kingmaker at the convention that chose Bill Davis, I could expect a reward. I was not disappointed. On March 1, when Davis announced his cabinet, I was named treasurer and minister of economics. This time, I did not ask for the weekend to think as I had when Robarts had offered me my first cabinet post.

MacNaughton, who had held the role under Robarts, had graciously offered to step aside in exchange for his former role of minister of highways, this time to include the department of transportation as well. Treasurer was the job I wanted, and definitely the number two spot in cabinet after Davis. Leslie Frost had been treasurer while he was prime minister. James Allan and then MacNaughton, both senior statesmen in the party, followed him. I was in good company.

In the Davis cabinet, only three ministers from the Robarts cabinet kept their positions. The rest were either new or received new roles. At cabinet meetings, Davis sat in the middle of the table with me to his right and Allan Lawrence, newly named attorney general, to his left. Despite my support for Davis on the final ballot, Allan and I got along well. His two main interests were justice and Toronto — not Metro Toronto, just the City of Toronto, the downtown core. His wife, Moira, was a far better political operative than he was.

The other leadership candidates were also rewarded with top spots: Bob Welch in education and Bert Lawrence in health. Bob Welch was a wonderful orator, but on many issues, you never really knew where he stood. This was a calculated action on his part; he always sought to find the middle ground. His strength as a compromiser was put to good use as House Leader during our two minority governments later in the decade. Bert Lawrence was intelligent and outspoken, but not the most practical of ministers. As part of the reorganization by Davis, all departments became ministries, and, in 1972, Lawrence, Bob Welch, and I were all elevated to the status of provincial secretaries or "super ministers" in a reorganized government.

Among the other appointees in 1971 was Tom Wells. He held broad views but too often simply reflected the opinions of his officials. When he was education minister, he never faced down the teachers' union as he should have. George Kerr was passionate about Burlington and contributed on a wide range of issues.

The three female ministers appointed by Davis over the years all did well. Margaret Birch, named Ontario's first female cabinet minister in 1972 as a minister without portfolio, was promoted in 1974 to provincial secretary for social development. She was generally quiet, but when she did speak, everyone listened. Bette Stephenson and Margaret Scrivener joined the Davis cabinet in 1975. Stephenson was strong, sensible, and treasurer for all too brief a time in the Frank Miller government. Scrivener served as minister of government services as well as minister of revenue.

With my gruff, blustering manner and booming voice, I may have intimidated some of the ministers, but not Scrivener. She would take me on in cabinet from time to time, but not as often as she did when she served on the Metropolitan Toronto Planning Board and I was minister of municipal affairs. Davis tolerated such arguments, but he preferred peace in the family, and most ministers took their cue from him. Scrivener was dropped from cabinet in a 1978 shuffle as the chemistry wasn't right.

Frank Miller was a nice guy and a right winger who was particularly bruised by hospital closures. As whip, Doug Kennedy did an excellent job of relaying the thoughts, moods, and concerns of caucus. Dennis Timbrell did a good job as my successor in energy (despite my interference) and an even better job in health. Roy McMurtry was a good attorney general, but that was it. He took little interest in government other than matters involving justice. He did not attend either caucus or cabinet on a regular basis. When he did show up, he was usually late. Lorne Henderson was a hog farmer and cracker-barrel politician who held numerous portfolios but is best remembered for two comments he made during cabinet meetings. Once, when he was reporting local feedback on some contentious matter, he said, "I have exposed myself all over the riding." As for keeping health-care costs in line, he said, "I'm opposed to detergent fees."

With these men and women, Bill Davis was able to stay in power through two minority governments, regain his majority, and last for fourteen years as premier. Few politicians of any stripe or jurisdiction in the modern era had his capacity for recovery and longevity. Davis is a straight arrow guided by his background as a United Church progressive. His great strength was knowing when to make a decision and when to delay, usually the latter. "Decisive he never was nor pretended to be, concluding early on in his twenty-five year political career that today's crisis could probably benefit most from a cooling off period rather than a quick solution," said Sally Barnes in her book *Bill: A Collection of Words and Pictures*. "He never dramatically killed ideas or projects with which he disagreed or he believed would not succeed; he just let them slowly suffocate while they waited for the required approval."[41]

I don't think Bill Davis has a mean bone in his body. On the political spectrum, he was slightly to the left of centre; ministers such as Roy McMurtry, Bob Elgie, and Larry Grossman were further to the left. Tom Wells was about in the same place on the spectrum as Davis, but the rest of us, me in particular, were somewhere to the right. There were times when Davis was too cautious for me, and we certainly didn't see eye-to-eye on every issue. But the fact that he kept such a diverse group working together as a team was his greatest strength and the reason for his durability. Few are the politicians as canny and accomplished as he. Whenever I was meeting with someone, if Bill Davis came into the room and joined the group, I always stood and called him "sir."

---

41 Barnes, p. 7.

11

Working with Bureaucrats

For a rock-ribbed Conservative like myself, the relentless growth of government was worrisome. The $300-million annual budget of 1949 under Leslie Frost had become $1 billion by the time John Robarts took office in 1961. When I was sworn in as treasurer and chairman of the Treasury Board, March 1, 1971, and delivered my first budget on April 26, annual spending had ballooned to $6 billion. From a handful of departments at Confederation, Ontario now had twenty-three different ministries. In a single decade, the number of civil servants had almost doubled from 32,000 in 1960 to 62,000 in 1970.

My deputy minister was Ian Macdonald, an economist and Rhodes scholar, who later served as president of York University. Macdonald was brilliant and had the great facility of being able to explain complex ideas to people like me — a politician, so, by definition, not brilliant. Macdonald and Rendall Dick, who succeeded him in 1974, built an intelligent, hard-working, and loyal team as a result of Robarts's demand for a civil service that was as good as, or better than, Ottawa's.

In the best tradition of the British and Canadian civil services, the minister decides the policy and the civil servant carries out that policy. As I said in a speech in 1968 describing my views on this relationship, "When a minister and his senior official disagree, the official should not resign but should set out his views clearly to his minister, then if after due consideration his views are overruled, he should do his level best to carry out the policy of the government even though he might not be in personal agreement."

I also told my staff, don't look to me for ideas. "That's your job. I may be capable of producing one in a hundred, if that. *You* bring them forward. It's my job to decide what we carry forward — what will sell — to Cabinet, to Caucus, to the public. But don't expect the politician to have all the ideas. I want bright people around me with bright ideas."[42]

They also put up with their minister's many foibles. When I wanted an answer, I didn't bother with the chain of command — I'd go straight to someone's office to get the information. That's not to say I was a micromanager. I needed not only to know if an idea would work politically, but also to see it from all sides, and I counted on the members of ministry to think that through. Just as important, they could see I worked hard, so they did, too.

In the run-up to each annual budget, even junior officers were included in all meetings — a suggestion made by Macdonald that I welcomed — so they could contribute from their areas of expertise. That made for crowded sessions, but budgets and budget speeches are pivotal points in the life of any government. In addition to the views of bureaucrats, we also sought those of individuals and outside groups. At the time, such consultations with chambers of commerce, investment bankers, and economists were unusual. Now, such representations are part of the planning for every budget in all jurisdictions.

There was one person I did not heed. Prior to my first budget, I was summoned to the premier's office. When I got there, it turned out to be Dalton Camp who had called. He said he was going to tell me how to write a budget. I didn't take too kindly to that. He also said he would advise on content. I didn't take too kindly to

---

42 Speech to the Institute of Public Administration of Canada, Toronto Group, Toronto, October 21, 1968, p. 11.

that, either. He suggested major spending on some project. I said we couldn't afford it. "Ministers of finance always say that," he said. Camp might have had the premier's ear, but he didn't command mine. I ignored his advice. Davis backed me up.

▼

My first budget speech was on Monday, April 26, 1971, at 8 p.m. I began with a reference to A. St. Clair Gordon, of Wallaceburg, who had been MPP for Kent West from 1934 to 1945. A Liberal, he and his wife were close friends of my parents, and he was my "Uncle Bill." Among the guests I invited that night were his granddaughter, Susan, and her husband, Douglas Bassett. As treasurer in the Mitch Hepburn government, Gordon had presented his budget on March 19, 1943. I was ten; the budget was $100 million.

Unemployment in 1972 was 4.9 per cent, so in my pre-election budget we tried to balance an expansionary policy to create jobs while at the same time controlling spending in education and the public service. I announced four objectives that, for the most part, set the tone for my entire time as treasurer. First, restore full employment and economic growth by encouraging private sector expansion; second, control public spending in order to restrain taxation levels and reduce inflationary pressures; third, advance municipal reforms in line with the long-term program we announced in 1969; and, fourth, realize greater Canadian participation and ownership in the economy.

I also declared war on the federal government. "Two things have become evident. First, the federal government is clearly bent on a course of greater centralization and concentration of power. Second, Ontario has been singled out for a reduced role in the building of our nation." As a result of inflation and Ottawa's decreased payments for shared-cost programs, higher budgetary costs were inevitable. Expenditures in my 1971 budget were up 10.7 per cent from the previous year.

In an attempt to control overall costs, I limited civil service salary increases to 5 per cent. I announced changes to the laws regarding takeovers, a stance I had promoted during my leadership campaign. U.S. firms enjoyed an advantage because they could deduct the interest cost of funds borrowed to buy shares in a Canadian firm. To level the playing field, we amended tax legislation to permit such deductions by Canadian companies. At the reception at the Albany Club after the speech, John Robarts told me, "It was a good budget, but your deficit was bigger than my first budget."

Politically, however, the budget was a success, as was the decision shortly after by Davis to halt further construction on the partially built Spadina Expressway meant to run from north Toronto through residential areas to the downtown core. In the election held on October 21, 1971, Davis's first as premier, we gained ten seats to win seventy-eight. I thought stopping Spadina was wrong. I believed in the principle of municipal autonomy, but Davis and the voters thought otherwise.

We were in the midst of a recession when I presented a mini-budget in December 1971, so my focus remained on getting the province's economy moving again. "It took almost four years after the last major recession to bring the economy back to full employment," I reminded the legislature.[43] To stimulate the economy, I cut income taxes by 3 per cent to put money in people's pockets and made $80 million available to municipalities and school boards for seasonal and temporary jobs.

▼

In January 1972, Davis followed a recommendation of the Committee on Government Productivity (COGP) and reduced the number of ministries from thirty to twenty-four. There were now two types of ministers, those with responsibilities for programs and four provincial secretaries, or super ministers, as we came to be known:

---

43 *Ottawa Journal*, December 21, 1971, p. 6.

Allan Lawrence in justice, Robert Welch in social development, Bert Lawrence in resources development, and I. Three of the four appointments of former leadership candidates didn't work out. They weren't given the powers they needed to be "super," and all announcements continued to be the responsibility of the individual ministers. Later that year, Allan Lawrence resigned to run federally. In 1974, Bert Lawrence left politics and returned to his Ottawa law practice. I don't think Bob Welch was ever truly happy in his role.

Unlike the other three, I enjoyed being a super minister. In addition to being treasurer, I also took back my previous duties as minister of municipal affairs and added minister of economics and intergovernmental affairs to my duties. Briefly, at one point, five deputy ministers reported to me: Ian Macdonald, Bill Palmer in municipal affairs, Carl Brannan and later Terk Bayly in Treasury Board, Bill Anderson in civil service, and Tom Eberlee in charge of COGP implementation.

I was clearly number two to the premier, and I enjoyed exercising the power entrusted to me. Not content with working fourteen to sixteen hours a day, I dictated a memo to my secretary, Mrs. Eaton, on March 22, 1972, to the effect that La Scala closed at 10:30 p.m. and could she please find out if Winston's, Julie's Mansion, or the Safari Lounge atop the Toronto-Dominion Centre stayed open later so I could work even longer over dinners.

During various times as treasurer, I had seven parliamentary assistants. They were Dick Beckett, Claude Bennett, Don Irvine, Keith Norton, Arthur Meen, George McCague, and George Ashe. Some ministers treated their parliamentary secretaries as executive assistants to do their bidding. Not I. Mine were intimately involved in my daily agenda and all decisions. All of them went on to hold their own cabinet posts.

In Treasury, there was also irreverent fun. Finance Minister John Turner came for a meeting in our boardroom one sultry summer's day. There was coffee available, but I asked if there was anything cold to drink. Duncan Allan, who later became deputy minister of agriculture, disappeared to the fourth floor and brought back a case of very cold beer. That would not have happened on Parliament Hill.

I found Turner and his deputy minister, Tom Shoyama, better to deal with than the previous deputy, Simon Reisman, who constantly shoved his smelly cigar in all of our faces. There were times when Reisman would speak as if he were the authority and the minister wasn't even there. I finally said, "Mr. Reisman, I'd really prefer to hear from the minister directly." In fairness, Reisman later played an important role in negotiating the Canada–U.S. Free Trade Agreement. Just ask him.

Turner and I hit it off. We held many productive meetings, one of which was at Château Montebello in Quebec with our wives. While Joyce and Geills were out cross-country skiing, we came to an agreement that meant Ottawa would allow an Ontario Tax Credit on the federal tax return.

On the spending side, I killed proposals I believed would be too costly. One such idea, recommended by the Ministry of Health, was a dental care program for children. I also beat back numerous costly ideas from my colleagues. Bert Lawrence wanted the government to buy the Blue Mountain ski resort near Collingwood from its owner Jozo Weider. It was a dumb plan, although I rejected it as gently as possible, telling Lawrence, "It would seem a great shame to me to be spending two and a half million dollars to buy something which is already available. With the enormous expense of skiing to the individual, I don't know whether we could justify running this sort of a park for skiers as a Provincial Park."[44] As a result of such watchfulness, the deficit fell during the two years following the 1972 budget.

I was not a tightwad on all topics. I took a trip to Japan in April 1972 to talk to Daiwa Bank about acting for Ontario. I could see there was a need to bolster Ontario's trade representation. Canada was buying about $800-million worth of goods annually from Japan with half coming to Ontario. Canada was selling a similar dollar amount to Japan each year, but only a small portion was from Ontario. "We are going to have to open more trade offices and be much more aggressive than we have been in the past," I wrote in a memo to John White,

---

44 Memo to Bert Lawrence, February 27, 1972.

then minister of industry and tourism. "What I am concerned about is, of course, our heavy dependence on the United States and our lack of penetration with so many other markets."[45]

These visits to foreign countries often allowed me to see people in a different light. On one trip to London, in the spring of 1971, my mother accompanied me in order to visit a relative. John and Norah Robarts were already there on a private visit, so one night they and my mother, along with our key Canadian advisors, Ted Medland of Wood Gundy, Bryce Farrill of McLeod Young Weir, and some others, all had dinner together at Don Luigi's on the King's Road. At the back of the restaurant were two Toronto bankers entertaining a couple of popsies. As the foursome passed our table on the way out, Medland and Farrill stood up, stopped them, and introduced them to everyone at our table, saying, "You know the former prime minister and Mrs. Robarts. And do meet the treasurer's mother." After they departed we all had a good laugh at their obvious embarrassment.

▼

Ontario's need for borrowing was modest in those days compared with today's debt load, now approaching $300 billion. We began issuing Ontario Treasury bills in September 1971 with a first auction of $10 million. I revelled in signing my name over the words "Treasurer of Ontario." To this day, old friends, former colleagues, and staff refer to me in their conversations and address me as "Treasurer." The continued use use of that title which goes back to 1867 (with a few interruptions) came to an abrupt end when Premier Bob Rae, named Floyd Laughren, Minister of Finance. Anyone can be a minister; there is only one Treasurer. Premier Peterson also did away with the title Sheriff, a storied designation dating back to the Magna Carta of 1215, calling them "court administrators" instead.

Ontario had previously been represented on Wall Street by First Boston, but the lead banker at that firm had it in his head that

45 Memo to John White, May 18, 1972.

he was ours for all eternity. Even after I had been appointed treasurer, he boasted that he would be continuing in his role. Said Charles MacNaughton: "You select Salomon Brothers, not that son of a bitch."

I had lunch with William Salomon, the top partner, who introduced me to Richard Schmeelk, the partner in charge of "Canadar," as Schmeelk pronounced it with his New York accent. I liked him, and he became our main contact in New York. I used to kid Schmeelk about how he never spent a dime when he was doing business in Canada. He would fly up and back on the same day. There was no hotel room, and we usually bought his lunch. Other than taxi fares to and from the airport, he left no money behind.

Over forty years, Schmeelk helped raise billions of dollars for the federal government, crown corporations, Ontario, several other provinces, and many corporations. Such was his reputation that he became known as Mr. Canada, the title of his 2007 memoirs. Sometimes when I travelled with Schmeelk, arrangements went awry. While we were in Austin, Texas, Schmeelk introduced me to the state treasurer, Warren Harding (not the U.S. president of the same name), who had succeeded Jesse James (not the Wild West gunman). Harding and James had once become so intoxicated while travelling by train that they were warned by the conductor about their loud behaviour. "Don't you know who we are?" they replied. "We're Jesse James and Warren G. Harding." The conductor thought they'd made up the names and promptly threw them off the train.

We urged Harding to allow Texas municipalities to purchase Hydro bonds by extolling such facts as the vast amounts of trade between our two countries and how we shared the world's longest undefended border. Harding was unimpressed, saying, "Down here, our border is with Mexico. Maybe we should be buying Mexican bonds."

Disappointed, we left his office only to discover our limo had disappeared along with our coats on what, for Texas, was a chilly day. Nobody had thought to write down a name or phone number. Finally, Ontario Hydro President Milan Nastich recalled that the car belonged to an undertaker. We looked up names in the Yellow Pages and were finally reunited with our driver and our belongings. The car had been needed for a funeral. For years after, I'd ask Schmeelk, "What *was* the name of that funeral parlour in Austin?"

The response to my speech in Dallas was kind under the circumstances. A follow-up note from the Canadian Consulate Office in Dallas said, "A complete lack of apparent reaction to the speech by either the audience or subsequently the press may have been as much attributable to a wait-and-see caution about Canada's political uncertainties, voiced in almost any discussion among the local investment community these days, as to any lack of luster in the content or delivery of the address."

After Schmeelk retired from Salomon Brothers, his interest in Canada continued. He founded CAI Capital Corporation with others, including David Culver, former CEO and Chairman of Alcan Aluminum Ltd., and Walter Wriston, former chairman of Citibank. CAI invested in and provided advice to diverse Canadian companies such as Country Style Food Services, owners of the donut chain of the same name, and Bio-Research Laboratories, formerly part of Connaught Labs.

In 1985, Schmeelk set up a $1-million fund (and later added another $1 million) to provide fellowships up to $40,000 over four years to middle managers willing to interrupt their careers for postgraduate studies. Schmeelk saw the awards as a way of strengthening relations between English and French Canada. Francophones attend the University of Western Ontario; Anglophones go to Laval. After thirty years, more than eighty scholarships have been awarded, a successful bridge between our two solitudes.

▼

As treasurer, you want to get spending right by balancing the demands of your cabinet colleagues and society as a whole with the reality of what is financially possible. In advance of the budget, there's a certain tension, even a frisson of excitement at times. What you're doing matters deeply to the economy in general and people's lives in particular. As if all that weren't enough, the political future of the government hinges on your efforts.

In the 1972 budget, my second, I was able to reduce the planned increase in provincial spending to just 4.5 per cent, well down from the previous year. At the same time, we increased revenue by setting higher taxes on beer, wine, cigarettes, liquor, and gasoline. I continued to limit growth in the public service to a 1 per cent gain on staff levels of 71,000 after a 2 per cent increase the previous year. Even that activity was not enough to stop an increase in the predicted deficit to $600 million, mainly because we were locked into grants to municipalities, hospitals, schools, and universities.

While it was the largest deficit ever for Ontario, it would have been far worse had I not resisted the siren call to increase public spending to boost the flagging economy. People cited economist John Maynard Keynes and his belief that governments should prime the pumps by spending more and incurring deeper deficits during difficult times. Not only did I not agree, I'd never even heard of the man. "It is not axiomatic that the only way out of any unemployment problem is through inflated public spending," I said. "The private sector is still the dominant part of our economy."[46]

There were other ministries larger than Treasury, but none as powerful. *Windsor Star* cartoonist Vic Roschkov drew me sitting on a throne, giving me the title "Lord Poobah, Duke of Chatham, Prince of Kent, Super Minister, King, Emperor."

Indeed, there was a risk in my taking on so much. On the one hand, the premier had rewarded me for my support. On the other hand, he may have been loading me down so I had no time to plot his overthrow and take his place. A *Globe and Mail* article published on July 7, 1972, quoted unnamed sources saying I was in over my head. The article went on to describe "the almost daily sight of Mr. Davis sitting benignly by while [McKeough] caught most of the opposition flak in the Legislature. Relations between the two men could never be described as close or even cordial."

---

46 *Ottawa Journal*, March 29, 1972, p. 6.

For the record, Bill Davis and I always got along well. Like Robarts before him, Davis knew I could manage my duties without his direct supervision. I accepted the compliments and the criticism, too. That's politics. However, my high-flying status didn't last. I was probably cruising for a fall.

12

▼

Honour Upheld

In 1972, a series of scandals embarrassed the Bill Davis government. The first began quietly enough when Ontario Hydro decided to build a new head office in order to save $1 million a year by owning rather than renting. Once Hydro had made that announcement, I told Hydro Chairman George Gathercole to involve the department of public works so government-bidding procedures were properly followed. Subsequently, during a trip to Japan, Gathercole spent considerable time telling me what a great proposal Ellis-Don had made, a conversation I conveniently forgot.

Hydro eventually awarded the $44-million contract to Canada Square Corp. Ltd., a development firm headed by Gerhard Moog, a friend of Premier Davis. Don Smith, who founded Ellis-Don Ltd., of London, Ontario, and who was well connected with both Liberals and Conservatives, complained his company's bid hadn't been given due consideration. John Cronyn, chairman of the Committee on Government Productivity and an Ellis-Don director, urged Smith not to make a fuss. Smith assumed Cronyn meant if he didn't shut up, he'd get no more provincial work, but that was not Cronyn's intent.

At one point, Joyce sent our friend Cronyn a note saying, "Keep your chin up. Better to be involved with Don Smith than Gerda Munsinger.

We love you!" I later admitted to the Select Committee investigating the contract that I knew Smith but added, "I'd be delighted if I didn't." The committee found no wrongdoing by Ontario Hydro.

The second scandal ensnared Dalton Bales. In 1969, while he was minister of labour, Bales and two associates paid $252,000 for ninety-nine acres of land near Markham, north of Toronto. The deal, revealed by the *Globe and Mail* on August 4, 1972, raised questions of whether Bales — who was by then attorney general — had been aware of any official zoning plans that might increase the property value. An official investigation found Bales had no insider knowledge. Even so, Bales turned over the land to a trustee to sell, with all profits donated to charity. Though Bales also offered to resign from cabinet, Davis asked him to remain, and he did. The third maladroit incident involved Bert Lawrence using a government plane to take his wife, family, and a government official to Cuba on what he claimed was a business trip. He survived, too.

On August 28, the *Globe and Mail* ran a story by John Zaritsky under the damning headline: "McKeough approved sub-division of land he had financial interest in." I had done nothing of the sort. As a family doing business in Chatham since 1847, we McKeoughs had long been investors in the community. It was, therefore, no departure when, in 1968, my sister, my brother, and I each put $4,050 into a new holding company, McKeough Investments Ltd., to bring together various family interests. We subsequently invested a further $15,000 for a one-third interest in Triple Ten Investments, giving me a one-ninth interest in Triple Ten. Triple Ten then became a 75 per cent owner in South Chatham Estates, which paid $375,000 for seventy-five acres of land in Chatham for a housing development. I took no part in any of those decisions.

Nor was I involved in 1969, when South Chatham Estates applied to the Ministry of Municipal Affairs to build a subdivision. As usual, ministry officials circulated the application to ten different agencies for review. After comments were received, the proposal was redesigned with a reduced number of lots as well as restrictions in accordance with conservation rules. As minister, I did not see, let alone approve of, either the initial proposal or the final plan. At no time was I consulted, nor did I take any steps to involve myself.

Nor was this subdivision any kind of furtive act; the ministry trumpeted the plan as number 2000 among the subdivisions created under the recently revised rules. I was informed that the celebrated plan was in Chatham, but I was not told of my ownership position. I did not personally sign this or any other similar document. My "signature" was one of many such rubber-stamped approvals that day and no different than that of the signature of the minister of transportation on a driver's licence.

Had I been asked to sign, I would have read it and realized the relevance. I read everything presented for my signature carefully. I once reviewed a letter that referred to my saying hello to a township reeve at a conference and mentioned how much I enjoyed meeting his wife. I sent the letter back for revision with the scrawled directive, "That was not his wife."

▼

On August 9, after the Bales incident, Premier Davis asked every cabinet minister to give him a list of all land, commercial property, and shares of private corporations they or members of their immediate families owned. My list of holdings was delivered to the premier's office on August 22 and went far beyond his request. I submitted nine detailed statements covering my affairs along with those of my wife, my children, my mother, my father's estate, and the estate of my maternal grandmother.

Chatham Mayor Doug Allin called me the next day to say Zaritsky was "snooping around" city hall about South Chatham Estates. Since I was leaving immediately for Europe and would be seeing Premier Davis during my trip, I took along a copy of my covering letter, but not the detailed statements, in case he had not seen my filing.

My first appointment was in Munich with Deutsche Bank on Friday, August 25, to finalize a fifteen-year 100-million deutsche marks (C$31 million) loan. Deutsche Bank didn't deal in eighths. They wanted 6.25 per cent interest even though they admitted 6 was more appropriate. Before I arrived for the signing, our advisors Ted Medland of Wood Gundy and Bryson Farrill of McLeod Young Weir beat up on Deutsche Bank, saying, "McKeough's just a new treasurer. Give him a break." I signed at 6 per cent!

Saturday I met with Premier Davis, gave him my covering letter, and orally outlined my holdings. That evening we attended the official opening of the 1972 Summer Olympics, games tragically marred by a terrorist attack and the deaths of eleven Israeli athletes and coaches. Sunday we flew to Zurich to finalize our first bond issue with the Union Bank of Switzerland (UBS). When we left the hotel room for dinner, someone mistakenly left the balcony doors open, and a violent rainstorm caused water damage in the room. It was as if nature was sending a warning something bad was about to happen.

On Monday, August 28, I called my deputy minister, Bill Palmer. He read me the *Globe* story which included extensive quotes from my brother Stewart saying I knew about the land deal. I also spoke with Joyce by phone. She was the first to say, "You know you'll have to resign." That night, for several hours, Ian Macdonald played devil's advocate with me at the hotel, putting forward arguments why I didn't need to resign. I was not convinced.

When I met with Davis to talk about the article, he did not seem upset with me. I signed the letter of intent with UBS for a $20-million loan, cancelled the rest of my appointments, and headed home with my aide Paul Little on Tuesday. When we arrived in Toronto, my staff arranged for me to use the stairs leading from the aircraft directly onto the tarmac in order avoid the media waiting in the terminal.

I was driven to the nearby lands and forests hangar and immediately took off for Chatham. There was some question as to whether I had cleared customs, but Little assured the media I had. On the plane to Chatham I found all the newspapers detailing my problem. Portions had already been read to me, but seeing everything in print was far worse. I was appalled. I cried half the way home.

At Bally McKeough the next morning, I looked out my window and saw a cluster of journalists standing on the driveway. I walked out to meet them and said, "It's not the first time my resignation has been called for and it won't be the last, I suppose."[47] I spent the morning receiving phone calls and telegrams, most of which said, "hang tough."

Among the callers was John Robarts who asked, "What are you doing?"

"Well, I'm thinking," I said.

"You'd better get down here to Toronto instead of sitting there and thinking."

Robarts invited me to his Westbury suite at 6 p.m. When I arrived at Queen's Park, reporters were everywhere looking for me, so I took to the tunnels connecting the government buildings and was able to get to his hotel unseen. When I arrived, I was probably 60 per cent leaning toward resigning. Robarts never said, "You should resign," but that was exactly what he was telling me. The needle moved to 80 per cent.

At 7 p.m. I arrived in my office in the Frost Building, where I joined Paul Little, Phil Lind, Ed Mahoney, Milt Farrow, and Eddie Goodman. After I heard their urgings to stay in office, I may have leaned that way, but only slightly. Still, I needed to make a statement. Farrow, who worked in the Ministry of Municipal Affairs, had provided a memo detailing the journey of a subdivision application on its way to approval. I dictated some paragraphs about my involvement in South Chatham Estates as well as my report on my holdings. Lind and Mahoney worked on the more difficult rhetoric of the concluding section. About 10 p.m., I decided I was no longer making a contribution, so I took some notes written by Lind and headed to my Toronto apartment.

After I left, Goodman said to Lind, "Something funny is going

---

47 *Ottawa Journal*, August 31, 1972, p. 29.

on here. I'm here to save Darcy, and I'm not sure he wants to be saved." With his trademark lisp, Goodman continued (referring to the trouble George Hees, a cabinet minister in the Diefenbaker government in the 1960s, had with Gerda Munsinger): "Heethy was fucking a whore. Not only was she a whore, she was a spy whore. We got Heethy off. Why can't we get Darcy off?"

The next morning, Thursday, August 31, as I sat on the toilet — where some of my best thinking gets done — I read Lind's notes. His concluding paragraph stood out: "Bearing in mind the facts and my role therein, my own honesty and integrity, the doubts which have been and no doubt will continue to be expressed, and most of all the principles in which I and my party believe, I have this morning submitted my resignation as a minister of the crown to the Premier." I decided my only course was resignation.

In my mind, a conflict of interest and the *appearance* of a conflict hold equal weight. In this case, there certainly was the appearance of a conflict. I was not going to let Premier Davis do what he did for Dalton Bales by urging me to stay. I held myself to my own higher standard; I knew when it was time to go. I had not done anything wrong, but a mistake had been made. I did not want the party or my leader in any way tarnished.

I slightly altered Phil's final few lines, and at 10:30 a.m. phoned Davis in London to tell him I intended to resign that morning. He did not try to change my mind. With the decision taken, Paul Little told Zaritsky of the *Globe* that the press conference that morning would be in Chatham. When I met the media at Queen's Park at 11:30 a.m., I had the pleasure of imagining Zaritsky, westbound somewhere on Highway 401, listening to me on the radio, far from the action. That was the only fun part of the day.

I made a thirteen-page detailed statement describing the lengthy subdivision approval process, how many parties were involved, how many changes were made along the way, and how the closest I ever got to any of it was my facsimile signature. "The fact remains that, regardless of my good intentions, an embarrassing situation has been created for me and for my colleagues in government, and doubts have been raised in the minds of some people in Ontario about the integrity of their representatives in government," I said. "I deeply regret that this has happened. I am satisfied that I, personally, have done nothing wrong. But the issue here is confidence in the integrity of the system. To my mind this is paramount. It is more important than any political party and more important than any individual in politics. I feel that I am guilty of no more than having made an error in judgment. Even my political opponents have not accused me of being dishonest.

"However, it is my conclusion that doubts have been raised and that these doubts may continue to be raised so long as I remain in this Ministry and Cabinet. Those who know me appreciate that I cannot live with these doubts for the months ahead. I cannot tolerate those doubts, knowing in my own mind that I do not deserve them."

Typical of the reaction to my declaration was that of Gordon Sinclair, a crusty curmudgeon, who gave his personal version of the news just before noon on Toronto radio station CFRB. That morning he was following bulletins coming over the wire from the press conference. At first he was derisive, saying this was just another case of a politician dodging his responsibility and refusing to come clean. Then, when he realized I was actually resigning, his tone changed abruptly on air, and he became almost lyrical about the example I was setting. When I learned later that Sinclair was on my side, I knew there would be many listeners who felt the same way.

For me, it was like losing an election. You have to be careful what you say in your concession speech. You don't want to sound morose or angry, and you certainly shouldn't blame your opponent for running a nasty campaign. Instead, you want to sound positive, because you're not making the last speech of that campaign; you're making the first speech of the next.

Among those who called to commiserate were John Turner; Robert Stanfield; Anglican Bishop Carmen Queen of Huron; and the Lieutenant Governor of Ontario, Ross Macdonald. I asked Macdonald why such a distinguished Liberal would worry about a Conservative in trouble. "One of my ministers has resigned," he said.

"That is of concern to me." I had a final drink with a few officials, packed up my desk, and headed home to Chatham.

▼

Prior to my statement, the *London Free Press* had denounced my actions in an editorial. "Mr. McKeough must have been singularly dull not to have understood the highly unethical position in which he put himself. His proper course would have been to have divested himself of his interest in the company involved before considering approval of the subdivision."[48]

The paper's views were transformed once I had resigned. "Though we are neither his supporters nor his opponents, we believe him. Indeed, several days before his resignation, an editorial in the *London Free Press* stressed that the McKeough family interests were well known in Kent County, to his political supporters and opponents alike. We did not then, and do not now, think Mr. McKeough was dishonest. As a member of the legislature, as a member of the cabinet and as a candidate for his party's leadership in 1971, Mr. McKeough has served the people of Ontario well."[49]

Even the *Globe and Mail* was gracious. "Mr. McKeough's resignation does him honour. He does not believe — and the evidence supports him — that he used his cabinet position to advance his personal prosperity."[50] Liberal Leader Robert Nixon, who had called for my resignation, now softened his views. "It had never been suggested that Mr. McKeough had in any way been guilty of dishonesty. His decision substantiates his reputation for integrity."[51] NDP leader Stephen Lewis went even further, allowing that he "could foresee Mr. McKeough being reappointed Provincial Treasurer within an appropriate absence of a year or two — probably before the next election."[52]

48 *London Free Press*, August 29, 1972
49 *London Free Press*, September 1, 1972.
50 *Globe and Mail*, September 1, 1972.
51 *Oshawa Times*, September 1, 1972.
52 *Kitchener-Waterloo Record*, August 31, 1972.

After returning from Europe, Premier Davis officially accepted my resignation. "The decision to accept Mr. McKeough's resignation does not in any way reflect upon his personal integrity, nor does it imply any misconduct on his part," he said. "Mr. McKeough's decision to submit his resignation exemplifies the high standards of personal and public responsibility which he has set for himself and with which I fully concur."

Davis replaced me as treasurer with the previous officeholder, Charles MacNaughton, and subsequently brought in tougher conflict rules for cabinet, calling for public disclosure of mortgages, stocks, and land; no longer permitting day-to-day business outside government; and ordering blind trusts to be administered by an independent trustee.

I did not blame anyone for my troubles, but when Paul Little next saw my brother Stewart, who had been quoted extensively in the initial *Globe* story saying I knew all about the subdivision, Little said to Stewart, "I'm the guy who told the press to go to hell — after you had told them everything else!"

The legislature was not sitting, so I was in Chatham with nothing much to do but work in the garden. My mother decided to get me some reading material from the library. She arrived at the librarian's desk with two piles of books, saying, "These are for me, those are for my son." The librarian pointed out she was over her limit and suggested that, if I was a member, the books meant for me could be taken out using my card. When the librarian looked in the files, there was no card in my name. Asked the librarian, "Does he own property in Chatham?" My mother laughed and replied, "That's why I'm taking out some books for him."

▾

That was a hard, dark time for me. I seriously considered leaving politics. I received a letter from Robarts saying, "Be of good heart — I am more than ever convinced that you did the right thing — and have left the way wide open for an honourable return to the world of public affairs."

If I were to stay in politics, I wanted to alter my work-life balance. I made a list about how I planned to slow my pace, spend Mondays and Fridays at home with family and constituents, be more political with caucus and riding associations, delegate more duties, take more personal time for books and movies, and space major speeches further apart.

It helped greatly that I received hundreds of letters from people who continued to think well of me despite my public humiliation. Three weeks after I resigned, I was able to give a speech with a thoughtful and optimistic tone. "I hope that those people who decide to serve the public interest will not be disheartened by setbacks. The knocks of public life can be hard, but life is too short for post-mortems. There is too much that needs to be done and can be done by each of us."[53]

I didn't give many interviews, but I did agree to go on Fraser Kelly's Sunday television show *Fraser Kelly Reports*. The *Globe* promoted the interview with a caricature by cartoonist Edward Franklin on the cover of its TV guide showing my face in the centre of a rose, with the clear implication I had come through smelling like the proverbial rose. After the taping, I gave Kelly a six-quart basket of tomatoes. Even in such circumstances, I was my father's son, sharing the Kent County bounty.

Charlie MacNaughton let me use his office in the main Legislative Building, next to the ladies' washroom. After hours, I used the ladies; the men's was miles away. On November 21, the first day of the next sitting, I attended caucus and received a welcome round of applause. I was assigned a front-row seat in the House, closest to Speaker Allan Reuter, the same spot occupied by Robarts after he had stepped down as premier.

Two weeks later, I was sitting in the House listening to NDP

---

53 Speech to the 13th Biennial Conference of the Province's Conservation Authorities, September 18, 1972.

leader Stephen Lewis carp about the investment tax credit I had introduced for corporations. Revenue Minister Allan Grossman said the cost to the Treasury was $27.5 million with more claims expected. Lewis jumped on the number, noting I had said it would cost $135 million.

"You were $100 million off," Lewis said, looking at me.

"You're in the nineteenth century," I shouted.

"No wonder they threw you out of cabinet," said Lewis. "You couldn't add."

I hollered a reply, but it got lost amid the bedlam and was not recorded by *Hansard*. "They both loved it," said the *Globe and Mail*. "The splendid bellow of Darcy McKeough was heard again in the Ontario Legislature yesterday."[54] I was back at work and feeling in fine form again.

---

54 *Globe and Mail,* December 7, 1972.

13
▾

Back in the Saddle

My energy connections went back a long way. When I started work at McKeough Sons after graduation from Western, I often saw the Scots-born Colonel Thomas Weir, Union Gas general manager and a director from 1943 to 1970, having lunch at the Kent Club. One bitter winter day, I remember saying the low temperatures must be good for Union Gas. "Nae, Darcy," he said, "it's the wund that makes it a good day." As long as I was an MPP, my biggest "constituent" was Union Gas, a large employer with head offices in Chatham.

Even after I resigned, Bruce Willson, the president of Union Gas, and Larry O'Connor, lawyer for the union, continued to keep me informed about the concerns of Union Gas and what they perceived to be Ontario's "inaction" in energy matters. I arranged several meetings for them with Minister of Energy and Resources Development Jack Simonett and Bill Davis.

I don't know who suggested there perhaps was a role in energy for me — probably Tom Kierans, a Toronto investment banker who was a long-time trusted advisor to me and to the government. My diary indicates he and I met with Davis on December 14, 1972, and that I met with Davis again on December 21. "He feels he cannot take me into the Cabinet at this time, will take me back as Treasurer in May or June," I wrote in my diary. "In the meantime, he asked me to take on an energy job, probably as a P. Asst. to him."

On January 15, 1973, Davis announced I would be his parliamentary assistant with special responsibility in the field of energy, a clear sign that all was forgiven. The terms of reference for my new role, effective the following month, included energy, Ontario Hydro, and relations with other governments on energy policy.

I also negotiated a novel pay arrangement that would never happen today. I had taken a reduction in annual pay of $21,000 when I resigned as minister. A parliamentary assistant was paid only an extra $5,000 on top of the regular MP's salary so I asked the party to make up the difference, which they did. I sent Bill Kelly a monthly invoice (taxable of course), which was paid by the Ontario Progressive Conservative Party.

Even prior to my resignation, I had taken an active role in energy by urging submissions to federal Energy Minister Joe Greene and by writing letters to Alberta Minister of Federal and Intergovernmental Affairs Don Getty which promoted a federal–provincial conference on energy policy.

Some other groundwork on the topic had already been laid by the Advisory Committee on Energy, chaired by J. J. Deutsch, principal of Queen's University. His findings, released the same day as my appointment, noted that the days of abundant and cheap energy were about to end. Ontario was dependent for 80 per cent of its energy on out-of-province resources, so any price increases would have a deleterious impact on industry and consumers.

At that point, the federal and provincial governments really had no energy policy except to create favourable business conditions for production, distribution, and export of oil and natural gas. One of my first tasks was to decide if the province should have a minister of energy, as recommended by Dr. Deutsch, a post not previously existing. The only related role was minister of energy resources with its responsibilities for conservation, the Ontario Water Resources Commission, and the Ontario Energy Board, which regulated the natural gas industry but not Ontario Hydro.

Ontario Hydro did not report through a minister until 1972, although government had some control. The prime minister appointed the chairman and the four board members, the treasurer had some oversight because the Province guaranteed their debt, and one of the Hydro board members was usually an MPP who inevitably was "consumed" by Hydro and became their spokesman. At various times, that person was Bob Macaulay, Bill Davis briefly, Bob Boyer for nearly ten years, and Arthur Evans.

In my new role, I gathered several people, including Dick Dillon, who was then the director of Task Force Hydro, an offshoot of the Committee on Government Productivity; Jim Smith, a Hydro veteran who worked for Dillon; Stuart Clarkson, who had been the executive director of the Deutsch Committee; Paul Little, a consultant; and Ralph Hedlin, who wrote speeches. Stewart's wife, Dorothy, had some fun writing a poem for my fortieth birthday that month:

> Again Darcy's traveling first class
> With the Hoipaloy and the Brass
> The reason of course is
> He's in Natural Resources
> With a tendency to pass a little gas

▾

As a first step, Premier Davis and I met with Alberta Premier Peter Lougheed, who told us natural gas prices could double. In addition, I met with federal Minister of Energy Donald Macdonald, executives at Imperial Oil, and other producers, as well as Pollution Probe. I also attended a lunchtime discussion session at Holy Trinity Church in Toronto to hear what consumers thought. There I spoke to Mel Watkins, leader of the Waffle movement that had broken away from the NDP. We agreed that, between us, our knowledge of energy would fill only a slim volume at that point. One thing was certain: while no one could predict, with any precision, how high energy prices would go, it was clear that increases would outstrip any rise in wages and would restrain economic growth in Ontario.

I did not seek to be minister of energy. In fact, rather than create another ministry, I thought we would be better off with a body of experts to develop research leading to an energy policy. "A group of thinkers rather than doers," was how I described it. As a result, in my June report to the premier, I recommended an Energy Secretariat reporting to the provincial secretary for resources development.

My report of sixty-two pages contained forty-six recommendations covering the importance of conservation, environmental protection, and the need for major capital investments by both the public and private sectors to increase the supply of energy. I conceded that the price of energy produced in Alberta should increase, saying, "The era of cheap energy has ended." I also recommended that Ontario build nuclear generators, invest in Alberta's oil sands, and help develop a national electricity grid to aid the smaller, power-poor provinces.

While I was agreeable to higher prices, I believed the consuming provinces must be protected against egregious increases. That led to my most controversial recommendation, my insistence that "the Government of Ontario should take such steps as are necessary to test the constitutionality of any actions by the Alberta government which are not in the national interests of Canada." As a manufacturing and consuming province, it was in Ontario's interest to keep prices as low as possible for as long as possible, but I could see rocky negotiations ahead with Alberta. Davis agreed with the broad sweep of my report.

Writing in the *London Free Press*, Harold Greer was also complimentary. "All in all, it represents an aggressive attempt, and the first of its kind, by an energy-short government to deal comprehensively with the energy crisis. The essential political fact of that crisis is that, barring some scientific miracle yet to be discovered, the supply, demand and price of energy have become and will remain the direct concern of government. Mr. McKeough, to his credit, has recognized and accepted it."[55]

---

55 *London Free Press*, June 12, 1973.

My fiercest critic was Stephen Lewis, yet I had developed a very unusual relationship with him. At root, we had little in common politically. As a leftist, he was on the other end of the spectrum. Our use of language was just as far apart. Where I was straightforward and plain, he would employ words like "milieu" and "persiflage" with which I was not familiar.

Still, I respected his intelligence, and I think he respected mine. Although we tangled in the legislature, over the years he sent me many handwritten notes. A year after I lost the leadership race in 1971, he had written, "You shouldn't be quite so smug about things. The future may dictate that you're demoted to the premiership." In the midst of the energy crisis, he wrote, "Darcy, you almost never lose and those you lose are fully recouped. Be patient, there'll be room at the top."

The *Globe* summed up the legislative sitting by saying, "[McKeough] quickly defined energy positions for Ontario in clear, toughly worded language. He is odds-on favourite to become the first head of the new ministry; if so, he should provide a real boost to a Cabinet that, on the whole, is sagging."[56] An editorial cartoon by Franklin in the *Globe* showed me as a brawny and naked Zeus with my vital parts adroitly covered by a trillium. The framed art still hangs in our kitchen. Of the many political images on display at Bally McKeough, that one has always attracted the most visitor attention.

▼

When Premier Davis asked me to be minister of energy on June 12, I was pleased to be invited back into cabinet, but I had some reluctance about the role. I countered with suggestions about what a cabinet shuffle could look like to make me treasurer again. If Energy were my only option, I wanted to be sure the position came with the same power and prestige as I had enjoyed before. I asked if I would again be listed second in the order of precedence, if I would

---

56 *Globe and Mail*, June 23, 1973.

be reappointed to the powerful Policy and Priorities Board, and if he would give me a free hand as minister. I also wanted a commitment from him on the timing of my move to Treasury. I didn't get that last item, but I was satisfied with the answers to the rest of my questions so, on June 29, I agreed to be minister of energy.

I arranged for offices in the Suncor building at the corner of Bay and Wellesley Streets, a block from Queen's Park, and recruited Richard Dillon as my deputy minister, a real catch. As founding dean of Engineering at the University of Western Ontario, Dick was close to John Robarts and John Cronyn. He was conscientious, inquisitive, hard working, and tough, but fun to be with. Dillon, in turn, recruited a staff of about twenty-five including Ben Wilson, from Management Board; Paul Cunningham, as administrator; Bruce MacOdrum, a Toronto lawyer and member of the Sierra Club; and Jim Smith, from Hydro. Paul Little returned as my executive assistant. I was also assigned a driver, Chuck Lamoureaux, who later went with me to Treasury and then on to the private sector at Union Gas. I was not one of those stuffy bosses who sat in the back seat. I always liked to be up front with Chuck where I was more comfortable and could refresh myself with a fifteen-minute nap en route.

The media, including my sometime nemesis, the *Globe and Mail*, was generally supportive. It reported: "Darcy McKeough was barely five minutes back in the Ontario Cabinet when Treasurer John White shouldered his way through well wishers and reporters. He stuck out his hand, slapped the McKeough back and grinned: 'Welcome back, young fella.' Politicians do a lot of hearty congratulating, but Mr. White probably really meant it this time. The return of Mr. McKeough should have the same effect on the Cabinet as a pep pill on a tiring athlete. Premier William Davis has indicated how important he regards Mr. McKeough's presence by immediately appointing him to the Policies and Priorities Board."[57]

▼

---

57 *Globe and Mail*, July 7, 1973.

During my eighteen months as minister of energy, one of my main goals was to restrain Ontario Hydro. Hydro thought they, not the government, ran the province. To be sure, they had created an enviable and reliable system. In the 1970s, Hydro had eight nuclear generators, four at Pickering and four at Bruce. Five of them ranked in the global top ten in terms of sustained output, a great credit to Atomic Energy of Canada Ltd. as the designer, but also to Hydro as the operator.

But Hydro was basically an engineering company and the board of directors, headed by George Gathercole, the chairman, existed only to serve the engineers — an ass-backwards approach if ever I saw one. Hydro staff and engineers did all the planning and strategizing, then sent their decisions to Gathercole to take to the board. Time and time again, once Gathercole had concluded his presentation, one of the tame directors would say, "Well, George, I think you have said it all." And that would be that. The board never discussed, altered, or sent back for reconsideration any staff proposal.

The unions further complicated matters. It wasn't just the demands of the Power Workers' Union, but also the Association of Hydro Engineers. In the 1970s, there were professionals at Hydro making more than $100,000 a year. Strikes and lockouts were not possible; management would never "run the store." Salaries just kept rising exponentially.

Even when it came to relatively minor matters, Hydro could be stubborn. At one point, Hydro wanted to expropriate some Kent County farmland in Raleigh and Harwich townships for eight miles of transmission tower lines. I urged them to use the Highway 401 right-of-way instead, which the province already owned. That way, they would save money and no farmers would lose land. Hydro claimed road salt in the winter would rust the towers. I finally won the argument; the towers were built where I suggested. Forty years later, they show no signs of rust.

Hydro couldn't even seem to figure out future needs. In 1977, Hydro predicted demand would grow by 7 per cent a year, an unimaginable prospect. At that rate, the system would have to double in size every ten years. My officials crunched the numbers and concluded

Off to Ridley College, St. Catharines, Ontario, in 1954, with my mother and sister, Ann.

In the cast of *The Importance of Being Earnest* for the Dramatic Society of Ridley College, 1948.
I played Lady Bracknell.

Receiving the Headmaster's prize from the Governor General, Lord Alexander, at Ridley in 1951.

With Ridley College's Upper School headmaster, Dr. J. R. Hamilton, 1951.

(*top left*) Officer cadet W. D. McKeough, University Naval Training Division, 1951; I later reached the rank of sub-lieutenant, RCNVR. (*top right*) With my mother in New York City in 1953. (*bottom left*) With Eunice Grindlay in *The Lady's Not for Burning*, Chatham Little Theatre, 1957. (*bottom right*) My father, Grant McKeough, c. 1960.

Joyce and me at the Toronto Hunt Club after our wedding,
at Trinity College Chapel, Toronto, on June 18, 1965.

Riding Western in the Arizona desert: Joyce's parents, Senator David Walker
and "Bunty" (Elizabeth); Joyce; and Joyce's brother and sister, David and Diane.

With John Robarts in Chatham, June 6, 1966, at the opening
of the new head office building of Union Gas.

Our son Jamie's christening, with John Robarts, October 7, 1966.

(*top*) My mother, Joyce, and me, on election night, October 17, 1967. (*bottom left*) Greeting the crowd at the leadership convention of February 12, 1971. (*bottom right*) A Donato cartoon that ran in the *Toronto Sun* on August 29, 1972, the day after the South Chatham story ran in the *Globe and Mail*.

(*top*) Joyce, Stewart, and Jamie with Prime Minister Diefenbaker in his parliamentary office, in 1972. (*bottom left*) Coming up smelling like a rose after my resignation: a Franklin cartoon that ran in the *Globe and Mail*, September 15, 1972. (*bottom right*) As Zeus, no less, tabling the Energy Report, June 7, 1973; a Franklin cartoon that ran on June 9 in the *Globe and Mail*.

(*top*) With Donald Macdonald (centre) and the Rt. Hon. Ted Heath, Prime Minister of Britain (right), at 10 Downing Street, in 1973. (*bottom*) Giving John Turner a copy of my budget, at a Federal-Provincial Conference of First Ministers in 1975. (*opposite*) On Budget Night, April 19, 1977, I relished saying, of the Opposition, "They are nothing more than the Parliamentary equivalent of a Gong Show over there" (a line given to me by my assistant Tom MacMillan).

If cutbacks fail, would the Premier consider annexing Alberta

(*top left*) This Franklin cartoon ran in the *Globe and Mail*, January 16, 1975, two days after I became Treasurer again, highlighting one of the problems with municipalities: Toronto's bylaw, advocated by Mayor Crombie, which banned new buildings higher than forty-five feet.

(*top right*) The restraint tours continued, hitting Metro Toronto and the hospitals in the pocketbook, leading to this Franklin cartoon in the *Globe and Mail*, March 3, 1976, captioned: "If cutbacks fail, would the Premier consider annexing Alberta?" (*bottom*) I took a crack at Joe Clark's policy of increasing the deficit in a speech at a party for Joyce and me on January 27, 1979, five months after my retirement. Later, Maureen Clark stayed overnight with us when giving a speech in Chatham. She was not amused to find this on the wall. The Mallette cartoon ran in the *Globe and Mail*, January 30, 1979.

Five Treasurers of Ontario: with me (left) are James Allan, Frank Miller, Charles MacNaughton, and John White, at a dinner I gave at the Toronto Club for Frank Miller in 1980.

The Davises and us, at the Stratford Festival, c. 1982.

A "board meeting," October 11, 1984, regarding the Leadership, held at
McLeod Young Weir: Paul Curley (left), John Thompson, Tom MacMillan,
Rendall Dick, Red Wilson, John Laschinger, me, Jim Hayhurst, Bill Watson, Kirk Foley,
Tom Kierans, Paul Little. Not attending were John Cronyn and Phil Lind.

A pen and ink drawing of me by Irma
Coucill, commissioned by Joyce in 1984,
when I was at Union Gas.

23/4/85

To Darcy McKeough, our shepherd who led us to battle against hemorrhaging deficits. On behalf of your compatriots at the BCNI
Tom d'Aquino

A Mallette cartoon that ran in *Canadian Business* in April 1985, in connection with my chairmanship of the Nielsen Task Force. A print of the cartoon was given to me by Tom D'Aquino, with the inscription, "To Darcy McKeough, our shepherd who led us to battle against hemorrhaging deficits. On behalf of your compatriots at the BCNI."

The *Globe and Mail* ran this Franklin cartoon on October 15, 1985, after I was fired by Union Gas.

(*top left*) My Union Gas portrait. (*top right*) With Governor General Ray Hnatyshyn, Rideau Hall, upon my investiture as an Officer of the Order of Canada, April 13, 1994. (*bottom*) With Brian Mulroney and Gord Bell, during a dinner at the Toronto Club, c. 1990.

(*top*) Joyce and Sir Neil Shaw with the Queen Mother at Titness, UK, June 8, 1997.
(*bottom right*) With the Queen, at Ontario Place, June 29, 1997. (*bottom left*) The *Toronto Sun*
ran this Dewar cartoon January 2, 2009, after we sold McKeough Supply Inc.
I don't know who the cartoon referred to, but it could have been me!

(*top*) Stew, Julia, Kate, Jamie, and Joyce with me at Bally McKeough, in 2009. (*bottom left*) Looking at our home, Bally McKeough, from Lake Erie in 2009. (*bottom right*) At our fiftieth wedding anniversary, the Toronto Club, June 18, 2015.

growth would be closer to 5 per cent. We ended up being right; Hydro was wrong. It was a crucial difference and meant we could spend a lot less. Hydro wouldn't listen and proposed a nuclear plant at Darlington with a capacity of three thousand five hundred megawatts, twice what Niagara Falls produced in hydroelectric power. Darlington was approved, even though the request never came before cabinet. I can only assume Premier Davis gave the go-ahead on his own.

Construction of Darlington finally began in 1981, long after I'd left Queen's Park. It fell far behind schedule and ended up costing $14 billion, more than three times the initial estimate of $4 billion. The first unit did not come on line until 1990 with two more units following in 1992–93. During the period from proposal to completion, there were no shortages and no brownouts. Hydro's earlier panic about the supply of electricity was unfounded.

While I constantly sought control of wayward spending, I also spent time on other issues affecting energy. One of my suggestions for energy conservation, making daylight saving time permanent, was based on my belief that Ontarians favoured such a step. A witty response came from none other than Robertson Davies, one of the country's greatest authors. "Daylight Saving Time is not very important, for the sun will continue in his old obstinate course, and we shall either go to work in the dark, or come home after work in the dark," he wrote in a letter to the editor of the *Globe and Mail*. "I confess that I like the latter course, as there is great beauty in dusk. But why must we be bamboozled with assertions that we have expressed ourselves in favour of something when it is clear that nobody has been asked, and nobody will be benefitted except a few thousand people involved in international business?"[58]

▼

Among Ontario's greatest energy assets was the CANDU (short for Canada Deuterium Uranium) reactor developed by Atomic Energy

---

58 Letters, December 15, 1973.

of Canada Ltd., as well as an abundance of the uranium required to run the reactors. I argued that the private sector should build nuclear plants (on the shores of Lake Superior was one of my suggestions) dedicated to selling electricity to the U.S. rather than export uranium. That way, we would employ Canadian technology, resources, and capital, and create jobs.

I also tried to sell CANDU in Britain and convinced federal Minister of Energy Donald Macdonald to join me on a three-day sales promotion trip in February 1974 that would include a meeting with Prime Minister Ted Heath. Our wives travelled with us, which initially caused a chill since Macdonald had defeated Joyce's father, David Walker, in the riding of Rosedale in 1962. However, everyone got along famously. Joyce and Don's wife, Ruth, went shopping together even though power curtailments meant the stores were dark and cold. Canadian High Commissioner Jake Warren accompanied Don and me to the 10 Downing Street meeting. At the end of the meeting, Heath allowed as how he would rather sell a British reactor to us than buy one of ours.

I'm not a nuclear engineer, but I did have three convictions. First, CANDU was a proven success. Second, it was the safest technology. And third, it wasn't being properly marketed around the world. In addition to personal sales calls, as minister of energy I urged the creation of a CANDU marketing corporation that would include private sector companies such as General Electric. I could never convince Hydro or AECL to come aboard. They saw no reason to promote their product. After I became treasurer again in 1975, I continued to push this idea through the two energy ministers succeeding me, Dennis Timbrell and Jim Taylor. I accomplished zilch. Hydro simply did not listen; they refused all advice.

Nuclear is a safe, reliable source of energy and, today, produces about half of Ontario's requirements. We should keep on building nuclear capacity, but if we do, it probably will not be with CANDU reactors. Although, in my view, the technology is superior, for some reason CANDU never caught on globally. All Hydro and AECL seemed to care about was that bigger was better. We went from 250-megawatt reactors to 500, 750, and 1,000. Undoubtedly the bigger the reactor, the less expensive it was to operate. But when something went wrong, a big part of the entire system went out of commission. In hindsight, more and smaller reactors might have been better.

Hydro also wasted time focusing on crazy ideas like buying Denison Mines Ltd., of Elliot Lake, in order to secure a fifty-year supply of uranium. The punitive cost of that idea scared the hell out of me. Hydro's growing indebtedness was already damaging the province's credit rating and driving up interest rates when I was treasurer again. They wanted to borrow $2 billion for 1977 alone. I set a cap of $1.5 billion for each of the next three years, but even then I was barely able to slow down, not stop, their extravagant expansion.

Long after I left government, I became involved with Ontario Hydro once again. In 1995, Premier Mike Harris asked Donald Macdonald, chairman of an advisory committee on competition in Ontario's electricity system, to review Hydro's future. Macdonald had been minister of national defence, energy, and finance in the Pierre Trudeau government and chaired the Royal Commission in the 1980s that led to free trade with the U.S.

I was a member of the committee along with Sylvia Sutherland, a two-term mayor of Peterborough and chair of the Ontario Municipal Electrical Association's environmental advisory committee; Jan Carr, vice-president, transmission and distribution division of Acres International Ltd., a consulting engineering firm; John Grant, former director and chief economist at investment bank Wood Gundy Inc.; Dr. Leonard Waverman, professor of economics and director, centre for international studies at the University of Toronto; and Robert Gillespie, chairman and CEO of General Electric Canada, a manufacturer of electrical products.

Our mandate was to find ways to end Ontario Hydro's monopoly by introducing competition into the Ontario electrical system. Despite having such major breaks as not paying income taxes, Hydro was mired in a financial mess with a hefty debt of $35 billion. Even the public relations department was bloated with a staff of more than one hundred. As part of our five-month study, we held public hearings, received submissions, and met with experts.

We recommended competing market units for power generation and independent entities for transmission. We urged that prices be set by the market, not by Ontario Hydro, a step we believed would reduce rates. Two years later, the Harris government finally took action by dividing Hydro into five parts, which included Ontario Power Generation in charge of generation and Hydro One running the transmission grid. Both were destined to be privatized, but the process was put on hold in 2003 by Ernie Eves, successor to Harris as premier.

Wrong-headed decisions have continued. The Dalton McGuinty government's move to close coal-fired plants and put the emphasis on wind and solar was a mistake. Such alternative sources of energy are far more expensive than coal, natural gas, or nuclear. A commitment to improved air quality is commendable, but Ohio and Michigan rely heavily on coal to produce electricity and are not closing their plants. Because of the prevailing southwest winds, we'll continue to have environmental problems in southern Ontario.

I look back with great remorse on my many and varied involvements with Ontario Hydro. The costs of inaction on a variety of fronts, combined with poor decisions taken by governments of all stripes, are visible on our monthly electricity bills. To this day, Hydro One remains an out-of-control crown corporation with a monopoly. When I started paying hydro bills at Bally McKeough in the mid 1960s, they were half my bill from Union Gas. Today, my hydro bill is three times larger than my gas charges. Sometimes, even an all-powerful Zeus can't get his way.

14

▼

The Energy Imperative

By 1972 Ontario, for more than a decade, had provided a guaranteed market and subsidized Alberta oil production to the tune of $70 million annually. Refineries in Sarnia and Port Credit paid more than refineries in Montreal or Saint John because they were fed by lower-priced oil from the Middle East or Venezuela. In November 1972, Alberta Premier Peter Lougheed said even such a sweetheart deal wasn't sufficient. He declared Alberta would double the price of natural gas, with more increases to come, meaning Ontario consumers and industries would spend an additional $52 million or more a year.

In my first speech on the topic as parliamentary assistant to the premier, on March 9, 1973, I noted that Ontario relied on out-of-province resources for 80 per cent of our energy needs. "There is no reason why Canada should be hurt industrially or in terms of jobs and job upgrading, or in its ability to compete in the world," I said. "I believe that, with the proper kind of national management, we can overcome what is termed an energy crisis and advance the industrial opportunity of this country."

I also believed that regulatory bodies such as the National Energy Board (NEB), where adversaries argued their differing views on prices, no longer functioned for the good of all sides. When I appeared before the NEB, the first time an Ontario minister had done so, I expressed our concern for the environment and the growing fear that natural gas would be in short supply.

I don't recall the ultimate NEB decision, and it doesn't matter. What I do remember was meeting with Robert Macaulay, our legal counsel, about my NEB appearance. When I expressed sympathy for the views — contrary to my own — expressed by TransCanada PipeLines, Macaulay, who had run against Robarts for leader, replied, "They're not down to their last fucking Learjet yet."[59]

Canada was the only country in the Western world that was self-sufficient in energy. Wasn't that a strength that could help all Canadians? Rather than rely on the NEB, I urged the federal government to join with all the provinces to protect producers and consumers alike. I urged a two-price system, one for exports and another for Canada, rather than subsidizing Alberta and the oil companies. Lougheed's immediate response to my idea was to declare that a "battle" had begun. He said, "It would appear that some other Canadians are asking Albertans to sell their natural resources below value as a cheap fuel for industry in other parts of Canada."[60]

Many such public statements were mere posturing. I had a number of meetings with Lougheed, who was likeable, laughed easily, and was a good listener. My sessions with him and his colleagues — Minister of Natural Resources Bill Dickie and Minister of Intergovernmental Affairs Don Getty — were always frank and friendly. We got along because I understood and agreed with their position in so far as it included letting markets function.

I was able to persuade Davis to be less of a politician and more of a statesman. "While the first responsibility of this government and this Legislature is to think of the people of Ontario," he told the legislature on June 7, 1973, "I am now urging that all of us think of the welfare of Canada. To think regionally or parochially is inappropriate in this context. To think of the short-term expedient is

59 Macaulay was later appointed chairman of the Ontario Energy Board on my recommendation to Premier Davis.
60 *Calgary Herald*, March 9, 1973.

to prejudice the long-term welfare of Canada."[61] But, while Davis "mainly" believed in markets, he was more of a Red Tory — someone who favoured government intervention — than I. Privately, he told me, "We could use a little aggression."

In September 1973, Ottawa embraced my suggestion for a two-price system by asking the oil companies to freeze Canadian prices voluntarily. At the same time, Ottawa brought in an export tax of forty cents per barrel on oil shipped to the U.S., then used those funds to subsidize prices in eastern Canada. On October 6, 1973, the energy crisis became a global issue after a coalition of Arab states invaded Israel. In the months that followed, as oil-producing Arab states embargoed oil exports and sent world prices higher, Ottawa hiked the Canadian export tax to $2.20. Without such a levy, the oil companies and Alberta would have enjoyed windfall gains, given that half of all Canadian production went to the U.S.

In November, I said in the legislature that all Canadians should share in the problem. "I think we in Ontario would certainly, for example, forgo Sunday driving to make sure there is heat in the homes of the province of Quebec — if it comes down to that." Outside the house, I admitted my comment was a bit facetious, then added, "If there is a shortage of heating in Quebec, then some public buildings will have to be closed in Ontario."[62]

I brought in conservation measures for provincial ministries and buildings as well as suggesting steps for citizens to save fuel. I estimated that, by reducing driving speeds, cutting back on lighting and heating, and buying more fuel-efficient cars, we could reduce total fuel consumption in Ontario by about 3.5 per cent.

▼

First ministers met in March 1974 without their respective energy ministers and advisors. They agreed the price of crude oil from

---

61 *Hansard*, p. 2784.
62 *Ottawa Journal*, November 7, 1973, p. 1.

Alberta and Saskatchewan would rise from $4 a barrel, where it had been frozen, to $6.50 a barrel at the wellhead. (The world price was $10.50.) Davis had wanted $6 so came away happy that the increase wasn't worse. But he had been misled. Nobody pointed out the difference between the wellhead price and the city gate price, which was higher. Davis also had not counted on the 12 per cent federal sales tax that added another nine cents a gallon. In all, he had missed about $300 million in additional costs. I like to think that, if my departmental advisors and I had also been present, we would have pointed out and avoided such hidden increases.

Ottawa and Alberta were on a mission to hike prices, supposedly to encourage more production, but the main outcome seemed to be more revenue for their coffers. "We accepted the increases in the price of natural gas — with modest protests because of the urgent need for securing additional supplies," I said in a speech in the legislature on December 19, 1974. "But then the producing provinces moved in, the federal government moved in and those dollars — paid by the consumers — were consumed. Are we to play the same scene a second time? Ontario is opposed to the jockeying up of natural gas and oil prices for the enrichment of governments at the expense of security of energy supply for our citizens."[63]

▼

Future supply was further threatened on December 4, 1974, when Atlantic Richfield Canada Ltd. pulled out of the Syncrude Canada Ltd. consortium that was building an extraction plant in Alberta's oil sands after estimated costs skyrocketed from $900 million to $2 billion. Atlantic Richfield, Imperial Oil, and Cities Service each held 30 per cent with Gulf Oil at 10 per cent. As a result, the deal needed a new partner and an injection of $600 million.

On January 24, 1975, by which time I had been reappointed treasurer, I flew to Edmonton with Dennis Timbrell — who had

---

63 *Hansard*, p. 6690.

replaced me in energy — and Dick Dillon, the deputy minister of energy, to confer with Lougheed. I agreed Ontario would be part of the solution if no new private sector partner came forward.

At a news conference following the meeting, I said Ontario was "not the saviour of this thing by ourselves or even a large new participant, if there is participation." I did indicate, however, that Ontario "has not closed any doors." Asked if Ontario would pick up Atlantic Richfield's 30 per cent share, I said, "Good Lord, no."[64]

But we were prepared to pick up a portion. On February 3, I flew to Winnipeg with Davis, Timbrell, Dillon, and Tom Kierans for a 9:30 a.m. meeting at the International Inn near the Winnipeg airport. Others present included the Alberta delegation led by Lougheed and the Ottawa contingent headed by Energy Minister Don Macdonald. The Syncrude owners were represented by Jack Armstrong of Imperial Oil, Bob Sellars of Canada-Cities Service Ltd., and Jerry McAfee of Gulf Oil Canada. Bill Daniel, CEO of Shell Canada, attended as a possible new participant but soon left when his demand for a guaranteed price on production was rejected.

Also present was Jean Chrétien, president of the Treasury Board, who later took sole credit for everyone's accomplishments. "It quickly became apparent that the deal was going nowhere," he wrote in his 1985 memoirs, *Straight from the Heart*. "Some partners were withdrawing, Ontario and Alberta were at each other's throats, and the discussions had deteriorated into confrontations. Since I was a neutral outsider, I was able to go back and forth among the players, particularly Lougheed and Davis, to work out an agreement. We got one by the end of the day, and I think my efforts on behalf of the West were noticed."[65]

That's not the way I remember it. Nor do I agree entirely with Don Macdonald's recollection of events. In his memoirs, *Thumper*, he paints Lougheed as a mean-spirited man who treated Davis badly. "Premier Lougheed was rude to Davis and dismissive of

64 *London Free Press*, January 25, 1975.
65 Chrétien, Jean, *Straight from the Heart* (Toronto: Key Porter, 1985), p. 157.

Ontario's offer. 'The chips at this table are one hundred million, not fifty. Perhaps you should withdraw and see if you can do better,'" wrote Macdonald of Lougheed's response to Ontario's $50-million first offer.[66]

I have no argument about the facts, but I never felt Lougheed acted rudely as described by Macdonald. Rather, I saw him as a damn good negotiator. Davis, Dillon, and I left the meeting room and caucused with Timbrell and Kierans. We agreed to increase our stake to $100 million, returned to the meeting, and the deal was done.

Ottawa contributed $300 million for a 15 per cent ownership position, and Alberta put in $200 million for 10 per cent interest. For our $100 million we owned 5 per cent. Once the three governments had committed a total of $600 million, the three private sector participants raised their total contribution from $1 billion to $1.4 billion to reach the $2 billion needed. I was proud to be a participant in that historic deal.

▼

On our way back to Toronto that evening, Davis, Kierans, and I talked about another deal that had been brought to us by Bryce Farrill of McLeod Young Weir. Gulf Canada, one of the participants in the Syncrude deal, was for sale. For $300 million we could buy a 60 per cent interest in Gulf that would have not only raised our stake in Syncrude, but also given us a bigger foothold in the oil and gas sector.

We considered the possibility seriously enough to give it a code name, Project Sutton, because Bryce, Tom, and I were all in love with Joan Sutton, the beautiful blonde columnist with the *Toronto Sun*. I felt we needed private sector partners to join us; none was interested, so the deal did not go ahead.

In 1978, we sold Ontario's portion of Syncrude for a $36-million

---

profit, but any profit was not the point. The most tangible result was the coming together of the private sector and three governments to create something for the good of all Canadians. Today Syncrude supplies half of Canada's oil production. Without Syncrude, we would all be a lot worse off.

Such deals were not easy for me ideologically. I'm generally not in favour of government investment; I constantly pushed the private sector to do its job. Only when the private sector refused to act on its own would I agree to even discuss the possibility of government participation.

Despite the many wrangles, my time in energy was busy and productive. In 1974 alone, I gave seventy-four speeches and made countless other public appearances. My only unmitigated disaster was agreeing to appear on Global TV's *The Great Debate* in front of a studio audience. The resolution was: "The energy crisis is a hoax perpetrated by the major oil companies." I was opposed to the motion. Arguing in favour was Ralph Nader, the American consumer advocate. Phil Lind warned me against taking on the high-profile Nader. I should have heeded him. "As a television debater, McKeough was a flop, the audience decided," said the *Toronto Star*. "They declared Nader the winner by 134 votes to 13. 'I'm surprised he got 13 votes,' one youth said on his way out."[67]

▼

Pricing and supply remained my concern during the rest of my time in office. In June 1975, Ottawa added a ten-cent-per-gallon excise tax on gasoline plus a tax on oil of $1.50 per barrel. In response, Davis asked the seven major oil companies to delay the increases until September 1. When they refused, he imposed a ninety-day freeze on gas and oil prices in Ontario.

In 1976, Ottawa decided Canadian prices should reach world prices within two to three years. Ontario proposed a blended-price

---

67 *Toronto Star*, January 1, 1974.

arrangement by which old oil that could be produced more cheaply would be priced lower than costly new oil. Our idea gained no traction. In July 1977, the feds increased the price in Canada by another $1 followed by a further $1 hike in January 1978.

The Progressive Conservative government of Joe Clark was little better when it came to considering consumers. In the December 1979 budget, Finance Minister John Crosbie announced an eighteen-cent tax on every gallon of gas. The government fell, Pierre Trudeau returned from retirement, and Canadians voted the Liberal Party back into office in the election of February 1980. Finally, in August 1980, the Trudeau government agreed to a version of the blended-price arrangement we had previously urged.

I fought hard for lower consumer prices right from the time I was parliamentary assistant to the premier through my years as treasurer until I resigned in 1978. But the truth is I never fully reconciled my economic concerns for business and residential users with my political belief that markets, not governments, should determine price and that higher prices would lead to greater exploration and development in Canada.

I was my own man, but I was always ready to listen and learn. I heard and heeded the Ontario electorate and my counterparts in other governments. But I make no apologies for the fact that I also respected the opinions of people in business. I believe mutual respect for the other point of view, and the relationships I built, contributed in some small way to the ultimate resolution.

▼

That relentless search for national energy solutions continued during my time after politics working in the private sector. As CEO of Union Gas, I helped orchestrate a two-day energy summit in November 1983 at the Niagara Institute in Niagara-on-the-Lake. The idea for such a public/private sector conclave came out of a meeting I'd had in May with Premier Lougheed. The key words used by Lougheed, who was in an expansive mood, were "Let's talk."

While it seemed like a straightforward idea, not everyone involved in energy had been talking to one another. My main role was to get both premiers Davis and Lougheed — who were not on good terms – to attend. I concluded such a meeting would best be conducted under the auspices of the Business Council on National Issues (BCNI), so I talked to Tom d'Aquino, CEO of BCNI, an organization of 150 chief executive officers. I had been a member since 1980. (The organization is now called the Canadian Council of Chief Executives.) He agreed to help and took on the specific task of convincing federal Minister of Energy Jean Chrétien to attend. Invitations were extended to a dozen ministers and officials from the three governments as well as two dozen CEOs from oil and gas, finance, and investment banking, including such leaders as Jean de Grandpré of Bell Canada Enterprises Inc., Jack Lawrence of Burns Fry Ltd., David Mitchell of Alberta Energy Co. Ltd., and Ced Ritchie of the Bank of Nova Scotia.

En route to the meeting in Niagara-on-the-Lake, Peter Lougheed stayed overnight at Bally McKeough. Joyce and I picked him up at the Chatham airport. We walked our property so he could stretch his legs, then had Stewart and Dorothy and Ann and George in for drinks. It was just the three of us for dinner with lively conversation that lasted until midnight.

In those days, I jogged six out of seven mornings a week, but I had already completed my run before Lougheed awoke, so he and Joyce went jogging together. It was a beautiful day at our end of the lake when Lougheed and I took off for Niagara by small plane. We flew low along the shoreline so I could show him some users of Alberta energy: the Nanticoke generating station, the Stelco steel mill, and the Texaco oil refinery. We then turned north up the Niagara River where, unfortunately, it was foggy and rainy so we couldn't see Niagara Falls, Ontario's major source of hydro-electric power.

The conference went well. I was surprised how readily all the participants set aside self-interest and agreed there was a benefit to be gained from a new strategy for a revitalized oil and gas sector. We appointed a task force headed by Don McIvor, CEO of Imperial Oil, to craft a statement with which we could all agree. With a consensus in sight, everyone met again in June 1984 at the Millcroft Inn in Alton, Ontario, to finalize what became known as *The Energy Imperative: A Perspective on Canadian Oil and Natural Gas Policy*. The next month, the Parliament of Canada was dissolved, and Brian Mulroney defeated Liberal Leader John Turner in the September 4 election.

The timing couldn't have been better. By then, all of our summit participants had signed *The Energy Imperative*, which was delivered to the incoming Minister of Energy, Pat Carney. Among the recommendations for a new oil and gas policy were: taxation based on profits instead of revenues; early deregulation of oil prices with deregulation of natural gas prices to follow; exploration and development incentives if necessary, using the tax system rather than grants; and an improved balance between Canadian participation and the need for continuing foreign investments.

Only when the document was made public did the world learn of our two meetings. We had managed to gather that sizeable and high-powered group twice without attracting any media attention. The Economic Council of Canada and others supported our conclusions, but it was Mulroney who slayed the dragons by killing the Foreign Investment Review Agency and the National Energy Program. BCNI took the credit, but as I look back, that summit at Niagara-on-the-Lake was one of my better moments. If I hadn't acted on Lougheed's "Let's talk" comment, who knows how long it would have taken to find an energy consensus involving so many players on the national stage?

During all the time since, little has been accomplished in the many related areas that concerned me. First, when economic times are good, there continues to be a shortage of labour skills in Alberta and no concerted effort to address the problem. Second, there is still no natural gas pipeline from the Arctic. Third, as debates and delays continue over bitumen pipelines from Alberta to Texas or the Pacific Coast, no one is pushing industry to build refineries in Alberta for export of finished products. Why wouldn't we do that? It would end much of the bickering and create jobs. Fourth, even with lower energy prices and a weaker Canadian dollar, manufacturing — the former engine of the Ontario economy — is in serious trouble. Ontario must adjust to this new reality by parlaying its strengths in financial services and mining, by upgrading skills, and by accepting reduced pension benefits and a lower wage scale in manufacturing than currently prevails. Those steps will be painful, but it's the best way forward.

15

▼

A Minority View

I felt relieved and redeemed when Premier Davis reappointed me treasurer in January 1975. This was where I belonged. Others agreed, including Norman Webster, the Queen's Park columnist for the *Globe and Mail*. He wrote: "On the day Winston Churchill was reappointed First Lord of the Admiralty, the same day Britain went to war against Nazi Germany, the message was sent around the Fleet: 'Winnie is back.' We wonder . . . is that telephone number which employees of the Ontario Ministry of Treasury, Economics and Intergovernmental Affairs dial for a recorded message on the latest news of their department repeating, 'Darcy is back?' Indeed he is."[68]

Politically, we were in trouble. A poll released that month had the Liberals at 41 per cent, the Conservatives at 31 per cent, and the NDP at 26 per cent. In one of the regular notes he sent to me in the House, Stephen Lewis predicted great things. "So there I was having a friendly — if rare — haircut at the King Edward, when the barber, scissors poised ominously over my left ear, announced that if Darcy McKeough were Premier, the Tories might survive . . . and what did I think? I think I should change barbers."

---

68 *Globe and Mail*, January 15, 1975.

The economy was suffering from stagflation, a combination of stagnant growth and rising inflation. The answer was to control spending, stimulate through the tax system, and follow solid principles of thrift and honesty — all while trying to reduce the deficit and encourage private sector activity. My budget of April 7, 1975, set out to do just that by reducing the size of the public sector by 6 per cent over six years. "I am convinced that one of the root causes of the current inflation problem in Canada is excessive government spending and unnecessary growth in the size and complexity of the public sector," I said in the budget speech. "This has shifted an increasing share of our total resources out of private production uses in the economy and has eroded the taxpayer's hard-earned income."[69]

In order to boost the economy, we lowered the retail sales tax from 7 per cent to 5 per cent for an eight-month period, eliminated the sales tax on production machinery and equipment, offered more tax credits for small business, and made available a $1,500 grant to first-time home buyers. As a result of the stimulus, I predicted a budget deficit of $1.2 billion, twice the previous record deficit of $625 million in 1971–72. "If one can point to a defining moment in postwar politics and the history of public policy and management in Ontario when the state 'changed its mind' . . . the 1975 budget would be a turning point," said a 2011 study published in *The Guardian*, an authoritative history of Ontario finance.[70]

▼

To bolster my departmental advisors, I reached beyond Queen's Park. Tom Kierans, who started in the investment business in 1962, was senior executive vice president and director at Pitfield, Mackay, Ross Ltd. in Toronto when I first met him. Tom grew up in a business and political environment as the son of Eric Kierans, an economist, business executive, and Liberal cabinet minister in both Quebec and

---

69 1975 Ontario Budget, p. 16.
70 Evans, Bryan and John Shields, "From Pragmatism to Neoliberalism," *The Guardian: Perspectives on the Ministry of Finance of Ontario* (Toronto: University of Toronto Press, 2011), p. 138.

Ottawa. Tom, who became a lifelong friend, is one of the brightest people I know, speaks his mind, and has an intimate knowledge of how public policy fits with the private sector.

Kierans left Bay Street to become an advisor to me for a few months when I returned to the role of treasurer. When he went back to investment banking after the 1975 budget, he wrote to me saying: "As you know, anyone who works on a successful budget tends to bask in the reflected glory, and in this case, I have come in for my share of compliments. Traditionally one demurs and sweepingly refers to the uncontested fact that 'it was the Treasurer's budget.' I never so reached, not only because of loyalty and tradition, but because the corollary is laughable. Darcy — I was there and I know that it bore your imprint and your imprint only. From start to finish you dominated it — not by authority but by superiority. The depth of your knowledge, your philosophical commitment to approach, your grasp and hold on detail and your administrative programming were overwhelming. It was a privilege to behold."[71]

In June 1975, the premier agreed to my idea for a Special Review Program to evaluate all provincial expenditures. This was not just some internal monitoring system set up for window dressing; it was a high-profile and proactive group and the first of many such bodies formed by government. I was chairman of the review with outside appointees Maxwell Henderson, former auditor-general of Canada; Robert Hurlbut, president of General Foods Ltd.; and Betty Kennedy, a highly respected broadcaster and commentator. Other members were Eric Winkler, chairman of the Management Board, as well as three senior deputy ministers: Rendall Dick, Jim Fleck, and Bill Anderson. Their report, tabled in November, recommended steps that would reduce spending by more than $3.6 billion over the next two years.

▼

71 Letter, May 15, 1975.

The election held on September 18, 1975, was a sharp rebuff. There were many reasons: the "scandals" and resignations, John White's aborted 7 per cent tax on heating, backlash from the Pickering airport, and regional government, but I think mostly it was just that, as a government, we were getting long in the tooth. The Progressive Conservative Party was reduced to a minority when our seat count fell from 78 in a 117-seat house to 51 in an expanded 125 seats. The NDP became the official Opposition, doubling their seats to 38, with the Liberals third at 35 seats. Liberal leader Robert Nixon resigned and was replaced by Stuart Smith, a Montreal-born psychiatrist. I won my seat, beating a local hotelkeeper who ran for the Liberals on a platform that included punishing juvenile delinquents with "three good whacks across the ass."

Strange as it may seem, I have to say that, compared with the opposition I faced during my efforts to bring about regional government, I had an easier time during my second period as treasurer. The Liberals had a consistent approach: more spending, less taxation. As a result, I always knew what their position would be. The NDP, on the other hand, were less concerned about taxation or revenues. One thing the NDP did well was work for the underdog in society.

God knows the NDP went off half-cocked at times, but just as Tories like Allan Grossman and John Yaremko pushed and prodded my party to act for the downtrodden, so did Stephen Lewis and the NDP of his era. All those forces helped make Ontario a better and more humane place.

Despite my cheese-paring ways, there were many times when I, too, helped the most needy. For example, in the 1975 budget I increased payments under the Provincial Guaranteed Annual Income System for more than 300,000 beneficiaries. The result was the highest guaranteed annual income for pensioners anywhere in Canada. No less a Red Tory than Hugh Segal, then a Davis advisor and now Master of Massey College, still sings my praises. "The Honourable Darcy McKeough, one of the most conservative finance ministers in the history of Ontario, pinstriped suit, Bank of Montreal tie, Toronto Club cufflinks, stood in his place in the Legislature and announced the Guaranteed Annual Income Supplement. And that took the level of poverty among seniors from 35 per cent to 3 per cent in two years,"[72] Segal told Anna Maria Tremonti on CBC's *The Current* in 2014.

I have no recollection what tie I wore, but I do know my wardrobe included neither a Bank of Montreal tie nor Toronto Club cufflinks. Segal, who is a Jew, used to kid me about the Kent Club in Chatham being N.J.A., meaning "No Jews Allowed." I have since joined the Toronto Club, but, at the time, the club did not allow politicians as members. As I pointed out to Hugh, it was N.P.A, "No Politicians Allowed." As for helping seniors, I happily plead guilty as charged.

▼

Prior to being reduced to a minority government, we had lost four by-elections, a beating that brought about changes in the premier's office. Entrepreneur Jim Fleck and former bureaucrat Malcolm Rowan departed and were replaced by the more politically astute Ed Stewart, who had been deputy minister of education when Davis was minister. Davis instituted a regular Tuesday-morning breakfast meeting at the Park Plaza Hotel to talk about policy.

At first, Davis was the only elected person present, but after the 1975 election, Eddie Goodman insisted some cabinet ministers and their deputies be included. I was an original invitee. Other regular participants over the years included Canadian Tire chairman Hugh Macaulay; Davis aide Clare Westcott; Party president David McFadden; Treasurer of the PC Party Bill Kelly; Norman Atkins of Camp Associates; Tom Kierans; and Segal, who had worked for Robert Stanfield and run twice federally before joining Davis.

The meetings, chaired by Stewart, lasted about ninety minutes. Topics could range from the disposal of uranium tailings in Elliott Lake to some newspaper story of the day. For the most part, Davis

---

72 *The Current*, CBC, June 30, 2014.

just listened like some wily sphinx. He had a sixth sense about which issues could be left alone without doing any political harm. No decisions were made at those meetings, but any ministers or deputy ministers who did not attend believed that they were. In retrospect, it was not a team-building exercise.

Some scenes from those Tuesday sessions ended up in Peter Raymont's excellent hour-long documentary, *The Art of the Possible*, released in 1978. Raymont aptly portrayed the mostly silent Davis, revealing little about his thoughts, while I was rambunctiously the opposite. In one of the scenes I respond to pressure from business to cut taxes and reduce unemployment by saying, "There is no incentive for me, other than on moral and Christian grounds, to worry about unemployment." Writing in the *Globe and Mail*, Peter Mosher declared, "Darcy McKeough emerged as the star of the National Film Board's $200,000 peek behind the closed doors of the Cabinet room. Some of the film's most interesting moments were the result of Mr. McKeough's strong personality."[73] You always knew where you stood with me.

I also gave advice in other ways. On September 24, 1975, I sent Davis a lengthy memo with a variety of ideas for changes in cabinet, how long the house should sit, and the timing of the next budget. Most important, I told Davis he should gather a dozen people for a meeting somewhere away from Queen's Park, to consider how we came to be in this minority situation and how we planned to win back public favour.

I assured Davis the problem was not his leadership. "Not one person that I have spoken to or has spoken to me has said anything about any change in leadership," I told him. "That's a good sign. We are a united party, but that talk will begin unless we appear to be listening." I was always loyal to my leader and never spent one minute trying to ease him out so I could step in.

A much smaller group than the Tuesday crowd met Thursday mornings to consider candidates for patronage appointments. I did

73 *Globe and Mail*, December 20, 1978.

not attend but regularly recommended people for specific roles. The full cabinet was involved in recommending lawyers for the honorific title of Queen's Counsel. The list was usually settled at a cabinet meeting just before Christmas. Discussions could become rollicking. The attorney general of the day always wanted to reduce the list, while some ministers tried to add names, and others worried about making appointments in ridings held by the Opposition.

My predecessor, George Parry, had, in his eighteen years as MPP, always looked after Tory lawyers in Kent. By comparison, I pushed for very few appointments. There were even occasions when I reached across party lines. One year, Doug Kerr, who was my father's lawyer and a Liberal, phoned to ask that his son, Brud Kerr, who was a Grit practising in London, be given a QC. I had no one to recommend from Kent that year and so put Kerr's name forward without bothering to consult the London PCs. To this day Tories in London must wonder how in the hell Brud Kerr (later a judge) received that title.

I applied the same non-partisan thinking to MPPs of other parties, as well as their offspring, even in cases where I crossed swords with an MPP in the House. In 1970, Morton Shulman, the crusading coroner who had been elected an NDP MPP in 1967, delivered a lengthy speech in the legislature about auto insurance. Once he'd concluded, he asked for a response from a cabinet minister, any cabinet minister. No one seemed willing, so I called out, "Sleazy Morty," and left it at that.

As a result, Shulman was no fan of mine, but over the years his view changed. "Darcy McKeough in those days was very strident and right wing and his current polish had yet to develop. The Darcy McKeough of today bears no resemblance to the man of 1970," wrote Shulman in 1979. "I have never seen a politician mellow and grow as Darcy has."[74]

To be sure, his more positive view may have been affected by how I handled the hiring of his daughter, Dianne, who applied for a government job using her married name, Saxe. When someone in

74 Shulman, Morton, *Member of the Legislature* (Toronto: Fitzhenry & Whiteside, 1979), pp. 90–91.

the department learned who she was, she was accused of duplicity for not revealing her relationship with her father. She was told she would need the minister's approval to get the job. As the minister involved, when asked, I said hiring her was fine with me. When next I saw Shulman, he offered his thanks. "Why Morty," I said, "if we didn't hire each others' children, who would?"

In most cases, we filled vacancies outside the civil service by rewarding party members in return for their loyalty and partisan efforts. In 1975, we appointed Elmer Bell, a former president of the Ontario Progressive Conservative Association, as chairman of the Ontario Police Commission. I remember George Hutchison, a reporter with the *London Free Press*, pressing me on Bell's credentials for the job. My view on these matters was simple. When two candidates for a role were of equal standing, if one was a Liberal and the other a Tory, you chose the Tory. "You don't hire your enemies," I told Hutchison. The other two political parties had no trouble following the same philosophy when they had the chance.

▼

On September 10, 1975, John Turner resigned as federal minister of finance. While the reasons for his departure weren't clear at the time, he had spent many frustrating and unsuccessful months trying to convince business and labour to voluntarily accept wage and price controls. When I spoke to him after he stepped down, he just sounded tired and fed up. I would get to know the feeling.

A week later, Margaret Thatcher, who earlier that year had been elected leader of the Conservative Party in Britain, visited Toronto to deliver a luncheon speech at the Empire Club. Davis was away, so I represented Ontario at the head table and had arranged for a meeting with her that afternoon. Rendall Dick and I met Thatcher and her husband, Denis, at the door of the Frost Building. Originally, we planned to serve tea to a gathering that would include people from her entourage and a few of my officials. At the last minute, the Iron Lady announced she wanted to see me alone. Pointing to the British consul-general who had arrived with her, she said, "Mr. Samples is a civil servant and I don't want him compromised."

For the next hour, Thatcher held forth to me about the economic situation in Britain in particular and the state of the world in general. I was amazed at her grasp of detail as she forcefully listed the problems Britain was facing and how the Labour government was tackling them. In the midst of a global recession, inflation in Britain was running at 25 per cent, a situation made worse by the fact Britain had to import half its food and most of its resources so was captive to external price pressures.

When we talked about leadership, she repeated a theme from her speech, saying leaders must be two or three years ahead of public opinion, be able to foresee dangers, and act in the best interests of the nation. "A leader must not follow public opinion from the back but lead from the front," she said. Her financial prescription sounded very similar to my own: don't spend more than you have. When growth stops and the economy slows down, spend even less. I came away inspired by Thatcher and with my beliefs about fiscal prudence reinforced. Viewed from up close, she was even more formidable than she appeared from afar. Fortunately, Joyce arrived and, along with Mr. Samples and Rendall Dick, we all had tea with Denis and Mrs. Thatcher, so we were able to see her more sociable side as well.

The following month, Canada was forced to take its own tough medicine against inflation. Although matters were not as serious as in Britain, inflation was running in the double digits and there were wage settlements in excess of 20 per cent. Pierre Trudeau announced a program of controls to cap wage and salary gains at 8 per cent in the first year, 6 per cent in the second, and 4 per cent in the third.

I fully supported his plans — conditional on phasing out the program by December 1978, as scheduled. I did not want such an intervention to become a permanent part of our lives. We responded in Ontario by reducing Hydro borrowing, extending the existing moratorium on civil service hiring, and freezing the salaries of senior bureaucrats. Controls worked. By May 1976, inflation had fallen to single-digit levels for the first time since February 1974.

Because we were a minority government, the political considerations for the budget of April 16, 1976, were more important than ever. There had been a period in March when it looked like the two Opposition parties would vote against the Speech from the Throne. Such a vote would have been a non-confidence matter; if we'd lost, the public would have been plunged into an April election — only five months after the last one. Fortunately, Liberal leader Stuart Smith backed off and the threat was postponed.

Budgets are also confidence matters. I needed to find more ways to save taxpayer dollars. That included rebuffing all appeals for spending. Metro Toronto Council, for example, was pleading for more money. I told its chairman, Paul Godfrey, "We've reached the limit. I wish we could be Lady Bountiful forever, but we can't."[75]

One idea I briefly considered was following the U.S. lead and making mortgage payments on housing tax deductible. Thank heaven we did not proceed. The idea might have been politically popular, but the cost to the Treasury would have been in the billions at a time when deficits were already too high.

As a theme, the budget focused on worthwhile programs while underlining the importance of a strong capitalist system in the global economy. "We have to face up to the fact that Canada is a small toad in a large pond, and we cannot compete without bigness. Consumers can be far better protected by more international competition than by any royal commissions inquiring into steel pricing or the concentration of corporate power," I said in a speech to the Toronto Society of Financial Analysts.[76] "We need to remind ourselves that public well-being has been largely financed by private sector wellbeing; that we have achieved our standard of living because we have encouraged investment, entrepreneurship, monetary reward, adequate profits, and individual initiative." Even in minority times, I stayed true to my beliefs and myself.

---

75 Hoy, Claire, *Toronto Sun*, February 4, 1976.
76 January 22, 1976.

16

▾

Balancing the Budget

In February 1976, the federal Progressive Conservative Party held a leadership convention to replace Robert Stanfield. Eddie Goodman, who supported Kingston MP and candidate Flora Macdonald, said he would also raise money for me if I ran. I had thought about it, but not seriously. I was happy where I was and did not have the facility in French I felt was necessary for that national role.

Before the convention, Joyce and I and the boys had breakfast in Toronto with Brian Mulroney, who had never held public office but looked like he could win the leadership. Davis told his ministers to be publicly neutral, and I was. I quietly voted for Joe Clark, the eventual winner on the fourth ballot, while Joyce rooted for Mulroney. As leader, Clark was a disappointment. He didn't listen to advice.

He also suffered from a fractious and disloyal caucus. In 1980, I urged him to be aggressive, call a leadership convention, and tell the party, "Put up or shut up." Instead, he waited until the scheduled leadership review in 1981, at which time 30 per cent voted for a review. He soldiered on until the next review, in 1983, when the numbers favouring a review rose slightly, to 33.1 per cent. Clark concluded that he couldn't continue and called a convention, which was won by Mulroney. By winning two majority governments, Mulroney accomplished more than any other prime minister since Sir John A. Macdonald. He had the courage to bring in the GST, stood tall against apartheid in South Africa, and signed the free trade deal with the U.S.

Aside from the truly enormous contributions he made to Canada, Mulroney was a wonderfully friendly, warm, and outgoing person. Joyce recalls an occasion at Pearson airport, on her way to catch a plane, when a loud voice boomed out, "Hello, Joyce McKeough." It was Brian, perched on a shoeshine chair, shouting to her across the terminal. Joyce has never forgotten that happy encounter.

The biggest fight I had over the April 1976 budget was with a mighty trio — Goodman, Hugh Macaulay, and Norman Atkins — who wanted to raise corporate income taxes: Davis settled the matter by siding with me. My budget speech urged spending restraint. "Governments cannot live on credit indefinitely any more than families can. No business can finance its essential expansion if governments crowd the financial markets and take all the money," I said, then promised Ontario would not require any public borrowing in 1976–77. By keeping expenditures to a 10 per cent increase with a 19 per cent bump in revenue because of stronger growth, I was able to announce, "The Ontario economy is back on trend."

We also predicted a drop in unemployment of half a percentage point, auto production up 20 per cent, and urban housing starts rising by 60 per cent. "Ontario has done a remarkable job in trimming the size of its bureaucracy, while the feds go happily on growing," wrote Norman Webster. "Ontario is holding down spending much better than Ottawa, and is bringing in new controls to block the little bureaucratic tricks that get around general edicts on restraint."[77]

In the House, Opposition leader Stuart Smith needled me incessantly. Provoked at one point, I said Smith had made an "an ass" of himself. Forced by Speaker Russell Rowe to retract, I said Smith was "not an ass, he's a fop," which I also had to retract. Outside the House, when I was asked the meaning of fop, I replied, "a fop is a well-dressed ass who drives two Datsuns." When it came time to

---

77 *Globe and Mail*, April 17, 1976.

vote on the budget, however, Smith and the Liberals supported us, so there was no snap election.

▼

Although I backed Ottawa's anti-inflation program, on other issues we were at odds. When Minister of National Health and Welfare Marc Lalonde released an Orange Paper proposing a form of guaranteed annual income, we made a stack of research material available to James Rusk of the *Globe and Mail* showing the high cost of such a program. Rusk wrote a hard-hitting series on the topic and the idea went nowhere.

As a long-time nationalist, I also worried about the ongoing impact of Ottawa's intrusive Foreign Investment Review Agency (FIRA). Established in 1973, FIRA created problems for the business community because of the lengthy wait times for decisions. I made four suggestions: FIRA should review only major deals; rules needed to be more transparent; FIRA's staff of 125 members should be reduced; and a Canadian firm acquiring another Canadian firm should be given extra time to complete a deal.

In recent years, we have seen a number of great Canadian companies disappear — Stelco, Dofasco, Noranda, Labatt's, Molson, Falconbridge, Inco — it's a long list. I think Ontario and Ottawa should have quietly urged some mergers between Canadian companies so they could bulk up for battle with global competitors. Having said that, I think we are better off with an open border that welcomes foreign investment and takeovers.

Our meetings with the federal government about foreign investment and other topics were often held in the conference centre across from the Château Laurier. I went out of my way, even in the good weather, to walk through the underground tunnel joining the two buildings because of the friendly commissionaire posted at one of the doors. Every time I passed he'd say, "Good morning, sir, one of the greatest." I could always feel myself purring with pleasure at his compliment until the occasion when he said, "Good morning, Mr. MacNaughton, one of the greatest." That brought me down to reality!

Once, while flying back from Ottawa on a government plane, there was an engine problem. The pilot spoke to my aide Tom MacMillan, who announced: "I have good news and I have bad news. The bad news is that we're going to have to shut down one of the engines. The good news is that this plane has two engines and can fly just fine on one." He then added, "Does anyone want another drink?" All three of the other passengers handed him their glasses. I was making changes to a speech draft and just kept on working.

After the plane landed safely in Toronto, I noticed the emergency vehicles nearby and asked, "What's all that about?" MacMillan said, "Did you not hear anything I said about the engine?" I then realized that I had been vaguely aware of the warning but was so busy his words hadn't really registered. "Some day, MacMillan," I said, "you'll learn what leadership is all about."

I was always intimately involved in my speeches. Some politicians just read what they're handed by staff. Not I. I'm responsible for my words. I would meet with Les Horswill, my speechwriter, a couple of weeks ahead of delivery and give him some ideas about topics. I might also say, "Let's have some fun with so-and-so." I'd see a draft after a few days, make written comments, and then we'd go back and forth through another few drafts until I was satisfied.

If I was speaking to the Guelph Rotary Club, I would also meet with the local riding executive to bring them up to date on what was happening at Queen's Park and learn where they stood on issues of the day. The grass roots need tending or they wither and die. I always carried a tall leather pocket folder containing cards on which I would write possible speech lines, somebody's birthday I heard about, or any undertaking I'd made. At the end of the day, I would give all the cards I'd stuffed in my suit pocket to my secretary to follow up.

I was always fact gathering, even from members of other parties. During one meeting with Jean Chrétien, then minister of Indian affairs and northern development, we talked about the difficulties facing our Native peoples. Said Chrétien, "The average Eskimo family has two children and one policy analyst."

▼

The election of René Lévesque as premier of Quebec in 1976 sent shock waves throughout Canada and the rest of the world. The threat of separation caused political instability and drove our dollar down thirteen cents against the U.S. dollar over the next two years. Inflation grew as the price of imports increased; foreign investors were leery of Canada's apparent instability. Premier Davis established a special cabinet committee to develop a policy response to Quebec's possible separation. With Davis as chairman, I was on the committee with Roy McMurtry, René Brunelle, Tom Wells, Bob Welch, and Frank Miller.

I also reached out on my own, establishing a good working relationship with Lévesque's Minister of Finance Jacques Parizeau and Minister of Intergovernmental Affairs Claude Morin, after inviting myself to a meeting with them in Quebec City within two weeks of the Parti Québécois (PQ) win. Parizeau was smart, a dandy, full of himself, and an aristocrat. His intelligence and style were such that I used to call him Canada's only professional finance minister. We got along well, and we both liked brandy. Morin was equally bright, but dour.

Despite our differences, we had a mutual interest against Ottawa's desire for greater centralization. Their answer, of course, went much further — get out. In response, I urged them to attend the finance ministers' meeting in December. They agreed and joined the other provincial ministers in common cause against Ottawa. In my view, if the ten provinces could agree on financial matters, then maybe we could all find agreement in other areas, including constitutional arrangements.

Pierre Trudeau had promised any tax reforms would not reduce provincial revenues but now was reneging. Our main battle was about a new revenue-sharing scheme foisted on us by Ottawa that would cost Ontario more than $300 million a year and force us to increase personal income tax by 10 per cent to replace the lost revenue.

We had already won 12.5 points of personal income tax and one point of corporate tax from Ottawa. We wanted four more points of personal tax; Ottawa was offering one point and some cash.

Despite the unusual provincial unanimity among finance ministers, federal finance minister Donald Macdonald refused to relent, and the issue was tossed to first ministers. I sent Davis to the first ministers' meeting with a card to place on the table in front of him that read: "Four points, don't forget." In the end, we got two points and some cash, a classic compromise. The federal government won greater control over finances while the provinces gained more flexibility when it came to the design and administration of health and education.

During a trip to England, France, Germany, and Switzerland in 1978, I sought to reassure investors about the unity of Canada and the outcome of any referendum that might be held. Because Parizeau had delivered a decent budget, and the PQ were turning out to be good managers and honest, too — something new in Quebec — Lévesque was a tough opponent. "This struggle over the integrity of our country may not be neat, dispassionate, or always played by the Marquis of Queensbury rules, but we are not dealing with a bunch of pirates either," I told the Canada–United Kingdom Chamber of Commerce. "Both sides are appealing within an orderly and open society for the loyalty of a free people. We are not refighting the Battle of the Plains of Abraham; Canada was not fashioned by a victorious empire but by the vision of free men."[78]

Quebec's délégué général in London, Gilles Loiselle, was scheduled to attend the event, so I sent him a copy of my remarks in advance. He was not perturbed, telling me, "If I had to walk out of every lunch at which someone said something unpleasant about Quebec, I'd never eat."[79]

---

78 *Globe and Mail*, January 19, 1978, p. 13.
79 *Globe and Mail*, September 9, 1978, p. 12.

Restraining spending and receiving a hearing in Ottawa remained my watchwords in preparation for the April 1977 budget, despite the fact we were still in a minority government. Early in February, when I met with ministers of finance, I urged Ottawa to lift controls on profits (in place since 1975) because I was looking for a boost from the private sector. "Governments do not create wealth or prosperity. The private sector does," I said in a February speech to Partnership for Prosperity, an economic conference called by Premier Davis. "Governments only create conditions — fiscal, legislative, regulatory, perhaps psychological — in which the private sector can go to work and make good things happen. There are three goals: jobs, price stability, and income security. Together these things not only mean growth but also a fair sharing of the benefits of growth."

Looking back, I think the 1977 budget was the best of the six budgets I presented because of its long-term direction. Rather than just look ahead one year, as the traditional budget does, I set out a three-year plan and forecast a balanced budget by 1981. To establish this bold goal, I had the support of the so-called Red Tory ministers. The media always made a fuss about how there were two wings in the party with the Red Tories seen as left-leaning politicians more interested in social programs than fiscal responsibility. In fact, most ministers were fiscally conservative. They believed in balancing the budget and paying down debt.

By now readers will have concluded that Norman Webster of the *Globe* was my favourite columnist. He was consistently the best commentator during my time in politics. He didn't always agree with me, but he did approve of this budget. "It was just two weeks ago that NDP leader Stephen Lewis described Treasurer Darcy McKeough as a man suffering from 'an almost terminal scrawniness of the imagination.' In his budget speech, Mr. McKeough exposed that for the canard it is."[80]

---

80 *Globe and Mail*, April 21, 1977.

Years later, Bryan Evans and John Shields concurred in their chapter in *The Guardian*. "With the aid of a Special Program Review, designed to help find ways to curtail government growth, the budgets of 1976 and 1977 revealed that Ontario indeed had turned a corner. Between 1975–6 and 1982–3, Ontario government expenditures as a percentage of [Gross Provincial Product] fell year after year."[81]

▼

Meanwhile, an election was in the wind. The polling looked good for us, and Eddie Goodman had convinced Marvin Shore, a Liberal MPP from London, to cross the floor. The Liberals under Stuart Smith seemed in disarray. They supported the budget, but when we tried to raise the ceiling on rent controls to 8 per cent from 6 per cent, we were defeated in the House. An election was called for June 9, 1977.

I spent half the election campaigning in other ridings, yet managed to win 46.5 per cent of the vote in my own constituency, the best since 1963, when there was no NDP candidate. The overall results, however, were little changed. We increased our share of the popular vote by three percentage points and picked up seven seats to hold fifty-eight, still five seats short of a majority.

The NDP dropped back to third place in the election. Stephen Lewis resigned as leader and was replaced by Michael Cassidy, first elected to the legislature from Ottawa Centre in 1971. I had a far different relationship with Cassidy than I'd had with Lewis. Recently, when Lewis was in Chatham giving a speech, he stayed overnight with us at Bally McKeough. I had no such bipartisan feelings for Cassidy. The day after Cassidy was elected leader he called me an economic primitive and a reactionary. I responded by calling him "the most sanctimonious and dogmatic politician in Ontario."[82] Our rapport never improved.

---

81 Dutil, Patrice, ed., *The Guardian*, p. 138.
82 *Globe and Mail*, April 7, 1978, p. 5.

The second minority provided new ammunition for my ongoing efforts to balance the budget. As Jonathan Manthorpe told his readers in the *Toronto Star* on September 3, 1977:

McKeough is no longer talking about saving paper clips, using envelopes twice, nor even of banning civil service hiring. What he is talking about now is ditching existing government programs, and his fellow ministers don't like it one bit. One of the problems is that McKeough, who has a Bismarckian approach to diplomacy, is not being very gentle with his cabinet brethren. All of them could accept the restraint program, which has been going on for a couple of years, but this is something else. "It seems to be a little less thoughtful than before," said one source. "It's really a broad-axe approach. It's a case of 'all right, everybody, cut off 10 per cent from your budget.'"

Aside from my spendthrift colleagues, another problem was the legacy left by my predecessor as treasurer, John White, in what became known as the Edmonton Commitment. In a 1973 tri-level conference in that city, White had made three promises. First, Ontario's financial transfers to local governments would grow at the same rate as total revenues. Second, municipal borrowing powers would be strengthened. Third, the province would pass along to the municipalities, dollar for dollar, any additional tax sharing by Ottawa with Ontario. There were several issues with those promises, including what was the proper base year, what should be included (teachers' pensions, for example, initially were not), and the fact the province's own spending was increasing at a much lower rate than foreseen by the Edmonton Commitment.

I could have repudiated the commitment but didn't. In a twelve-city tour in September 1977 to explain why municipal councils and school boards would be receiving less in transfer payments than they expected, I used my own cost-cutting measures as an example of what others should be doing. I was aiming for a 3 per cent reduction in senior management positions on top of the 7 per cent cuts of the previous two years.

I also indicated there were rebates and other payments to the municipalities that should be included in the calculation but had not been in the past. Even with my proposed changes, Metro Toronto, for example, was getting 8.3 per cent more in grants than in the previous year. At the same time, Ontario government spending was rising only 6.3 per cent, so we were paying them more than was provided for in the formula. There was some grumbling, but the municipalities eventually fell into line. Restraint was the order of the day.

▼

Jean Chrétien replaced Donald Macdonald as federal finance minister in September 1977. Chrétien seemed more pragmatic than Macdonald, so I concluded he would be more open to my ideas. At an October 1977 meeting of finance ministers, I urged a reduction in the retail sales tax by all provinces as the best way to encourage consumer spending and boost the economy. Ottawa would compensate the provinces for the lost revenue.

In his first budget in April 1978, Chrétien followed my advice and then took all the credit. In his book *Straight from the Heart*, he says he rejected doing anything with the federal sales tax and decided a coordinated approach was the answer instead. "My plan was to consult with all the provinces before the budget and get them to agree to lower their sales taxes in return for financial compensation from Ottawa."[83] Sounds exactly like my plan.

In fact, Chrétien called me to help persuade some of the finance ministers to go along with the idea. Chrétien, Parizeau, and I met for dinner at the Hotel Bonaventure in Montreal. I thought the deal was done; Parizeau was onside. But once the tax cuts were announced, Quebec kicked up a fuss until a truce was struck. Writes Chrétien: "I could have called Darcy McKeough to be my witness, but that

---

83 Chrétien, Jean, *Straight from the Heart*, pp. 103–104.

would have put him in a difficult position: he was an Ontario Tory, and the federal Tories were making so much hay out of my discomfort. Though he didn't volunteer to intervene publicly, I was told that he informed both Joe Clark and René Lévesque that Chrétien was right, that Parizeau had shaken hands on a deal."[84] I have no recollection of this. I might have contacted Clark — but Lévesque? Hardly. All I know is it was Ontario's idea, we made it possible, and I regard my initiative as one of the public policy changes about which I am most proud.

I was also an early supporter of free trade with the U.S. In 1977, U.S. Ambassador Tom Enders urged a trade pact between Canada and the U.S. that would go further than the tariff cuts required by international agreements. I could see the benefits, but I also knew we needed to get our own act together first. "I think that's a good starting offer: but where is the Canadian position?" I said in a November 1977 speech. "Do we really have as clear an idea of what we want from the Americans as they have of their own interests? I think not. We have a collection of regional interests but no common position."[85]

It took another dozen years before the Canada–U.S. Free Trade Agreement was finally launched. And, wonder of wonders, there is even some talk that Canada may one day change its protectionist supply management system. To this day, the federal government's out-of-date policies keep dairy and poultry prices too high and foreign competitors at bay. If and when those restrictions are eventually lifted, I will be the first to shout, "Hallelujah!" But no politician can expect support for his every idea, as I was about to discover when I tried to raise Ontario Health Insurance Plan premiums.

84 Ibid., p. 107.
85 Speech to the Conference Board of Canada, Montreal, November 16, 1977.

17

▾

The End of Days

Health-care spending was a priority as I prepared for the 1978 budget. Per person medical visits were up 20 per cent in four years, and the rate of admission to hospitals was rising twice as fast as the growth in population. In order to bolster revenue and cover some of the growing costs, I proposed a 37.5 per cent increase in Ontario Health Insurance Plan (OHIP) premiums. That meant an individual paid $6 more a month for a total of $22, and $12 more, $44 a month, for a family. Even with the higher rates, premiums covered only one-third of costs; government paid the rest.

As for cost cutting, I had done everything I could, including a reduction of 1,350 civil servants over three years. Spending was projected to rise 7 per cent, less than the previous year's 9.1 per cent. Still, the budget would result in my fourth deficit in a row greater than $1 billion.

As usual, Premier Davis came to Treasury for his budget briefing. In all my time as treasurer, he never actually said yes or no to any aspect of any budget. A portion of that February meeting appeared in Peter Raymont's *The Art of the Possible*, including the part when I pointed to the OHIP increases and said, "That's the only one I think we'll hear anything about."[86] How right he was!

Next came a briefing with some of my closest advisors: Phil Lind, John Cronyn, John Thompson, Kirk Foley, Jim Hayhurst, and Tom Kierans. Cronyn and I got into an argument about nothing very serious, then I blew my top when Lind suggested the party at the Albany Club after the budget speech should feature a pay bar. My argumentative reaction to old friends told me I had been in the job too long. Either I was not listening to people, or I had simply become arrogant.

When I delivered the budget on March 7, a printed French version was made available, and I read a paragraph in French. "Finally, the production of an Ontario budget in French for the first time since Confederation was a nice touch, as was the Treasurer's one halting paragraph in *la belle langue*. Not too much was made of it; it just happened; and that was exactly right," wrote Norman Webster.[87] I was, and remain, very proud of that step in the right direction.

At first, my budget seemed to be a success. We won a non-confidence vote in the House with Liberal support. But the premium hike was referred to the Standing Committee on Social Development. The committee, with an Opposition majority, voted 7 to 5 to have the increase withdrawn.

Stephen Lewis was no longer an MPP, but he wrote regularly for the *Toronto Star*. In a column, he reminded me we had first been elected in 1963 and heckled other MPPs mercilessly. Then he wrote, "Well, Darcy, nearly 15 years have passed and it's time to tone things down. All that whooping and stomping and lubricating your lungs in the Legislature; it's just not good for your reputation. I don't mind when you do it to me because we understand each other — a little wink after question period, or a midnight drink at La Scala, and everything's back on track. But those other guys on the opposition benches don't quite feel it that way. You see — if I may presume on

86 *Globe and Mail*, December 20, 1978.
87 *Globe and Mail*, March 9, 1978.

our friendship — you just must do some very speedy mellowing. Not as much as I did over the years — I mellowed my way right out of the leadership. But at least enough to save your job. It's called compromise, moderation, flexibility."[88]

Lewis was right. I had to act or we would have an unwanted election. I cut the proposed hike in half to 18.75 per cent. To make up for the $271 million in foregone revenue, I pulled funds from other programs and raised corporate taxes by 1 per cent. In the vote that followed, we survived, supported by the Liberals. "My principles are intact," I bravely said. "I don't feel limp or weakened."[89]

▼

In fact, for a year I had been coasting rather than creating. I was worn out and frustrated over the rejection by caucus and cabinet of a series of local government reforms. I was also upset by my inability to bring about the market value assessment I had been promoting since 1969.

Beyond such specific issues, I was bored. I attended too many meetings where I said to myself, "God, I've heard all this before." There were times I would doze. I realized I wasn't going anywhere because the premier wasn't going anywhere. I had always been loyal and remained so; I would never have tried to push out Premier Davis. But I came to the conclusion that, if I couldn't be premier, I should resign.

On June 1, I delivered a handwritten letter to the premier's office that said:

Dear Bill:

It has been nearly 15 years now since I was first elected to the Legislature, and for nearly eleven of those years, I have had the

88 *Toronto Star*, April 23, 1978.
89 *Globe and Mail*, April 26, 1978, p. 5.

great privilege of serving in the Executive Council — for 4½ years under John and 6½ years under you. It's a long time and although at 45, I feel that I'm not old, I sure as hell feel that I have been doing what I have been doing for a long enough time. Frankly, I am tired and although the summer will cure that problem, I am run down in terms of ideas and enthusiasm and probably ambition and zeal. A change is needed for me personally; what that will be I don't know; I will be surprised though if Joyce, the boys and I don't benefit from some new challenge — whatever it may turn out to be. If our party is to continue to govern then we have to constantly renew our ranks; whether my departure will spur some of the other "old timers" (and some not so old), I don't know but I would be hopeful that the example might give you some elbow room. I wouldn't be honest if I denied that the events of this spring have not influenced my decision. The fact is however that the thinking has been in my mind (and Joyce's) for some time; the recognition of my need for a change has however been brought home by facing up to the fact that I have lost some of the knack (or luck) which I may have had in meeting and handling current problems and needs.

I told the premier my resignation was effective June 26 because the following day the cabinet would begin the 1979 budget process, by which time a new treasurer should be in place. I concluded by saying:

All of this has not been arrived at lightly, nor does my decision in any way reflect on the government, my colleagues or our party. For all three my respect, loyalty and support have only strengthened over these last months and years. My reason basically is personal and that perhaps is a good way to end this letter — simply expressing to you my warmest personal regards and affection together with my warm thanks for all your leadership and support and most of all for your great friendship.

A week went by before I finally heard from Davis, who said we would talk in four days. The day Davis responded, I announced in the House that I was indefinitely postponing market value assessment. I was either crazy to have promoted property tax reform or way ahead of my time. When action was finally taken in 1998, I appeared before a legislative committee studying the bill and said, "My only regret is that the provincial treasurer twenty years ago didn't have intestinal fortitude to do what this bill is now doing."

Even with those changes, distortions remain. Bally McKeough has a 2014 market assessment of $700,000. I pay property tax of $10,658 or 15.2 per cent of assessed value. Our Toronto condo was assessed in 2014 at $561,500 with taxes of $4,060 or 7.2 per cent, less than half the tax rate of Bally McKeough. Many Toronto properties are taxed at even lower rates. My message to Toronto is this: Quit bitching, stop asking Queen's Park for more money, and bring your property tax rates up to the same level as other municipalities. Your books will be balanced, and you'll be able to pay for current programs and afford new ones.

▼

Bill Davis did not meet with me on the day he promised to discuss my resignation. It was always difficult to get an answer from him. As treasurer, I would send, before any meeting with him, a list of topics to be discussed with ten or twelve headings and just a word or two about each. I'd go down the list with him in person. If he didn't make any comment on a specific item after fifteen or twenty seconds, I would assume that he was okay, and I'd move on.

After the House rose for the summer, I remained in limbo. Except for a two-day staff meeting in July, I spent most of my time that month at home with family, playing tennis and barbecuing. That same month, Ford Motor Co. pitted Windsor, Ontario, against Lima, Ohio, to squeeze the best government incentive for a new $500-million engine plant and its 2,600 jobs. I was dead-set against a subsidy bidding war, but Ontario offered $28 million and Ottawa added $40 million, enough to win.

Finally, a lunch was set with Davis for August 15. Immediately before that, we spent several days together at a federal–provincial meeting in Regina during which he never mentioned my resignation. My only insight came from John Cronyn, who seemed to have been designated to tell me Davis would not be resigning in the near future.

When Davis and I finally met for lunch, at La Scala on August 15, it was more than ten weeks since I had submitted my resignation. After the soup course, he said, "I'm not going." I replied, "Well, then I am." He tried to talk me out of it, but I was adamant. It was time to get on with the rest of my life. I paid for lunch, Davis drove me back to my office, and I drafted a statement he approved later that day.

I flew to Chatham to tell my riding executive, and then my mother, that I was resigning both as provincial treasurer and MPP for Chatham-Kent. Informing everybody came as a great relief to me. I didn't realize just how long I had been agonizing over this decision. I swam, then had dinner, all with the phone off the hook so no one could reach me.

The next day, I held a news conference in Chatham at 8:30 a.m. for local media and then flew to Toronto to meet the Queen's Park press at 11:30. In my brief statement, I said: "I have served my riding for fifteen years and in the Cabinet of Ontario for eleven years; I believe I still have a lot of energy and I want to keep growing. It's time for a change for me personally. Frankly, I am excited by the opportunity of building a new career. I do not resent for a moment the demands of public life. Indeed, my family has always supported me, and I am indebted for their understanding and assistance. The political arena has been good to me, and I leave with a sense of deep appreciation and accomplishment. I believe politics must be a place for builders, and I believe we are building well in Ontario. Our province has changed immensely over the last decade, and government has had to make changes to protect and enhance those things we cherish. I have been able to help in that process, and I am proud of the reforms that are in place."

Among the reforms I listed as accomplishments were economic renewal, greater government efficiencies, and setting the path to a balanced budget. As for the future, I said I was open to just about anything except politics. I noted I no longer would sit as an MPP because I wanted a clean break, adding, "I have too much respect for the taxpayers to expect them to subsidize me during a job search."

Someone asked if I was retiring for the same reason as Donald Macdonald, who had done so as federal finance minster a year earlier because, as he put it, he didn't have the "royal jelly" to be prime minister. My problem was "too much royal jelly," I said. "I don't think anybody who seriously goes into public life doesn't harbour ambition to get the top job. Sure, I was disappointed seven years ago, and I suppose always will be. I'd be dishonest if I didn't say I would have like to have been top."[90]

I dropped in briefly on cabinet to say my goodbyes. The members were gracious, but some of them were probably glad to see me go. One of my last acts was arguing for a hold-the-line 6.3 per cent increase in spending during the next budget year. Others in cabinet wanted more. In order to stifle their demands, I used the figure in a speech, sent the *Toronto Star* an advance copy, and made sure there was a stack of newspapers available at the next cabinet meeting with the page one headline trumpeting the ceiling. My ceiling.

I invited about fifty people to my office for a farewell drink. At the same time, the annual parade to mark the opening day of the Canadian National Exhibition was wending its way south past the legislature and then down University Avenue. Said Eddie Goodman, as he stood on the small balcony watching the clowns and bands, "Leave it to Darcy to arrange a parade on the day of his resignation."

Fifteen minutes after my press conference was over, Davis named Frank Miller, formerly minister of natural resources, as my replacement. I understood the need to demonstrate continuity, but I have to say I was miffed when the spotlight was so quickly swung away from my departure. I did not attend Miller's 12:30 p.m. swearing-in ceremony, although I did call on him the following day to wish him well with his reduced workload. As treasurer he lost responsibility

---

90 *Globe and Mail*, August 17, 1978, p. 5.

for intergovernmental affairs, municipal affairs, and housing. Miller soon changed the year he planned to balance the budget from my 1981 to his 1984.

One of the first well-wishers to call me was Jacques Parizeau. Liberal leader David Peterson described my resignation as "a serious blow to the government of Ontario and to the Conservative Party. He single-handedly represented the government's image of management competence."[91] Hugh Windsor, who had just taken over from Norman Webster as Queen's Park columnist for the *Globe*, compared my resignation with John Turner's in 1975, noting we were about the same age at the time of departure — Turner was forty-six, I was forty-five. "Both were considered heirs apparent and yet both quit, leaving a cloud of ambiguity swirling around their departures, including the possibility they will be back some day. Both seem to have left because the way to the top job was blocked, at least temporarily."[92]

Even the *Toronto Star* expressed regret. "We frequently disagreed with Darcy McKeough. But his departure from Ontario politics leaves a void that will be hard to fill."[93] The *Globe* praised my achievements in an editorial. "He cut government spending in Ontario and he hollered at the top of his considerable lungs for the cutting of government spending in Canada. He even told Ottawa how to do it, as flamboyantly as he told the Ontario Legislature."[94]

That weekend Joyce and I entertained house guests in what was an annual gathering of close friends at Bally McKeough: Phil and Anne Lind, Tom and Inta Kierans, and Tom and Pam MacMillan. Now that I was out of the public eye, MacMillan brought t-shirts he had printed that said: "Darcy Who?" Someone suggested I should take no phone calls unless it was one of three people with a job offer: Ian Sinclair, Chairman and CEO of Canadian Pacific Ltd.; Conrad Black, Chairman of Argus Corp. Ltd.; or a representative from the College of Cardinals in Rome.

91 *Toronto Star*, August 17, 1978, p. A20.
92 *Globe and Mail*, August 29, 1978, p. 7.
93 *Toronto Star*, April 21, 1978.
94 *Globe and Mail*, August 17, 1978.

When Joe Clark, the leader of the Opposition, called, Joyce answered and said I couldn't come to the phone because I was playing tennis. "Darcy's winning out there, and Darcy never quits when he's winning," she said. Later, when I called Clark back, he asked me to run federally. He even had a riding in mind for me, but I told him I had no interest.

Now that I was in private life, my special MPP plates had to be returned. But my new set said NSF-198 — the three worst letters in finance: non-sufficient funds. I exchanged them for something less descriptive. For the moment I might have been the poorer for leaving politics, but not that poor.

Three hundred Treasury staff held a farewell party for me in September at St. Lawrence Hall in downtown Toronto. Included in the gifts was a collection of my budgets labelled "Fiscal Fantasies: A Collection of Short Stories by Darcy McKeough." They also presented me with a red-leather binder entitled *The Unpublished Sayings of Chairman McKeough*. On the cover was a cartoon of me as a duck, looking nonchalant and smoking my pipe. Underwater my agitating legs were visibly entangled in red tape. One of the best quotes, which I may or may not have said, came when I was being briefed on ministry spending about to be scrutinized by a legislative committee to which I had been summoned. "Always tell me the truth," I said. "Then I'll know what I'm changing."

I was also given a copy of Adam Smith's *The Wealth of Nations*, first published in the eighteenth century, with the explanation, "We won't be needing this anymore because we are moving on to twentieth-century economists." For my part, I told them I hadn't yet calculated the pawnshop value of all their gifts. And since there still was some summer left, and I was looking for paid work, I was available to cut lawns. On a more serious note, I said I didn't think Davis should have stripped away so many responsibilities from Treasurer Miller, but added, "Everybody's entitled to make their own mistakes."

Others agreed. "TEIGA seemed to work exceptionally well and is fondly remembered as a 'golden age' by many of its employees," said a chapter on Treasury by Luc Bernier and Joseph Facal in *The*

Guardian, "The Ontario Ministry of Finance as an Exception in Canadian Public Administration." "Though the Ontario TEIGA was only temporary, it remains a fascinating example of public administration innovation and policy entrepreneurship."[95]

One of the gifts I did keep, and which is displayed to this day in the library at Bally McKeough, was a large granite millstone, complete with chain, to wear around my neck. It's inscribed "Edmonton and a balanced budget. Je maintiendrai." I will maintain. Even if I torpedoed the Edmonton Commitment, that was indeed my motto at Treasury. I may not have always made friends, but I was consistent in my beliefs.

In an era when big governments thought they could do anything and afford everything, I knew that wasn't possible. Governments in general today try to be more careful with the taxpayer's money. In that regard, I was ahead of my time. I believe my approach was prescient and practical.

That same month, Bill Davis announced he was staying on as leader until the next election, which he did not intend to call until 1981. My riding association held a dinner, attended by Bill and Kathy Davis, to honour Joyce and me. "I look back on the last fifteen years with happiness and, immodestly, with some pride," I said in my speech. "Happy because I have worked under, with, and for so many wonderful people, colleagues, staff, constituents. Proud because of a number of things which have been accomplished during that time: highways and bridges, flood control works, dikes, a parkway, and a community college. These are material things. There is also the feeling of satisfaction of having been able to assist so many people, young and old, with their problems."

I also said I would continue to speak out on public issues, predicting Ontario could look forward to steady growth in incomes, jobs, an ability to help the less fortunate, and the pursuit of cultural and athletic excellence. "But we will do all these things only if we remember the lessons we have so painfully learned in the seventies:

---

95 Dutil, ed., *The Guardian*, pp. 221–22.

that there are no free lunches, that too large expectations by individuals and governments have been major causes of inflation and hence have caused problems in balance of payments and our financial stability generally."

Andy Watson, a provincial agricultural representative, was nominated to replace me in the Chatham-Kent by-election on October 19. He won and served two terms. Moreover, his election broke a jinx. Until then, the Davis government had lost all the by-elections it called — Huron, St. George, Stormont, and Carleton East — and won none back in succeeding elections. Before Watson was sworn in, my last official act was to sit with him in the gallery of the legislature, where I beamed and smiled and crowed a bit.

18

▼

The Constitution and Other Reforms

Lord knows I am not a lawyer, let alone a constitutional lawyer, but during my time in office I was part of some historic constitutional events in Canada. Originally we were "The Dominion of Canada," which, of course, came from Psalm 72, "He shall have dominion also from sea to sea." Then some jackass proposed, and in an unguarded moment the Parliament of Canada passed, a bill dropping the word Dominion. What a shame!

There were two parts to the historic equation: first, the law and the constitution, and second, the fiscal arrangements between the Dominion of Canada and the provinces.

I was involved with both. There were even occasions when I made common cause with Jacques Parizeau and the Parti Québécois to battle the federal government's ongoing seizure of fiscal powers. As I regularly reminded Ottawa, "We were here first." There was an Upper Canada and a Lower Canada before there was a Canada.

But, to begin at the beginning, in the history of conquests it has to be said that, after General James Wolfe captured Quebec City in 1759, the defeated were, by any standard, well treated. The positions of the Roman Catholic Church and French civil law were respected and honoured; a succession of British Governors were magnanimous victors. But the American War of Independence and the War of 1812 cast a long shadow over the future of British North America.

Among my famous maternal forebears was Jonathan Sewell III, my great-great-great-grandfather. Born in Cambridge, Massachusetts, in 1766, he was bilingual, a Loyalist who fled the American Revolution, sat in the Legislative Assembly of Lower Canada, and was appointed Chief Justice of Lower Canada in 1808.

Sewell was among the first to react to the American threat. In 1814 he proposed a Representative Assembly composed of Upper and Lower Canada, New Brunswick, Nova Scotia, Prince Edward Island, and Cape Breton. Sewell had the support of Edward, the Duke of Kent, but Queen Victoria later said the time was not right. It would take until 1867 before Sir John A. Macdonald accomplished the feat of Confederation.

Given that accord, what went wrong with French–English relations? Louis Riel, conscription in two world wars, the emergence of Toronto over Montreal as the nation's financial centre, the understandable desire to preserve French language and culture, and the diminution of the Catholic Church in Quebec as a stabilizing, conservative force were major factors. Admittedly, this list is an overly simplistic description of how we arrived at Quebec nationalism as declared in 1962 by Quebec Premier Jean Lesage's slogan *Maîtres chez nous* (Masters in our own house) and his successor, Daniel Johnson, whose 1965 book was entitled *Égalité ou Indépendance* (Equality or Independence).

With Expo 67 in Montreal such an international success, those were heady days. In a speech to the Rotary Club of Chatham on September 13, 1967, I approvingly quoted Peter C. Newman, who wrote in the *Toronto Star*, "This is the greatest thing we have ever done as a nation. Can we ever be the same again?" I went on to say, "This is one of those events which marks a change in the course of history, and which constitutes a milestone in the development of our country."

Constitutional debate took an arduous path from John Robarts and his Confederation of Tomorrow conference in 1967 to Pierre

Trudeau and the Victoria Charter of 1971. I was in Victoria when Trudeau brought Margaret, his new wife of three months, there. We were all enchanted by her beauty, poise, and warmth. British Columbia Premier W. A. C. Bennett, the conference host, was a bit of a hypocrite. He didn't drink but built a magnificent Government House in Victoria for wining and dining. Bennett took everyone on a cruise on the Straits of Juan de Fuca on a boat that carried no booze. Fortunately, the irrepressible Duncan Allan had stocked our cabin, so we became the locus of happy hour. As the *Telegram* reported: "The bottles were just nicely opened in the Ontario cabin when Mr. Bennett invited Premier William Davis to a coffee party in his suite. As the chagrined Mr. Davis headed for the door, Treasurer Darcy McKeough slapped him on the back and said with a grin: 'Bill, for the first time I'm glad you won the leadership.'"[96]

The Victoria Charter agreed to by first ministers would have brought home the British North America Act with an amending formula, but Quebec Premier Robert Bourassa asked if he could consult his cabinet. After he returned home, he found widespread anger and disapproval. Quebec wanted control of social programs but wanted them paid for by Ottawa. Bourassa told Trudeau he could not sell the Victoria Charter. The deal was off. Bourassa might have been a fine man, but he was not, on that occasion, a great leader.[97]

Trudeau had said that, if the Victoria Charter were rejected, the constitutional process would be postponed indefinitely, and that's what happened. No constitutional effort ever got as close to an agreement again as the Victoria Charter.

Many public servants and political leaders played a positive role. First and foremost, I would cite all members of TEIGA, particularly Ian MacDonald, Rendall Dick, and Don Stevenson. Their basic thrust was, "What is good for Canada is good for Ontario." I also salute the efforts of Peter Lougheed, Don Getty, Duff Roblin,

96 *Telegram*, June 30, 1971.
97 For a more detailed explanation, see John English, *Just Watch Me: The Life of Pierre Elliott Trudeau, 1968–2000* (Toronto: Knopf Canada, 2009), pp. 135–40.

182   THE DUKE OF KENT

Richard Hatfield, Marcel Bélanger, Jean Charest, and most of my colleagues in cabinet in both the Robarts and Davis administrations.

I made every effort to help by hosting Quebec politicians who visited Toronto, such as Quebec Finance Minister Raymond Garneau. Garneau was as committed a Canadian as I have met. In 1978, I arranged a summer job at Ontario Place for his son Jean-François, who visited Bally McKeough for a weekend.

I also urged Davis to consider making a greater commitment to bilingualism in Ontario as a show of support for Quebec. Davis carried on the Robarts policy — where the numbers warranted — of making French-language services available in the courts and in certain ministries without legislation. Both saw anything more as politically divisive.

I found out much later that, had he believed he could have overcome the political reality, Davis would have legislated official bilingualism. In 1985, by which time we had both left office, we had lunch at Winston's. We began by discussing his about-face when he'd declared full financial support for the Roman Catholic school system just before resigning in 1984. In so doing, he reversed his 1971 decision against funding. Stopping Spadina aside, we won the 1971 election because that decision appealed to our Protestant voters.

I told him his switch had amazed me because the ministry of education believed in only one system. Davis, of course, had been minister of education, and his deputy Ed Stewart joined the premier's office. Stewart was strongly opposed to supporting separate schools. I used to accuse him of being the last Orangeman! Davis said I was wrong about Ed Stewart, but I doubt it.

Davis insisted that, when he became premier, equality for separate schools was one of his three goals. His second was patriating the constitution. At that point, I groaned and asked, "What was the third?" When he replied, "Official bilingualism," I said, "I was right to get out when I did." Despite the worthy nature of those ambitions, any one of them would have torn apart the Tory party and made it impossible for us to get anything done as a government amid the resulting controversy.

The Davis decision on extending funding beyond grade ten to grade thirteen, after years of lobbying by Archbishop of Toronto Gerald Emmett Carter, was supported by all parties. But it was unpopular with some Tories who likely stayed home in the 1985 election rather than vote for Frank Miller. Such an attitude helped bring about the defeat of Miller and the rise of David Peterson to the premier's office. I remain convinced that Davis either should not have made the decision or should have seen it through himself by continuing as leader.

▼

In office, I was often frustrated by the amount of time given over to the Constitution. "Let us not forget — and let the Government of Canada not forget — that there are other regional issues that require attention," I said in a speech to the Association of Municipalities on September 8, 1976. "We must not allow ourselves to become so obsessed with the symbolic issues — such as those which centre on French–English relationships — that we neglect other issues which deserve just as much attention."

Nor did I hesitate to take on Parizeau. I pointed out to him that only British Columbia and Ontario put more money into Confederation than they took out. By itself, Ontario gave $26 billion over sixteen years, money that was shared by Quebec and the other provinces. On April 25, 1977, when I introduced Parizeau at an Ontario Economic Council conference in Toronto, I did not let the moment pass. I told the audience that, during a recent meeting of finance ministers, I had been asked by a reporter why the PQ government, aimed at taking Quebec out of Canada, would bother sending a representative to such a meeting. Said I, "Jacques' answer was if you decide to order a new car you still have to tune the old one until the new one is ready. My reply to that was I thought neither of us could afford to order a new car."[98]

---

98 *Hamilton Spectator*, April 26, 1977.

In 1977, Trudeau tried to stall Quebec's ambitions by appointing John Robarts and Jean-Luc Pépin, an academic and former federal minister, to head the Task Force on Unity. After two years of hearings, their findings included entrenching language rights in the Constitution, reducing federal powers, and reforming the Senate.

Trudeau ignored the recommendations and continued to meddle in provincial matters.

▼

Pierre Trudeau defeated Joe Clark in the February 1980 election, and René Lévesque lost his first referendum 60 to 40 that May. In November 1981, when Ottawa and the provinces met, ten of the eleven participants agreed to a Charter of Rights and decided to ask the parliament of the United Kingdom to patriate the constitution with an amending formula and a notwithstanding clause. Quebec did not agree. I had left politics, but had I been there, my advice to Premier Davis would have been, "Ontario should not agree unless Quebec agrees."

When Brian Mulroney was prime minister, he tried to bring in Quebec with the Meech Lake Accord of 1987. As a member of the Business Council on National Issues, I did what I could, but all to no avail. Newfoundland and Manitoba refused to approve the agreement. Trudeau's supreme ego was a large factor in the defeat of Meech. I know of no other instance in Canada, the U.K., or the U.S. in which a former prime minister or president interfered so blatantly in their country's affairs after leaving office. The other leaders all chose to be statesmen, but not Trudeau.

Mulroney tried again with a referendum to be held following an agreement at the Charlottetown Conference in 1992. "Yes" committees were formed in all the provinces. Ontario's non-partisan effort was co-chaired by three former lieutenant governors: John Black Aird, Lincoln Alexander, and Pauline McGibbon. Premier Bob Rae asked me to serve as a vice-chairman on the Ontario committee. I made a number of speeches, but Charlottetown was defeated on October 26, 1992, although Ontario, bless her heart, narrowly voted yes.

The issue continued to dominate public debate in Canada after Parizeau became premier of Quebec in 1994. On October 30, 1995, Quebec held a second referendum on sovereignty and the "good guys" won, but barely, with 50.58 per cent of the vote, a majority of just 54,288 votes out of 4.8 million cast.

In 2000, Prime Minister Jean Chrétien passed the Clarity Act setting out the conditions that would apply to negotiations following a vote to secede. Was that a smart move? I have never been able to decide. Since then, little has happened, thank goodness. The crushing defeat of PQ Premier Pauline Marois by Philippe Couillard and the Liberals in 2014 seems to have settled the question for now. But those of us who have been active on this file know the debate has faded before and then returned with a vengeance.

▼

Other much-needed reforms are also on hold. Any movement toward Senate reform has evaporated after allegations about the expense account practices of certain senators. Those who would abolish the Senate are wrong. We need a chamber of sober second thought. The Bank Act has regularly been improved by the Senate Banking Committee, to cite just one example. As for term limits, I'm in favour, but why not for members of the House of Commons as well?

Even if there is no full reform, the Senate must at least become more responsive to the provinces. When vacancies occur, the provinces should recommend candidates — based on an election if they choose — and the Government of Canada should appoint from that list. No constitutional amendment would be required for that major step.

I also believe we should preserve our relationship with the monarch. Even those who are opposed say we should wait until the death of Queen Elizabeth to become a republic. It's not on! The provinces will never agree. I like the fact that the sovereign, the governor general, and the lieutenant governors in our system are separate and apart from politics. As Winston Churchill said, "When we win a war, we say, 'God Save the Queen'; when we lose a war, we say, 'Sack the Prime Minister!'"

Proportional representation is another idea that regularly comes up, but I prefer the current first-past-the-post system. Any preferential system would turn a minority government with less than 50 per cent of the vote into a majority government. In my view, whether a leader has 38 per cent or 52 per cent, he or she always has one eye on the next election, which means the ongoing opinion of the people does matter. Having been part of both majority and minority governments, I believe leaders do listen and learn. To be sure, that does not include everybody. Ernie Jackson and John Robarts were great friends but in some ways were polar opposites. I recall Robarts once saying, "We are a great people's party." To which Jackson added, "If we could just get rid of the fucking people."

▼

I would also like to get rid of the centralizers. Canada was created in 1867 by a compromise between those Fathers of Confederation who wanted a strong central government and those who sought a more decentralized model. The British North America Act brought together four disparate colonies followed by six more. Measured by today's standards, the centralizers lost. They got control only of foreign affairs, the post office, part of the courts and jail system, defence, tariffs, and customs. All else remained with the provinces — in particular, education, health and welfare, and taxation. That latter list now falls within Ottawa's expanded purview.

The provinces loaned their taxing powers to Ottawa during the First World War and never got those powers back. The resulting revenue has allowed the federal government to interject itself deliberately into former areas of provincial jurisdiction. The Canada Health Act is the most blatant example. "When he was asked about his disappointments in office, Robarts listed his failure to stop the federal medicare plan and his concern about the effect that the federal tax reform proposals would have on the Ontario economy," wrote Robarts's biographer, A. K. McDougall.[99]

For me, medicare was blackmail. Once Ottawa found health care too expensive, they reduced the money but kept control of the rules. As a result, accountability is blurred. If the wait time for a hip replacement is too long, who's to blame? The hospital, a municipal responsibility? The province that funds the hospital? Or the federal government that partially pays but sets the rules?

Moreover, there is ongoing tension between Canada and the provinces, particularly the haves versus the have-nots. The friction is most keenly felt in Quebec, where a lack of resources to carry out their role under the BNA Act has contributed to separatist feelings.

There are two alternatives. First, amend the BNA Act to transfer some of the responsibilities to Ottawa. Or second, stick to the BNA and give the provinces taxing power to pay for their responsibilities while Ottawa ceases to meddle, interfere, bribe, and confuse. Amending the constitution is a non-starter. A determination to adhere to our respective BNA responsibilities is possible.

In my time, we promoted various routes including a transfer of tax points to the province in order to fund health care. Ottawa, assisted by the have-not provinces, refused. We also advocated "disentanglement," a solution that would mean the government closest to those on the receiving end should handle delivery of the service. I continued to advocate this approach after I left office. In an Empire Club speech in 1982, I said, "We now have eleven departments of labour, eleven departments of agriculture, eleven of industry, eleven of corrections, and the list goes on. In almost every case, we need either one department, with its head office in Ottawa, or ten, one in each of the provinces. We do not need eleven. We must get away from the confusion, the cross purposes, the waste, and the sheer ineffectiveness that comes from having eleven."[100]

---

99 McDougall, A. K., *John P. Robarts: His Life and Government* (Toronto: University of Toronto Press, 1986), p. 259.
100 Speech to the Empire Club of Canada, March 4, 1982.

In my perhaps slightly utopian world, Ottawa would get out of employment insurance, roads, urban transit, and food inspection, among many other areas. Perhaps if Ottawa were to assume post-secondary education and manpower, then in the name of fiscal balance, the provinces could take over health. The provinces could focus on people-oriented areas while Ottawa looked after business regulation, securities markets, and environmental protection. To pay for all this, the provinces would stop collecting corporate income tax in return for a bigger share of personal income tax.

In 1947, public sector spending in Canada amounted to 24 per cent of the economy. Today, if you include the spending of government-owned enterprises, it's twice that. For every percentage point of public sector spending we were able to cut in my utopia, we'd save more than a billion dollars. To quote Everett Dirksen, the Republican senator from Illinois, "A billion here, a billion there, and pretty soon you're talking real money."

▼

Some steps toward my utopia have been taken by others. Ontario Premier Mike Harris moved primary and secondary education away from the municipalities to a provincial responsibility. He also ended road grants to municipalities, thereby forcing municipalities to determine their own priorities. Prime Minister Stephen Harper declared that federal contributions to health will be limited to the growth in inflation, a step that demonstrates his respect for provincial responsibility under the BNA Act. The result is that the provinces will have more ability to innovate.

As for how to control health-care costs, I must admit I have no better answers than anyone else. We should look at deterrent fees and two-tier systems like those in Britain and France. There also needs to be more transparency. When someone checks out of a hospital, there should be a bill showing the gross cost less what's covered by health insurance. David Peterson abolished OHIP premiums in

1990, thereby removing one way of reminding taxpayers that health care isn't free. That was a dumb move.

Another seemingly intractable problem is our Native peoples, highlighted in 2012 by the sad story about Attawapiskat First Nation, where so much federal government money appears to have been wasted. If Aboriginal peoples are ever to move into the mainstream, perhaps the province or municipality in which they are located should look after their education and health care.

Equalization, the process of making payments to provinces with tax revenues below the national average, is equally fraught. Ontario is today a recipient of equalization, something I thought would never happen. Over-equalization can hinder internal migration by people who work part of the year and collect insurance for the rest. I seldom compliment our neighbours, but the lack of equalization in the United States has encouraged internal migration, generally to the greater benefit of the whole. In Canada we should be promoting a similar free flow.

For Ontario, with its enormous deficit and prospects for slow growth at best, the soundest solution is for Ottawa to transfer more tax points so the provinces can cover their biggest constitutional responsibility, health care. If not that, there are other possibilities. Federal Finance Minister Jim Flaherty twice reduced the GST, once in 2006 and again in 2008, taking the federal portion down from 7 per cent to 5 per cent. Ontario Premier Dalton McGuinty should have moved in and raised the provincial sales tax by an equivalent amount. McGuinty missed the perfect opportunity to follow my golden rule: the government that does the spending also does the taxing.

19

▾

Behind Boardroom Doors

I had been the king of the castle in Toronto, overseeing billions of taxpayer dollars. As a private citizen, I missed the challenge of being scrummed by the media, tilting with opponents in the legislature, and meeting business and political leaders across Canada and in other countries. I felt fulfilled in politics because of what I believed I had accomplished. On my retirement I received more than five hundred letters of gratitude and best wishes.

Some politicians don't bother to keep in touch with former colleagues, but I've always been a different kind of cat. I like to see everybody, hear how they're doing, share a few war stories, thank them for what we accomplished, and honour those who have passed away. I've hosted many such gatherings over the years, most recently in 2014, when I invited two dozen former colleagues from TEIGA for lunch at the Toronto Club. They came from all over southern Ontario — as far away as Cobourg in the east, Oakville in the west, and Alliston to the north.

These are my memoirs, but none of it would have been possible without the diligent work of many dedicated people. While being a minister of the Crown may look like a solo flight, it is anything but, and I had the best possible help along the way. As for any mistakes

I made, those were mine and mine alone. That's what ministerial responsibility meant in that era, just like the sign on the desk of President Harry Truman said: The buck stops here.

The great thing about democracy is how otherwise powerful people can be reduced to trolling for votes in a bowling alley. What I did not miss were the petty, sometimes childish, political intrigues. And Joyce and I had to attend far too many functions when we'd rather have been home with our boys.

Joyce was never just the dedicated spouse sitting demurely on stage with me. Her political father once told her, "You can be the grovelling wife or you can make it work for you." Joyce took the latter route. She was always her own person, not waiting on the doorstep for me to come home. During elections, however, no one worked harder than Joyce. Beyond that, her extensive volunteer work included fundraising campaigns for the Heart and Stroke Foundation; Branksome Hall; and the Toronto Garden Club, sponsors of the annual Canada Blooms show.

When I resigned from office, TVOntario's Isabel Bassett interviewed Joyce and asked, "What do you miss about politics?" Replied Joyce, "*Nothing*. We had that life, and I loved it, and now we've moved on." Joyce was always fully supportive, ever gracious, and the most politically astute person I know.

Stewart, born in 1966, and Jamie, born in 1968, are the loves of our lives. We are grateful for their excellent education at Harwich-Raleigh School in Blenheim. They thrived at Ridley, where they made loyal, lifelong friends. Stew excelled on the cultural front, and Jamie was a member of the Ridley heavy eight rowing team that brought home gold in two consecutive years at the prestigious Henley Royal Regatta in England.

Stew is now the Senior Advisor leading corporate development efforts in California and New York for Susan G. Komen. The organization has raised more than $2.5 billion for breast cancer research. Jamie, a graduate of the University of British Columbia, married Julia Rastall. They live in Vancouver with their daughter,

Kate Reagan McKeough. Jamie sells portfolio and macro strategy research for Pavilion Global Markets Ltd.

▼

A few days after resigning, I had a previously scheduled lunch with Ced Ritchie, Chairman, President, and Chief Executive Officer of the Bank of Nova Scotia. Ritchie was a diehard Liberal, but he made three generous offers. I could be a director of the bank, an officer at the bank, or receive the bank's backing if I decided to start something on my own. I never took Ritchie up on any of his proposals, but I left that lunch in the full knowledge I would succeed admirably in my new life.

I worked from my office at McKeough Sons in Chatham, but also from a downtown Toronto office courtesy of John Thompson. The CEOs of three trust companies and two banks offered me positions on their boards of directors, but I had not heard from CIBC, our family bank since 1871. I ran into Charlie MacNaughton, who was on the Bank of Montreal board, and mentioned this incongruity. Soon after, CIBC Chairman and CEO Russ Harrison and President Don Fullerton invited me to lunch and asked me to be a director. I accepted and turned down the other invitations.

Monthly meetings of the CIBC board began at 11 a.m. and were over in time for 12:30 p.m. lunch preceded by champagne cocktails. Fellow board member John Robarts told me that little happened at the full board meetings; the much smaller executive committee made the important decisions. He also told me the bank spent $10,000 a year on cigars, some of which he and I enjoyed.

Fellow director Conrad Black would always arrive ten or fifteen minutes late. He would enter the room and pause to see where a seat had been saved for him. After a few minutes, he would intervene and say something profound. After Bill Davis resigned as premier, he also joined the CIBC board. When the banks began talking about selling life insurance in the branches, financial advisors already in the insurance business actively lobbied Ottawa against allowing such competition. Robarts, Davis, and I urged CIBC to fight back by joining with all banks in mobilizing the thousands of local bank managers across the country, but no such coordinated campaign ever occurred. It took years for the banks to gain approval to sell insurance, and even then only in offices separate from the branches.

CIBC was a more political place than Queen's Park. At one point, Russ Harrison appointed Don Fullerton CEO and then deposed him. At an audit committee meeting that I chaired not long after, we approved the quarterly statement and press release. By the time the full board met the following day, Harrison — who had not been at the audit committee meeting — had added $50 million to the earnings and changed the press release. Whether he was right or not doesn't matter. His overruling of the audit committee was inappropriate.

In response, Fullerton invited several directors to his house. We decided to fire Harrison and name Fullerton as Chairman and CEO. Our mistake was in leaving Harrison on the board. Until Harrison eventually retired, I don't think he and Fullerton so much as acknowledged each other at board meetings. The atmosphere was poisonous.

In 1999, when John Hunkin succeeded Al Flood as Chairman and CEO, another director, Jalynn Bennett, and I met with Hunkin. We told him the board needed a lead director or a non-executive chairman. We also said the executive committee should be eliminated with work spread to the other committees. We further urged that former CEOs should not continue sitting on the board. Some of our recommendations were accepted: the executive committee was discontinued, and a lead director, Bill Etherington, was appointed and later named chair.

CIBC management took on too many risky loans resulting in costly write-offs. The board mostly went along; we should have reined them in. As a result, from being the second biggest of the Big Five banks, CIBC sank to last.

At Numac Oil & Gas, where I also served as a director, CEO Bill McGregor was so efficient that the longest meeting I ever attended lasted all of eight and a half minutes. McGregor, an oil patch pioneer, had integrity and guts. He followed folksy business sayings such as "Bite off more than you can chew, then chew like hell." In 1992, McGregor was replaced by his son Stewart, a mistake as far as I was concerned. The company never did as well as when Bill McGregor was in charge.

Matters came to a head at a board meeting in Palm Springs on February 27, 1998. Stewart was a golfer; this was our second board meeting in the desert. The meeting started at 8 a.m., and at noon, directors wanted to continue. Stewart did not; he had a 12:30 tee time. That belled the cat! At the next board meeting, Stewart McGregor was gone.

In the first few years after leaving Queen's Park, I also accepted board appointments from Hal Jackman at Algoma Central Railway, Neil Shaw at Redpath Industries Ltd., Bill Campbell at Consumers Glass Co., and Alf Powis at Noranda Mines Ltd. Because of my time in government, I was regarded as someone who could make a contribution. I never saw these appointments as payoffs, but it's for others to decide how much I contributed. I did not lobby governments, nor did I allow my name to be used by foreign countries seeking to lend funds to Ontario.

In 1986, I joined the board of Massey-Ferguson Ltd., one among the many companies acquired by Conrad Black when he bought Argus Corp. in 1978. Black installed Victor Rice as CEO and then left. We directors served under sufferance; Rice was a much better talker than a listener.

The company was doing less business in farm machinery and more in auto parts, so the name was changed, to Varity Corp. Rice wanted to move corporate headquarters to the U.S. for tax reasons. He should have located near Detroit, close to the Big Three automakers. Instead, in 1991, Rice chose Buffalo, a city that just happened to be near his summer home in Niagara-on-the-Lake. Hal Jackman and Red Wilson resigned in protest. The rest of us supported Rice.

Varity was my second-best paying board after CIBC and required the least number of meetings each year, only five or six as opposed to CIBC's thirty. Rice always chose five-star locations for board meetings, at Arizona spas or British country house hotels. Varity was acquired by Lucas Industries in 1996, and Lucas Varity in turn was bought by TRW Automotive in 1999. Varity directors had agreed to take reduced compensation. In return, the company agreed to donate $1 million to charities designated by each director. TRW reneged on the deal. I had to write apologetic letters to the University of Western Ontario, Robarts Research Institute, and the Stratford Festival withdrawing my promised bequests.

My other boards included Canada Development Investment Corp. (where I was chairman), CPL Long Term Care Real Estate Investment Trust, Sceptre Resources Ltd., Global Stone Corp., InterTAN Canada Ltd., Cameco Corp., Mediacom Inc., and St. Marys Cement Corp.

My record as director was twenty-six years with Canadian General Tower Ltd., an auto parts company based in Cambridge, Ontario, owned by the Chaplin family. Jim Chaplin was a friend from Ridley; we were each other's best man. I served until the company was sold in 2012, my last board role.

In some cases (St. Marys Cement Corp. and Medicacom Inc. are two examples), my time was relatively brief because the firm was acquired. I quit after a few meetings of Canadian General Investments Ltd. because the chairman, Colonel Max Meighen, practised too much nepotism for my liking. I also turned down offers. I was asked to join the Bell Canada board but declined. I felt it would be disloyal to my friend Phil Lind, who worked at Rogers, a Bell competitor.

These days, board work is more onerous, so people say five boards is plenty. I disagree. For most of my time as a director, I was on twice that many and was always well briefed, vigilant, and challenging. Anyone who knows me would be surprised if I were anything less. I served with an interconnected group composed of some of the same directors: Jalynn Bennett, Ralph Barford, Merv Lahn, Peter Lougheed, John Turner, Doug Bassett, and Dick Sharpe. I often got appointed because I was part of the "network." I don't think that's wrong. You are nominated by people who know you and, in turn, you nominate others you know, like, and respect. Director selection has since been taken over by search firms charging huge fees. I'm not sure we're further ahead.

I believed then, and I believe now, that the main job of a director is to hire and, if necessary, fire the CEO. Directors set the broad strategies, policies, and goals, often on the recommendation of management, and they provide advice in the form of their experience and wisdom. However, directors should not conduct hands-on, day-to-day administration.

I also believe a majority of directors should be independent of management; a majority shareholder should not dominate a board; the dual-share structure, where some shareholders don't have a full vote, should be ended; and executive compensation should be publicly reported as a lump sum, not on a name-by-name basis. In terms of size, ten or twelve directors is about right and means there isn't a two-tier problem, with some directors "in the know" and others who are second-class citizens.

In terms of compensation, I worry about the growing gap between the top and the bottom. The push to pay CEOs more and more was led by consultants who said the CEO had to be paid the same as a competitor or it would be embarrassing. Boards too often went along. Pay should be tied to performance. I am not, however, a fan of enforced rules or even guidelines for corporate governance. It all boils down to applying common-sense thinking.

▼

I was also part of a task force established immediately after the election of the Mulroney government in September 1984. Chaired by Deputy Prime Minister Erik Nielsen, the objective was to eliminate program duplication, reduce red tape, improve efficiency, and save money. About a thousand federal programs worth $90 billion, administered by 126 departments involving 170,000 employees, were identified for review. My role was to advise the government on the recommendations made by the private sector teams before those recommendations went to cabinet. I worked closely with Philip Aspinall of Coopers & Lybrand's Montreal office, who was chairman of the private sector advisory committee, Peter Harder, Nielsen's executive assistant, and Peter Meyboom, former deputy secretary of the Treasury Board.

In the end, advisors included more than a hundred senior executives (each of whom were paid $1, suitably framed), a similar number of federal civil servants, and forty-two experts from provincial governments and academe. In March 1986, Nielsen delivered a twenty-one-volume report that detailed possible savings of up to $10 billion a year. I had been quoted as saying, "There would be blood on the floor."[101] There was, maybe not enough, but I believe the committee's work created the realization among civil servants that programs need to be regularly reviewed rather than automatically renewed.

One of my longest-serving activities is helping Ridley College. I was asked to join the Board of Governors and attended my first meeting on December 13, 1978. There's hardly been a day since when I didn't do something for my alma mater. In 1979, I was appointed to the executive committee, and from 1983 to 1989 I chaired a campaign that raised more than $15 million to split between the endowment fund and the Second Century Building, which has classrooms, up-to-date labs, and a theatre. We also built a new headmaster's house; the former house became the residence of the Gooderham West housemaster. School House, a residence, was turned into offices.

To achieve our fundraising goal, Headmaster Jere Packard and I attended thirty-five receptions in Canada, the United States, Bermuda, Nassau, Hong Kong, and Tokyo. Not all our efforts were successful. In one case, we approached a firm with Ridley connections about donating a grand piano worth $50,000. In response, the

---

101 *Globe and Mail*, April 21, 1986.

company asked to borrow a painting to use in conjunction with their centennial celebrations. We immediately agreed. Some months later, by way of thanks, they sent not a cheque for $50,000 but a coffee mug carrying the company name and hundredth anniversary designation.

I still attend two or three of the quarterly meetings each year to keep in touch. Stewart and Jamie both were at Ridley, Stewart from 1979 to 1985 and Jamie from 1982 to 1986. They, like me, profited enormously from their time there, and both have given to the school in return. Recently an endowment was created in my name to encourage debating and public speaking, two of my many student pursuits.

Another labour of love was the Robarts Research Institute in London, conceived by Dr. Charles Drake, a renowned neurosurgeon, and Dr. Henry (Barney) Barnett, an equally prominent heart and stroke scientist. Allyn Taylor, the honorary chairman of Canada Trust Co., Richard Ivey, and I approached Bill Davis in 1983, and he agreed to honour, with government support, Robarts, who had died the previous year. The $12-million Institute opened in 1986, and I helped raise a further $13 million for scientific research.

When Robarts's second wife decided to sell some of his possessions, I joined with others to raise the money to buy his Companion of the Order of Canada medal for display in the lobby of the Institute.[102] We also provided a silver tray and a Bible from his swearing-in ceremony. Robarts's daughter Robin donated her father's miniatures of medals received during the Second World War. We held a celebratory luncheon that included port and cigars — perhaps not the most appropriate for a medical institution, but John Robarts would have approved.

▼

In the midst of my busy new life, on Thanksgiving Monday, October 8, 1984, Bill Davis announced he was stepping down as leader. My

102 It was renamed the Robarts Research Institute in 2005.

home phone rang constantly with callers wondering whether I would be running to replace him. When Davis called to talk about his departure, he said, "Thank you for making the last thirteen years possible."

I told him Joyce and I were headed to Bermuda for a ten-day holiday that Friday. He did not specifically urge me to run, but he did say he wanted to talk again after we returned. Peter Lougheed was more blunt. "As a friend, I have no advice," he said. "But as a citizen, I want you to feel my pressure in Bermuda."

A group quickly formed to promote my candidacy. They included John Cronyn, Paul Curley, John Thompson, Paul Little, Tom MacMillan, Kirk Foley, Phil Lind, John Laschinger, Jim Hayhurst, Bill Watson, Rendall Dick, Tom Kierans, and Red Wilson. When we met that Thursday, about half the group thought I should run. The other half was in favour, with qualifications, or against.

In Bermuda, I made a list of reasons to run and another list of why it would be a bad idea. On the "pro" side, I wrote that I was the best available candidate and could bring about real change because, like Brian Mulroney, who had been sworn in as prime minister the previous month, I had business experience that would be helpful. Other positive factors included the fact that my former political network was eager, raising money would be no problem, and I was happiest when I was in the thick of things.

The list of "cons" was equally persuasive. I worried about being "rusty" like John Turner, who re-entered politics, ran against Mulroney, and fared badly. There also might be a perception among delegates that I had abandoned the party. Regional government, tax reform, and OHIP increases could come back to haunt me. Finally, I liked what I was doing and would be taking a huge pay cut to go back into politics. Between my boards and my CEO role at Union Gas (described in the next chapter), I was earning more than $300,000 a year. The bottom line was: how badly did I want the job of party leader?

A diary kept by my sister-in-law Dorothy during the 1971 leadership campaign played a major role in my decision. She'd given me the diary right after the convention, but I had not read it until that point. I'd forgotten some of what it recounted: The plane that almost crashed in Lake Superior. And the time we were on our way to Timmins, ran into a dreadful storm, and the pilot kept saying we would be landing at Muskoka airport near Bracebridge, but we were about a hundred miles away from where we were supposed to be and he didn't seem to know exactly what would happen next.

I didn't miss the eighteen-hour days of politics. In the private sector, I still worked hard, but not like I used to. My weekends were my own. I wasn't attending a banquet at the Legion hall or in a nursing home visiting an old soul who had just turned ninety and didn't know why I was there any more than I did.

Still, there were moments when I said to myself, "Everything is goofed up. If I were in charge, how much better things would be." The decision was not easy. In my office was photo of myself in full rhetorical flight with the caption, "McQ the best premier Ontario never had." However, after careful consideration of all aspects, I decided I would not run for leader.

On October 25, I met with Davis, then the press, but did not reveal my decision. Five days later, I called a news conference to announce I was not running. "A variety of personal considerations have entered into my decision, not the least of which is that I am quite committed to and thoroughly enjoying my present responsibilities." I said I would attend the leadership convention set for January 1985 but would not endorse any particular candidate.

A 1974 interview with Joan Sutton may help explain my state of mind. I was just making my way back into cabinet from my 1972 resignation when Sutton asked me, if Davis stepped down, would I run again, only three years after he'd beaten me for the leadership. "Yes, I would, although I'd like it to happen overnight without having to go through the process. But, I could just as easily walk away from it completely."[103] Well, in 1984 I again realized I could walk away. And I did.

---

103 *Toronto Sun*, September 22, 1974.

20

▼

Hostile Takeover

A series of roles on various boards, interesting though the people and issues were, would never have been enough for me. When I left politics, I wanted to run something. Bill Watson and John Cronyn, both directors of Chatham-based Union Gas Ltd., advised me to "go slow" as I looked for a full-time position as chief executive officer. They obviously had something in mind.

I joined the Union Gas board in June 1979. The directors were restless; profits had been declining for several years. CEO Bill Stewart resigned that summer. The board appointed a search committee, and in September I was named president and CEO. To celebrate, Joyce and I invited forty-six directors and members of Union Gas management to dinner at Bally McKeough. With Winston's catering, it felt like old times.

Incorporated in 1911, Union Gas was a utility company with 2,200 employees that distributed natural gas to 440,000 residential, commercial, and industrial customers in southwestern Ontario. I soon realized the biggest problem was that too many senior people had a "utility mentality." They were neither innovative nor hard working. No matter what time I departed head office at the end of the day, I was often the last one to leave.

My first recruit was Paul Little, a chartered accountant who had worked with me at Treasury, then went on to management roles at John Labatt Ltd. and Allpak Ltd., both in London, Ontario. Little became vice-president, finance and corporate development. I also promoted Stephen Bellringer, a seventeen-year employee, to president and chief operating officer. I shook up the financial end, too. We switched advisors from Dominion Securities and A. E. Ames to McLeod Young Weir Ltd. and Wood Gundy.

In addition to the stodgy corporate culture, we had four problems: a mixed bag of energy holdings in Western Canada; a money-losing realty and land development subsidiary, Major Holdings & Developments Ltd.; a long-term deal that locked us into buying high-priced synthetic natural gas from Petrosar Ltd., of Sarnia, Ontario; and depressed corporate earnings.

To further diversify our business in Western Canada, in May 1980 Union Gas bought 500,000 shares of Numac Oil & Gas Ltd., an Edmonton-based energy exploration company, for $20.5 million. We also bought another 500,000 shares of Numac from Allpak in return for $8 million in cash and 1 million treasury shares of Union Gas.

With holdings of about 20 per cent in Numac, we were now the largest shareholders. Allpak Chairman Richard Ivey and Numac President Bill McGregor joined the Union Gas board. As part of the deal, Precambrian Shield Resources Ltd., of Edmonton, in which Numac was a substantial shareholder, began managing and expanding our Western Canadian interests.

Because of high interest rates and a slump in real estate activity, Major Holdings, of Waterloo, Ontario, was suffering through the worst recession since the 1930s. In 1982, we wound up the company, sold the land, and took our losses.

Until the energy crisis of the early 1970s, Union Gas had been in a straightforward business: buy natural gas from Western Canada, store it in underground tanks, and then distribute the gas to customers. When oil prices quadrupled, Union Gas signed a fifteen-year deal to buy synthetic natural gas from Petrosar, thereby locking up a sure source of supply at a fixed price. But the continuing rise in world energy prices meant more exploration and additional supply in Canada. By 1981, we were paying Petrosar twice the cost of natural gas on the open market. We found a buyer in the U.S. for some of the expensive gas but were able only to reduce our losses, not offset them totally. We even sold a portion of the gas back to Petrosar for less than we paid. Eventually the Ontario Energy Board (OEB) allowed us to pass along some of the extra costs to customers.

I also continued my cost-cutting Treasury ways. We got out of the money-losing appliance sales business and, in 1982, I reduced the number of employees by about a hundred through a voluntary retirement scheme. As a result of all our efforts, profits improved dramatically. By 1984, we were in such good shape we did not even need to apply to the OEB for a rate increase. I also expanded the stock savings plan so all employees could participate and become shareholders. Eight hundred employees took up the offer in the first year.

My boldest step was to create a holding company, Union Enterprises Ltd. (UEL), with Union Gas as a subsidiary, thus giving us more freedom to acquire businesses outside the regulated gas environment. While UEL became our strategic expansionary strength, it was also our Achilles heel because we were no longer protected by the Ontario law that limited ownership of a utility by any one shareholder to 20 per cent. Because UEL was a holding company, anyone could acquire control. I had created the circumstances for my own exit.

▼

Many CEOs have poor communications skills. That was not a problem for me. I continued to give public speeches because I firmly believed business leaders should have views on the issues of the day. "Cost is not nearly as important as supply," I told the Hamilton Canadian Club in November 1980. "Energy self-reliance is not primarily a financial question. It is a political question; it is a public health and safety question; and it is an industrial strategy question. In stark and simple terms, lack of adequate supplies is the greatest disaster. Higher prices are preferable to shortages of oil." I no longer regarded myself as a partisan and felt comfortable opposing Premier Davis's call for lower energy prices.

Brascan Ltd., the holding company of Peter and Edward Bronfman, was our largest shareholder with a 16 per cent ownership position bought in 1980 through its subsidiary GLN Investments. As a result, two Brascan executives, President and CEO Trevor Eyton and Senior Vice-President Robert Dunford, were on our board. They were pleasant enough fellows, but I can't say they either helped or hindered the firm. I always assumed that Jack Cockwell, chief operating officer for the Bronfmans, was the mastermind behind the scenes.

At one point, Brascan wanted to sell its holdings. We thought that meant they had lost interest in Union Gas, but apparently that was not the case. In January 1985, two blocks of UEL shares — a total of 4.5 million shares — changed hands at $13 at a time when our shares were trading at $11. Lawyer Eddie Goodman phoned to say he represented the buyer, Unicorp Canada Corp., of Toronto. Unicorp was controlled by financier George Mann, a real estate and stock market entrepreneur, and run by its president, James Leech, a former officer in the Royal 22nd Regiment (the Van Doos). Unicorp had grown quickly, from $41 million in assets in 1978 to $480 million in 1984, mostly through U.S. real estate deals.

Brascan had agreed to sell Unicorp its 16 per cent stake, giving Unicorp a total of almost 30 per cent of the shares of UEL. Leech was quoted in news reports as saying he could work with me despite the fact that the two of us had never even spoken.

According to Goodman, Unicorp would be launching a takeover bid. Only upstart Robert Campeau's failed attempt to buy Royal Trustco in 1980 would rival what happened next. In that case, Campeau ran afoul of the Canadian Establishment. I found myself equally alone, facing the powerful Bronfman empire. The headline on a story by Hugh Anderson in the Montreal *Gazette* captured the tumult of events: "What a rumble we have here."[104]

To increase its holdings, Unicorp paid select institutional sellers

---

104 *Gazette*, February 8, 1985, p. C1.

as much as $13.25 per share in cash, then offered the remaining share-holders the equivalent of only $12.62 a share. Moreover, rather than cash, sellers at that lower price would receive for each UEL share a complex combination of one preferred share, the promise of a larger annual dividend, plus half a warrant to buy a non-voting Unicorp share at some unspecified point in the future.

Unicorp cut some unusual deals along the acquisition trail. When they bought Brascan's 16 per cent stake, Brascan agreed it would not back out of the sale even if some other firm, a "white knight," came along with a better offer. "To put it bluntly, white knight profits go to us," Jim Leech told a meeting of financial ana-lysts.[105] Why, I wondered, would Brascan give up the potential for more money? Was Unicorp just a stalking horse for Brascan? We asked for a hearing by the Ontario Securities Commission (OSC) to provide some answers. I also tried to raise political awareness and create further pressure points against the attempted takeover by meeting with Frank Miller, who had just been chosen leader of the Ontario Progressive Conservative Party and premier.

▼

The OSC hearing began on Friday, February 8, continued through Saturday, and ran for a week. I spent that first weekend in Chatham working from my office accompanied by Homer, our cocker spaniel, curled up on a cozy rug at my feet. As Joyce said, "If George Mann's going to own the rug, then let Homer do a job on it first."

The hearings found some irregularities. William Rogan, presi-dent of an investment counselling firm, testified that he had received a call from Gordon Capital, the broker acting for Unicorp, saying an offer for Union was imminent. Rogan was also told the day of the call was "the last day I could sell my shares for $13 cash and the follow-up was coming and would not be as attractive."[106] Despite

105   *Globe and Mail*, February 6, 1985.
106   *Globe and Mail*, February 11, 1985.

this and other damaging testimony, the OSC ruled against us and allowed the bid to proceed. Our board of directors formally rejected the offer as underpriced and unfair.

Ontario Energy Minister George Ashe called for a hearing by the Ontario Energy Board, but, overall, support from the government was not as helpful as it could have been. In a somewhat similar situation in 1970, when Consumers' Gas Co. made an offer to acquire Union Gas, the Ontario government effectively stopped that deal. Frank Miller could have done the same this time, but did not. He flat-out refused to see me after my first visit.

The plain truth was, with Bill Davis gone, I had fewer friends in government. David Weldon was Frank Miller's chief fundraiser; his firm, Midland Doherty Ltd., was one of two investment dealers working for Unicorp. Peter and Edward Bronfman were supporters of Larry Grossman, the treasurer.

I tried to find my own white knight to make a counter-offer but had no success despite meetings with companies in Canada and the U.S. as diverse as Rothmans, Dominion Foundries and Steel Ltd., and Pacific Gas and Electric Co. An emissary from Paul Reichmann suggested a merger with one of his companies, but they wanted a high price to avoid a writedown, so there was no deal.

On March 7, we took a new tactic by paying $125 million for Burns Foods Ltd., a Calgary-based food processing company. That acquisition gave us an additional $2.5 billion in sales and 5,700 more employees at such companies as Burns Meats Ltd., Palm Dairies, and food service company Scott National Co., not to mention two more planes and seven pilots. More importantly, because we issued 10 million new treasury shares to complete the deal, Unicorp's percentage ownership of UEL was diluted.

In takeover parlance, we had just bought some "shark repellent" in the form of a company we hoped Unicorp had no interest in, causing them to back away or reduce their demands. To that end, I offered Mann and Leech two or three seats on our board as long as they would vote only a reduced portion of their holdings. They declined. At the same time, we appealed the OSC decision permitting the Unicorp bid to proceed. We also spent about $1 million in newspaper ads, as did the other side, to deliver our opposing messages directly to shareholders. Most business deals are done without such fanfare; in this case we wanted to create a fuss.

Despite our best efforts, some of my friends abandoned me. On March 12 Hal Jackman, the majority owner of National Victoria and Grey Trust Co., sold his corporate holdings of 1.9 million shares of Union Gas to Unicorp. By March 15, Unicorp owned 60 per cent of our shares or 48 per cent of the votes, after taking the preferred shares into account. I knew the game was over. We had lost.

Joyce and the boys were skiing in Zürs, Austria. I was supposed to have gone with them but couldn't. The only relief that weekend came when the phone at Bally McKeough didn't work and no one could reach me.

My sole remaining strategy was to sue for peace, end the acrimony, and try to get back to running the business. I met with George Mann and Jim Leech to discuss the makeup of the board and management under new ownership. We agreed Unicorp would have a majority of eleven directors on an expanded UEL board of twenty. Burns Foods got three seats and previous directors were reduced to six: Ralph Barford, George Blumenauer, Merv Lahn, Bill McGregor, David Waldon, and me. I stayed on as chairman, CEO, and president with George Mann as chairman of the executive committee. Unicorp also gained a majority of directors on the Union Gas board.

There was some collateral damage. In the provincial election on May 2, Premier Miller was reduced to a minority. My successor as MPP, Andy Watson, lost in Chatham-Kent, a riding we had held for forty years. There were likely many reasons for Watson's defeat, but one of them was the government's inaction to save Union Gas, the largest employer in Chatham.

▼

Unicorp's victory was complete, but the unfairness of it all still troubled me. Large institutional shareholders got cash at top prices. Smaller shareholders received low-rated preferred shares or sold on the open market for less money. Before the takeover, there were 14,600 Union Gas shareholders, each of whom owned fewer than 5,000 shares. After all the institutions had done their trading and taken their profits, there were still 14,100 of those individual shareholders.

I wasn't alone in my concern. "The normal folk are beginning to see themselves as second stringers in the games the big boys play, at least compared to heavy hitters like the financial generals in the service of Edward and Peter Bronfman, and the tough smart fellows at Gordon Capital Corp., or other movers and shakers," wrote Dunnery Best in the *Financial Post*. "This may be eventually translated into a reluctance to put money into the Canadian stock market. After all the investment industry depends on confidence and honesty to prosper. It must look fair, as well as be fair. The rules must be the same for everyone, and enforcement must be even-handed and prompt."[107]

I was also upset that Eddie Goodman, my long-time colleague-in-arms at Queen's Park, acted for Unicorp and against me. (We remained friends. It's hard not to get along with Eddie. But still, I was pissed off.) As for Hal Jackman selling his Union Gas shares, I subsequently resigned from his Algoma Central board on the grounds that, if he had no confidence in me, then I shouldn't be among his directors. Jackman never understood my reasoning and several times asked me to rejoin his board. For him, the sale was just business; for me, it was personal.

When I next met George Mann and Jim Leech, we agreed to sell Numac and parts of Burns Foods, acquire more complementary utility businesses, and hire a president who would become a chief operating officer. But that agreement was soon swept aside by their plan to merge Unicorp and Union Enterprises, a step that would eliminate some executives, alter the roles of others, pay the minority shareholders $12.50 in cash per share, and strip me of my president and CEO titles.

---

107 *Financial Post*, April 20, 1985.

Neither Leech nor Mann had ever run anything; they just seemed slick and interfering rather than able to devise a thoughtful new business strategy. I responded to Leech's $12.50 offer by asking for $14 a share. On August 2 Mann compromised at $13, and all parties shook hands. Four days later he reneged on the deal.

I told Mann there were now three options: Unicorp could accept the original $14 offer, UEL could buy out Unicorp, or we somehow would make the existing situation work. I also laid out a multi-year strategy with me as CEO. Mann's response was to head off in an entirely different direction. He now wanted to sell all of Burns Foods and buy Northland Bank!

With the battle lines drawn, the question was: Who was running the company, George Mann or I? During the standoff period that fall, I came to an agreement with Arthur Child of Burns that he would relinquish his president and CEO titles but continue as chairman. Mann wanted me to become president of Burns; I disagreed, saying we should promote from within or find someone who knew that business well. Mann saw all of this as a breakdown in communications and indicated in an October 21 memo to me that Unicorp was prepared to neither sell Union Enterprises nor buy out the minority shareholders. Oh, and by the way, he wanted my resignation.

The showdown came the next day at a UEL board meeting. I took the directors through a lengthy list of all I had accomplished. I presented a plan to sell parts of Burns as well as combine Burns and UEL executives to save money, all while remaining as CEO. Mann countered with a motion to remove me from office. Since his appointees dominated the board, the vote was a foregone conclusion. I was fired as chairman, president, and CEO of UEL but allowed to stay on as chairman of Union Gas until the annual meeting in June 1986.

My departure was eased by a settlement equivalent to two years' salary. A note from Merv Lahn captured the sentiment held by many. "Despite all the adversities — particularly Unicorp — you have stood tall, never compromised integrity and led incisively. You have accomplished what many thought was nigh impossible. Congratulations."

Two regulatory hearings substantiated my concerns about fairness toward the minority shareholders. The Ontario Energy Board (OEB) heard thirty witnesses over twenty-six days, agreed with me that Union shareholders had been poorly treated, and recommended legislative changes to give the OEB wider authority in such circumstances. Testimony before the Ontario Securities Commission revealed that four companies in the Brascan orbit held fully three-quarters of all the Unicorp shares issued in the bid to acquire UEL. Obviously, Brascan officials had a "hard-on" for Union Gas, something they had denied but which I had assumed was the case all along.

The behind-the-scenes cabal was evident to the media. "If revenge is a dish best served cold, then Edper Enterprises impresario Jack Cockwell is surely enjoying an al fresco meal at Darcy McKeough's expense. With last week's restructuring of Unicorp Canada Corp., Cockwell finally gained the control position at Union Gas that he was denied by McKeough eight years ago," said the *Financial Times*. "Back then, Cockwell arranged for a subsidiary of his Brascan Ltd. to buy a 16 per cent block of the energy utility. McKeough wouldn't listen to Cockwell's ideas, however, and for his bad manners lost Union in a 1985 hostile takeover that became infamous for its dirty play and behind-closed-doors finagling. The winner was George Mann's Unicorp Canada Corp. — but Jack Cockwell sat in the catbird seat."[108]

The OSC also agreed that shareholders had been treated unfairly. In a negotiated settlement with the OSC, Gordon Capital was ordered not to take part in any takeovers for sixty days and told to pay minority shareholders $7.1 million, the equivalent of 40 cents a share.

Today, Union Gas is alive and well as part of Spectra Energy Corp. of Houston. Spectra is run by CEO Greg Ebel, a Canadian who lived in Chatham while running Union Gas during his climb to the top. While I didn't remain CEO as long as I would have liked,

---

108 *Financial Times*, November 20, 1988.

I accomplished a lot. During my five years at the helm, annual revenue and market value both more than doubled. My mother, who died in 1990, always said, "Your best days were when you were at Union Gas." Mothers are always right.

21

▼

The Sugar House

After I was fired from Union Gas in 1985, I received various feelers from Queen's Park and Ottawa but nothing that interested me. I wanted to remain in the private sector. I registered with Herman Smith, the executive search firm, to get my name circulating again. One of my U.S. boards made noises about asking me to resign, but in the end I retained all my directorships despite my very public lynching.

Among my first board appointments after leaving politics in 1978 was Redpath Industries Ltd., a company with nineteenth-century roots in Montreal as a cane sugar refiner. A successor operation, Canada and Dominion Sugar Co. Ltd., refined sugar cane in Montreal and beet sugar in Chatham and Wallaceburg. After the firm's new refinery opened on the Toronto waterfront in 1959, Chatham was closed in 1960, then Wallaceburg in 1968. Despite Herculean efforts, sufficient acreage of beets could not be contracted.

As had been the case with Union Gas, I knew one of the leaders of what was locally called "the sugar house." Bill McGregor was a friend of my parents, and after he retired we visited him in Miami where he lived in an oceanside hotel and surrounded himself with card tables covered in graphs of sugar prices.

In 1959, Tate & Lyle PLC, based in London, England, acquired a majority interest in Canada and Dominion and, in 1973, changed the name back to the historic Redpath. In 1980, the Montreal refinery was closed, leaving only the Toronto operations.

Neil Shaw, a long-time friend, had worked his way up to chairman and CEO of Tate & Lyle. In 1981, Shaw sought a Canadian CEO for Redpath. I suggested L. R. "Red" Wilson, who for the three previous years had been Ontario deputy minister of industry and tourism. Wilson was hired, one of the best recommendations I've ever made. I took over as Redpath chairman when Conrad Harrington retired from the board in 1982.

Another Redpath director was Paul Martin, who later resigned to run for parliament and became prime minister. At board dinners, with spouses present, I would rise and say something like, "Unaccustomed as I am to public speaking, I'd like to call on Paul Martin to bring greetings from the Liberal Party of Canada." Paul and his wife Sheila used to say that, of all the corporate functions they attended, the Redpath dinners were the best.

My association with Tate & Lyle opened a glorious window on British life and aristocracy. The annual meeting in London, to which the chairman of Redpath was invited, was held at the Marriott Hotel on Grosvenor Square and featured hampers of products on display. The black-tie dinner drew 150 to the ballroom of the Savoy Hotel, and latterly, the Berkeley Hotel. The first chairman during that period was George Jellicoe, the second Earl Jellicoe, who was in the House of Lords for sixty-eight years. Next was Robert Haslam, chairman successively of British Steel Corp. and British Coal Corp. Knighted in 1985, Haslam was created a life peer in 1990, taking the title Baron Haslam.

Red Wilson would host a pub lunch at The Boot and Flogger in Southwark near London Bridge. Shaw gave dinner parties for out-of-towners at the company's Thames River offices on the aptly named Sugar Quay. Joyce and I always stayed at a residence owned by Tate & Lyle on Cadogan Square in Knightsbridge, a ten-minute walk from

Harrods. Staff brought the full English breakfast to our room. Our partially consumed bottles of Beefeater gin and Martini and Rossi vermouth were carefully stored and returned the following year.

We always stayed for a week, went for long walks, watched Margaret Thatcher during Question Period in the House of Commons, toured the National Galley and the Tate, and saw West End theatre starring the likes of Sir Alec Guinness and Vanessa Redgrave. One year we cheered on Jamie when he rowed for Ridley at the Henley Royal Regatta.

Neil Shaw, who was knighted in 1994, was the instigator of a most memorable occasion in 1997. He called on May 24 to ask, "Would we come to lunch with the Queen Mother on June 8?" Yes, we would! At ninety-six, the Queen Mother was hale, hearty, and a wonderful conversationalist during lunch with a dozen of us at the Shaw residence in Titness Park, Ascot.

The Queen Mother died in 2002 at the age of 101. When I spoke at the service of Thanksgiving at Christ Church in Chatham, I shared my special memories of that grand woman. In my remarks, I said that at the Shaws' we'd talked about the 1939 Royal Tour of what she called "lovely Canada." At one small town, she and King George VI met the mayor. They commented that mayors usually wore their chains of office and he wasn't wearing his. The mayor replied that he "only wore it on important occasions." The Queen Mother told us she and the King laughed about that comment all across Canada.

▼

My Redpath office on the twenty-eighth floor of the Royal Bank building offered a panoramic view of the refining operations and storage silos on Toronto's waterfront. In 1988, Red Wilson and I switched roles; he became chairman and I took over as president and CEO. As Trevor Eyton, my former foe, put it, "Presidents usually become chairman. You're doing it the other way." We made that unusual exchange because Wilson was slated to run Tate & Lyle

North America as well as take on additional duties as chairman of A. E. Staley Manufacturing Co., of Decatur, Illinois, the producer of corn sweeteners and food starches recently acquired by Tate & Lyle.

Wilson suggested, given my increased workload, that Joyce and I should move to Toronto. We weren't about to give up Bally McKeough, so we bought a pied-à-terre on Front Street near the St. Lawrence Market, just a ten-minute walk to the office.

During my time as CEO, we acquired Amstar Sugar Corp., the largest cane sugar refiner in the U.S., with headquarters in Stamford, Connecticut, and operations in Brooklyn, Baltimore, and New Orleans. Redpath and Tate & Lyle were joint owners in the US$315-million deal that made us North America's largest sugar refiner. With the Canada–U.S. Free Trade Agreement just coming into effect, we were well positioned.

I was hardly launched as CEO when Neil Shaw told Wilson and me, while we were in London in January 1989, that the strategic focus of Tate & Lyle was changing. They had decided to concentrate on their core business of sugar and starch through Staley, acquire the minority interest in Redpath, and sell off all the non-sugar companies including Redpath's earlier diversification into auto parts and packaging.

The decision came as a surprise to both Wilson and me. From a business perspective, it was certainly the right decision, but I would be out of a job. Shaw asked Wilson to move to London with Tate & Lyle, but he decided to remain in Canada and joined the Bank of Nova Scotia as vice-chairman. He lasted about a year, concluded he wasn't cut out for banking, and, in 1990, became president and COO of BCE Inc., Canada's largest telecommunications company.

I served as non-executive chairman of Redpath through 1990 as the company was wound down. I received a pension that started in 1998 when I turned sixty-five, but the real legacy for me from my time at Redpath was our deepened friendships with the Shaws and the Wilsons.

▼

I moved my Toronto office across King Street to the Scotiabank building, home of the Canada Development Investment Corp. (CDIC), where I was a part-time chairman of the Mulroney government's vehicle for privatizing crown corporations. Prior to my arrival, CDIC sold de Havilland Aircraft of Canada Ltd. and Teleglobe Canada, among others. CDIC had a small staff that included Annette Verschuren who went on to great things as president of The Home Depot Canada.

My first big sale was Canada Development Corp., holder of the government's interest in Petro-Canada. The $361-million deal went through despite almost being sideswiped by Black Monday, October 19, 1987, when global stock markets crashed. I remained a director until 1993 when the newly elected Jean Chrétien replaced me with a Liberal appointee.

In 1987, I also became treasurer of the Canadian Alliance for Trade and Opportunities, an umbrella group flowing from the Royal Commission chaired by Donald Macdonald that recommended Canada–U.S. free trade. With co-chairs Macdonald and Peter Lougheed, I raised money so we could promote to Canadians the benefits of free trade. I gave about two dozen speeches and a similar number of media interviews, reminding audiences nearly 80 per cent of Canada's trade was with the U.S. "Our most promising alternative is to build on success, to assure ongoing and expanded access to the market we know best and where our track record is outstanding," I told a meeting of the Association of Municipalities of Ontario.

As the issue began to dominate the 1988 federal election, opponents of free trade included Liberal Leader John Turner, Ontario Premier David Peterson, and organized labour. "During the election campaign, business leaders spoke out bluntly and purchased ads in favour of the trade agreement. Their support was unprecedented and effective," wrote Prime Minister Brian Mulroney in his memoirs.[109]

When Mulroney won his second term, on November 21, 1988, I told the *London Free Press*, "It was the consumer who won last

109 Mulroney, Brian, *Memoirs: 1939–1993* (Toronto: McClelland & Stewart, 2007), p. 633.

Monday night, make no bones about it. But the most important thing is there was a majority. Minority governments cost too much. It's an awful thing for me to admit, and I choke when I say it, but a Liberal majority would have been better than a minority government of any kind."[110]

▼

With the Canada–U.S. free trade pact successfully launched, the Mulroney government established the Select Auto Panel with me as Canadian co-chairman. The U.S. co-chairman was Peter Peterson, chairman of the Blackstone Group LP and a former commerce secretary in the Nixon administration. The thirty-member group had fifteen appointees from each country. American members included General Motors chairman Roger Smith and United Auto Workers president Owen Bieber. Canada's representatives included Moe Closs, CEO of Chrysler Canada Ltd., and Bob White, president of the Canadian Auto Workers Union.

The panel was neither a policy-making nor a negotiating group; it was a forum for the exchange of ideas and information. We were to build on the success of the Auto Pact with a focus on employment, labour skills, technology, and competitiveness. But one of the principal items on the U.S. agenda was to increase the minimum North American–produced content of vehicles qualifying for free trade between the two countries from 50 per cent to 60 per cent. I worried that the higher level flew in the face of free trade by creating barriers, not pulling them down.

My view did not prevail. The panel voted for the increase with Ford and Chrysler's Canadian representatives on the U.S. side. Trade Minister John Crosbie correctly rejected the recommendation, arguing that such an increase would put Asian automotive transplants in Canada at a serious disadvantage because they could lose their free-trade status.

---

110 *London Free Press*, November 28, 1988.

I thought everyone was missing the mark by getting entangled in this debate when the very competitiveness of the North American industry was at stake. More and more consumers were choosing foreign cars over the Big Three. The U.S. panel members all seemed to have their heads in the sand — the very reason the Big Three were in trouble in the first place.

In the end, all the panel did was "rag the puck" for three years. But free trade and free markets eventually worked. With so many foreign firms building plants in the U.S., there is now a realization in that country that the auto sector goes beyond the Big Three. I still get angry when I hear about the hefty subsidies required to lure manufacturing plants, most recently in 2014 when Ford sought $700 million in government financial help for a new $2-billion engine plant. Windsor lost out to Mexico. Someone should convene a meeting that includes all the involved jurisdictions and say, "No one can afford these subsidies; let's find a way to achieve a level playing field."

▼

I'm a long-time fan of the Stratford Festival, but my time as a member of the Board of Governors was strained and stressful. In the 1953 inaugural year, when I was twenty, I saw *Richard III* in the tent that served as the first theatre. I went with my mother and Colonel Grant Thompson and his wife, Win, who were staying at Erie Beach for the summer. We drove, stopping on a side road for martinis and sandwiches, attended the evening performance, and were home by 2 a.m. I've never missed a year since, so when I was asked in 1979 to join the board, I was happy to accept.

The board was mired in controversy. Artistic Director Robin Phillips was forever threatening to resign. At the all-day annual meeting in 1980 when the directors finally accepted his resignation, there was a terrible row during which actor Richard Monette called us all "bastards."

John Hirsch, a brilliant director who also had a very difficult personality, succeeded Phillips. Hirsch would arrive at board meetings where everyone was in a pleasant mood and, within two minutes, have aroused the ire of us all. In 1984, Stratford's *The Mikado* was among the first productions at the grand reopening of The Old Vic in London, lovingly restored by Toronto entrepreneur Ed Mirvish. We attended in the presence of Princess Anne. The only man not wearing the requisite black tie was Hirsch.

Stratford's shows were artistically stellar but financially disastrous. In 1984, when I was treasurer, we went $800,000 over budget and suffered a $1-million box office shortfall. By then I was on track to become president of Stratford, but my 1985 departure from Union Gas meant I no longer had the necessary corporate clout, so I went off the board. I briefly served as a director of the Stratford Foundation, but concluded the Foundation existed to serve the Festival rather than respect the wishes of donors, so I left it, too.

Throughout my life, my church has always been important to me. In addition to being a warden at Christ Church and a delegate to the Synods of Huron, for twenty-five years I was a member of the investment subcommittee of the Administration and Finance Committee of the Diocese of Huron. For ten years I was chairman of that key body supervising the investment funds of the diocese, the pension funds, and a long list of parish endowments.

My two biggest accomplishments were, first, to move the diocese out of mortgages — good return but no growth — into a portfolio of bonds and equities, and, second, to gather together in an annual report the various components of the endowment — showing gains and losses — as a way of encouraging further giving. I also chaired two campaigns that raised more than $20 million for Huron College in London. For my efforts, I received an honorary doctorate of divinity from Huron in 2003.

▼

Harbourfront was another arrow in my quiver of public service. In 1990, Minister of Public Works Elmer MacKay asked me for a report on Harbourfront, one hundred acres of land on the Toronto waterfront between York and Bathurst Streets which the government of Pierre Trudeau had purchased in 1972. Ottawa created the Harbourfront Corporation for the purpose of developing, managing, and operating the site, as well as to promote programs of a cultural, recreational, and educational nature for the public.

There's no question Harbourfront became a successful "people place." By the late 1980s, there were 3.5 million visitors annually. But some of the development was disastrous and included ugly high-rise apartment blocks for assisted housing. In fairness to Harbourfront, this was dictated by the City of Toronto, but how much better it would have been if the waterfront development had been more high-brow like Miami Beach or Chicago. The greater proceeds from land sales would have allowed for more assisted housing elsewhere. Nor did the Gardiner Expressway help. The elevated six-lane highway had created a barrier between Harbourfront and the rest of the city.

Prior to my appointment, there were several studies including one by former Toronto mayor David Crombie, who recommended splitting the programming and development functions. Crombie's 1989 findings also provided for the transfer of forty-one acres to the city for parks and $25 million for improvements at the water's edge. The recommendations also would have allowed Harbourfront to continue its development activities. There was tentative harmony between Ottawa and Toronto, but the province of Ontario disagreed with Crombie and imposed a development freeze until a consensus could be reached.

The province initiated another study, this one by former Treasury colleague Duncan Allan. His report, submitted in March 1990, had four objectives: guarantee that future development should not further restrict public access; provide sufficient program funding without federal money; ensure fair treatment for the City of Toronto regarding parkland; and settle all commercial arrangements with private developers.

With this burdened background, I was appointed, in April 1990, as Ottawa's representative to assess, mediate, and make recommendations on the provincial report. After six months of study, I urged the dismantling of Harbourfront, the sale of assets, and continuation of recreational and cultural programs backed by an endowment fund financed from land sales. I also proposed restricting all development to the north side of Queen's Quay while leaving ample parkland, open space, and ready public access to Lake Ontario.

The Harbourfront board, led by Chairman Norman Seagram and General Manager William Boyle, were not convinced their programs would be properly funded, so they fought a rearguard action that delayed approvals. The next four years became a quagmire of meetings among developers and all three levels of government.

The election of Jean Chrétien as prime minister brought an end to my involvement and the appointment of a new chairman, David Foran Ellis. My hope and expectation was that an $80-million endowment fund would generate an annual payout of about $9 million for Harbourfront programs. By then, however, a recession had arrived. The two properties to be sold to provide for the endowment were no longer as valuable. The new chairman recommended continued funding from Ottawa for Harbourfront. I was disappointed with the outcome. The opportunity had existed to create a Toronto waterfront to rival Chicago's Lake Shore Drive. Feuding among the various parties had wasted so much time.

Tearing down the Gardiner Expressway, as has been proposed, will not provide relief. To move the same amount of traffic, only tunnelling would work, and that's too expensive. Just ask Boston. Well-lit and attractive pedestrian walkways on Yonge and York Streets may help, as will the newly erected buildings for the 2015 Pan American Games, but I'm afraid our best chance for waterfront livability was lost long ago.

▼

These days, my most time-consuming pursuit, and the one that has become my ongoing passion, is genealogical research, or what I call "treeing." I have assembled forty four-inch-thick three-ring binders, filled four filing cabinets, and have numerous shelves loaded to capacity with the history of McKeough Supply and Bally McKeough, as well as the family trees of McKeough, my grandmother McKeough's family, and Joyce's family. Helping with all of this was my long-time secretary Louise Anderson, who retired in 1993. Deb Prosser took over and continues to work with me in my home office at Bally McKeough in what was formerly my father's basement billiard room and then became Stewart and Jamie's playroom.

Hardly a day goes by without some treeing activity such as a birth, death, or a letter from someone with information that takes me farther back in time. The process has led me to erect plaques and new grave markers, as well as print copies of specific trees for family reunions, and deposit material in the Archives of Ontario. The bigger question is why? First of all, it's fun and often you end up helping others trace their ancestors. Second, until you know where you've come from, you can never fully understand yourself. We are all part of a continuum that leads from the distant past inexorably toward a more promising future.

22

▼

A Life Well Lived

Of all the corporate and political donnybrooks in which I was involved, none was more difficult than my relationship with my brother, Stewart. After our parents died, Stewart, Ann, and I each held a one-third interest in the family plumbing and heating business. Our board of directors included Stewart and his wife Dorothy, Ann and her husband George, and Joyce and me.

While I was in politics and through the 1980s, the family business did well under Stewart's leadership. In 1988, annual sales peaked at $14 million. By 1990, however, with a recession settling in, the company was losing money. The London branch was unionized, the managers were discouraged, and board meetings could be rancorous.

We urged Stewart to sell the business while there was still some value remaining, but he wouldn't listen. What finally brought matters to a head was his decision in 1991 to hire new auditors, despite the fact that four among the six directors were happy with the existing firm, Price Waterhouse. That July, we called a board meeting and dismissed Stewart.

I took over as chairman and president with Grant McTavish, a consultant recommended by Price Waterhouse, as general manager.

Downsizing was the only answer. We sold the steel business and reduced the number of branches from five to three. Sales fell to $5.2 million in 1993. At that point, McTavish said he had done all he could, so we appointed Rick Elliott, formerly manager of our Hamilton branch, as general manager, and Bob Davis, previously in charge of London, as purchasing manager.

Once Stewart had departed, I tried to buy him out. Discussions would ebb and flow, or turn to him wanting to buy me out. By 1994, the business was improving. Annual sales had risen to $6.6 million, and we were profitable again. Stewart recommended selling to a firm in Kitchener, Ontario. Although the deal didn't go through, their offer provided a valuation for our business, and Stewart agreed to sell me his one-third share. Elliott was appointed president and CEO; I remained as chairman. Ann and I gave Elliott an option for 10 per cent of the business, leaving me with 60 per cent and Ann with 30 per cent.

In 2008, the company, by then called McKeough Supply Inc., was healthy again with eight branches, eighty-five employees, and annual sales of $35.5 million, for which most of the credit goes to Rick Elliott. I was seventy-five and Ann was eighty-four. The fifth generation was not interested in the business, so we made the painful decision to sell after 161 years of family ownership. The buyer was Emco Corp., of London, Ontario. Based on what I'd paid for Stewart's shares fourteen years earlier, the value of the company had grown fourfold, a handsome return on my investment.

▼

The most definitive feature article ever written about me was "What Makes the Mighty Darcy Run?" published in the October 8, 1977, issue of *Financial Post Magazine*. The author of the piece, which stretched over six pages, was Ian Brown, now with the *Globe and Mail* and TVOntario. "The oddest thing about researching the McKeough profile was that nearly all McKeough's friends knew about me," wrote Brown in an introduction. "I made numerous calls thinking I might for once catch someone off guard. Time and again it was 'I heard you might call.'"

At first Brown assumed my assistant Tom MacMillan was letting people know it was fine with me for them to talk to Brown. However, during the period Brown was gathering information, I ran into a *Financial Post* editor and said Brown kept coming up with people I hadn't thought to call. "I realized then," wrote Brown, "how much loyal orchestration was going on. How would he know I'd called people unless they always called him afterwards?"

I suppose there was some orchestration. The point is that I never discouraged anyone from talking. Brown came to Chatham, attended many events in which I was involved, and interviewed anyone he wanted. Access was not an issue.

But even after all that research, Brown's thesis ended up to be off the mark. He quoted Stephen Lewis as saying about me, "I used to think he had progressive twitches. I was wrong. He's an unrepentant reactionary." Brown concluded I should follow my "progressive twitches" rather than remain true to my conservative core, or I would find that the times had passed me by.

In the more than three decades since the story appeared, most people in politics have moved to the right, where I was positioned all along. Today's voters prefer leaders who are fiscally conservative, have a social conscience, and promote business innovation over government intervention.

Brown was, however, accurate about my other traits: I'm a workaholic, detail oriented, garrulous, and loyal, and someone who prefers to be surrounded by bright people. The reason I never became party leader had nothing to do with my character, my values, or my views. In one relevant aspect, politics has not changed since I won election as an MPP in the first place. Everything depends on good luck and good timing. If Bill Davis had been ready to retire in 1978, I would have stayed in politics and likely would have been chosen leader and premier by the party. But luck and timing were not with me.

I've often wondered how I would have stacked up against other leaders. Among provincial premiers, John Robarts was the best. Bill Davis had the right instincts. He was overly pragmatic, but he won elections and that's what matters. I voted for Frank Miller at the 1985 leadership convention, only to see him last less than five months. I'd like to think I would have done better as premier in that spring election than Miller, but perhaps I, too, would have fallen to the Liberal–NDP coalition that formed. After more than four decades of Tory rule, maybe the voters simply wanted change.

The Tories did not regain power until Mike Harris was premier from 1995 to 2002. I would not have had the balls to carry out his Common Sense Revolution. I was a right winger, but not that far to the right. Harris asked me to vet all incoming Tory MPPs to uncover any past problems. To do so, I worked with Jim Baillie from the Torys law firm and Rob Prichard, president of the University of Toronto. A team of lawyers used detailed questionnaires; accountants scoured tax returns. My job was to quiz the MPPs after the preliminary interviews and ask as a final question, "Is there anything else the premier-elect should know?" In a couple of instances there was. We reported all concerns to Harris. I also told him about several MPPs who particularly impressed me.

Looking at other leaders, in Opposition David Peterson was to the right of Genghis Khan. In government, he and his treasurer, Robert Nixon, moved way to the left. Bob Rae learned what he needed to do too late and lost the premiership. Peter Lougheed had the best balance of all. Brian Mulroney left a mark on history matched by few others. Jean Chrétien would never have survived as long as he did without Bank of Canada Governor David Dodge and Finance Minister Paul Martin there to save his ass. As a former prime minister, Pierre Trudeau should have kept his mouth shut on the Constitution.

When Hugh Segal phoned in 1998 asking for my help in his run for leader of the federal Progressive Conservative Party, I said,

"Hugh, do you really think the party — let alone the country — is ready for an overweight, never elected, balding, Jewish leader?" I didn't think it was a terrific idea, but I said I would back him if he ran. I made some calls, hosted a fundraiser, plus another event to help Segal pay down his considerable debt after Joe Clark won. As a compassionate conservative, Segal would have made a great leader. He served with distinction in the Senate from 2005 to 2014 and is now Master of Massey College. Stephen Harper should have listened more closely to him.

I have also helped friends in other parties, on occasion. I sent a cheque to Roy Romanow when he was running for NDP leader in Saskatchewan in 1987 on his way to becoming premier in 1991. Another cheque went to Gerry Regan's defence fund after the former Nova Scotia Liberal premier was accused in 1995 of various sex-related charges dating back decades. He was acquitted on all counts.

Meanwhile, the old crowd is dying off. Of the 108 members in the twenty-seventh Legislative Assembly of Ontario when I arrived in 1963, only six are still alive: Gord Carton, Bill Davis, Alan Eagleson, Stephen Lewis, Bob Nixon, and me. I think few would disagree with me when I say Ontario has lost its position as the leading economic power and main force for unity in Canada as it was in my day.

The media's relentless focus on gossip and the brevity of TV clips are part of the problem, but, in fairness, that's what attracts an audience. The sophisticated tools, focus groups, polling, and the necessity to raise large amounts of money have all contributed to make the political scene much more partisan and mean-spirited.

The Big Five banks used to support the political process by giving the same amount to both major parties. They felt their encouragement was part of good citizenship and good government. This was equally true of trade union support for the NDP. Big donations are now illegal, replaced by more modest amounts from individual voters. I have, for years, supported my party both federally and provincially to the maximum allowed, and I'm delighted to do so. But the wording used in today's appeals from all political parties has nothing to do with sound policies or support for the democratic system. Instead, the missives are baldly partisan and aimed squarely at opponents. Parties have far too much money to pay for the attack ads that I deplore.

Even all these years later, I am still asked. "Do you miss being in government?" Now that I'm in my eighties, I say no, but for a long time I said, "No, it's not like it used to be." In that regard, I was just like my Aunt Floy, who lived in Britain and would say after the Second World War, "It's not like it used to be, but nothing is." In our day, we got things done and had fun, relations were civil, and the nastiness that now prevails in Ottawa and Queen's Park was not present.

The best part of being in politics was the power. In Steve Paikin's excellent book *Public Triumph, Private Tragedy*, he quotes John Robarts in response to the question "What do you miss?" put to him by Toronto Blue Jays President Paul Beeston: "Paul, the power! At that time you could get anywhere. Doors were open for you. You will not ever understand, unless you were in the position, how much power there is."[III]

I, too, liked the power. I first learned the power of being treasurer just after I was appointed in 1971. A large employer was about to be put into bankruptcy (and justifiably so) by the Royal Bank. I phoned the Royal's Chairman and CEO, Earle McLaughlin, and asked if I could come and see him. (Later, when I was more confident and my sense of entitlement had grown, I would likely have summoned McLaughlin to my office.) I told him it would be helpful if the bankruptcy proceedings could be slowed for a few months. I didn't say so, but I meant until after the coming election. McLaughlin immediately understood and agreed. I was able to tell the premier about my good deed.

But even at my peak, my power flowed in large measure from the premier of the day, first from Robarts and then from Davis. Both would have made outstanding leaders of the federal Progressive

III Paikin, Steve, *Public Triumph, Private Tragedy: The Double Life of John P. Robarts* (Toronto: Viking, 2005), p. 167.

Conservative Party, although Robarts never had the same aspirations as Davis. If Robarts had run for federal leader in 1967, he would have easily defeated the other leading candidates, Robert Stanfield and Duff Roblin.

Davis came very close to running federally in 1983. I was asked to sound out Peter Lougheed about a Davis candidacy. Lougheed happened to be in Toronto and was booked to appear on *Canada AM*. I picked him up at his hotel and drove him to the television studio in northeast Toronto for the interview. On the way back, I asked for his views if Davis ran. "I'm not inclined to support," said Lougheed. I reported the conversation; Davis stayed put.

But my pleasure in politics came not just from the power but also the perks. I didn't pay for most meals at La Scala or anywhere else. Either my guests or my staff picked up the check. There were government planes, first- or business-class air travel, a car and driver. If I felt like walking the forty minutes from my apartment to Queen's Park in the morning, my driver would ferry my briefcase for me.

The media and editorial cartoonists tried to ensure that all of this didn't go to my head, not always with success. Today, there are more humbling reminders. I was recently in my doctor's waiting room when my ears perked up at the mention of Monte McNaughton, the Progressive Conservative MPP for Lambton-Kent-Middlesex who was running to replace Tim Hudak as Ontario leader. The man I overheard went on to tell his wife he had read an article saying, "Monte was endorsed by Darcy McKeough, who has been out of politics for thirty-six years." The man then paused and added, "He didn't do much when he was there."

I waited for someone in the room to spring to my defence, but no one did. Then I hoped, when my turn came to see the doctor, that they'd announce my name, but they just called my number. The moment came and went. Memories dim. Legacies fade. Immortality is well nigh impossible.

▼

When Jamie was young and first went to school in Blenheim, he attended on Mondays, Wednesdays, and Fridays. He called his off days — Tuesdays and Thursdays — "my every other day." I find I now have more "every other days" than I used to. My only political activity is meeting with a few "old farts." In addition to my regular lunches with former Treasury people, for more than forty years I've continued to arrange an annual pre-Christmas lunch at the Toronto Club to honour the memory of John Robarts. Robarts hosted the original lunch at The Ports of Call, now long gone. John Cronyn, Don Early, and I took over after Robarts died.

The occasion is serious, but the tone is light. I might start the proceedings by saying something like, "I'm going to read a long grace. You can all doze off." There is a ritual of rivalries and ribald remarks that bounce back and forth across the table like tennis balls over the net. Attendance has included such denizens of those days as Eddie Goodman, Richard Rohmer, Richard Dillon, Tom Kierans, Douglas Bassett, Red Wilson, and Ernie Jackson. Every year the turnout grows smaller as people pass away.

Another similar event is a lunch organized four times a year by Alan Eagleson, my first seatmate in the legislature. In 1988, Eagleson pleaded guilty to fraud and served six months in jail. Among his constant friends who attend are John Turner, the Very Reverend Douglas Stoute, Bill Davis, Andy Brandt, Paul Godfrey, Gord Carton, and Roy McMurtry. Many of us sent letters to the court extolling Eagleson's character in the hopes of reducing the sentence. "If I was ever down and out, and down to my last dollar," I wrote, "Alan would be the first person I would call for help, knowing full well that the answer would be, 'How can I help?'" Eagleson remains undaunted and unrepentant.

▼

These days at 6 p.m. in the good weather I'm usually on the terrace at Bally McKeough, having a martini or two, reading a book, usually history or a biography. But sometimes I just sit and sip, enjoy the view, and reflect on a life well lived. Among my many activities, the most enjoyable was treasurer. There was nobility in that office. I felt a fiduciary responsibility for the people of Ontario.

People have called me privileged, as if that were some stain upon my soul. I worked hard for everything I got. I worked harder for everything in which I believed. The only real privilege in my life was the privilege of public service. I felt a duty to return to society some of what I had been given, to work for a better world. I tried to make a difference as a politician, corporate director, fundraiser for various causes, and through my church.

On April 13, 1994, I was invested as an Officer of the Order of Canada. The citation reads: "Following many years in politics and public life, he returned to the private sector where his experience and energy led to successful business ventures and fund-raising efforts on behalf of educational, medical, research and cultural institutions. The John P. Robarts Research Institute and Ridley College, in particular, have benefitted from his commitment and expertise."

I have never been a milquetoast man. I can still get worked up about the foolishness of the supply management system, excessive health-care costs, and teachers' unions. If you were on my team or I was on yours, you had my undivided attention, my unvarnished views, and never an unfinished project. Some would say I was too impatient, but I always took enough time to hear all sides before deciding where I stood. Once I knew where I wanted to go, I'd do my damnedest to get the job done. There were occasions when I'm sure I drove others to distraction, but I never abandoned the field when I knew in my heart I was right. I'd always think: just one more speech, one more discussion over dinner with someone who disagreed, or a new strategy to steer things straight, and I'd be home free. I didn't win every battle; no one does. But time has proven me right more often than not.

I enjoyed my years running businesses and being on boards, but it's the legacy I helped create through politics — efficient regional government and fairer property taxes — that lives on. For me, politics was always about improving the public welfare of citizens.

Politicians require not only ideas and policies, but also morals and scruples to define their behaviour. I can hold my head high and say I always acted with honour even — perhaps especially — when accused of wrongdoing. Today's lesser-light politicians would do well to follow my lead. If that sounds smug, so be it. Honesty and high ethical standards have always been among my best qualities.

Moreover, I was nothing if I was not consistent. I followed the same lodestar throughout my political career: interference with the private sector is most effective when kept to a minimum. "In serving the public interest we should remember that we are not the be-all and end-all; that the public gets along pretty well without our help; that every day of the week people are gainfully employed; that people make this country move, this province tick, with a very minimum of interference from us," I said in a speech in 1968 and believe still. "People are living happy useful lives and they do so without often having the hand of big brother rest on their shoulders. We have a proven system — a minimum of government interference. I would hesitate to promote the idea in your mind or in my mind that the system should be any other way."[112]

I was fortunate always to have around me a fan club in Kent County and at Queen's Park, people who made politics fun and life worth living. I wish I could have been premier at some point, but as I look back with a glad heart and a clear conscience, I am content.

I conclude with a few phrases from the Book of Common Prayer, ones I have requested be read when my time comes. "When we shall have served thee in our generation, we may be gathered unto our fathers, having the testimony of a good conscience; in the communion of the Catholic Church; in the confidence of a certain faith; in the comfort of a reasonable, religious, and holy hope; in favour with thee our God; and in perfect charity with the world."

That is my hope; that is my faith.

---

112 Speech to the Institute of Public Administration of Canada, Toronto Regional Group, Toronto, October 21, 1968, p. 22.

Appendix

Extract from a Speech by the Hon. W. Darcy McKeough to the Government Relations Club at the School of Business Administration, University of Western Ontario, March 5, 1985

I won't make any extravagant claims [about the Nielsen Task Force on Program Review] at this point, but I believe that the outcome will be a government program structure that will be less intimidating and confusing, less costly, more efficient, and more adaptable to changing situations. I believe one of the big bonuses is that dozens of men and women from inside and outside the public service will have worked closely together, gotten to know each other, and learned a great deal about how the other half lives, works, and thinks. Anyone who has participated can't help but come out of the experience a better-rounded, more aware, more capable executive, regardless of the sector in which the capabilities are put to use in the future.

I should warn you of one thing, however. The purpose of the task force is not to make government run just like a business. It is part of the private sector mindset in Canada that, if only government were run by business people in the same way as businesses are run, all would be well, taxes would fall, waste would disappear, and efficiency would reign. When people tell me government should be run like business, I'm tempted to reply that business should be run like a business. By that I mean that I have yet to find a perfectly run business. Businesses do not consistently apply in their daily affairs the principles you are or were exposed to in the School of Business Administration at the University of Western Ontario. Bureaucracies are not confined to government — they exist and do their mysterious thing in every large organization, public or private. Empire-building, backward vision, paper-pushing, and risk-avoidance thrive, often to the detriment of a firm's shareholders and customers.

I started out as a businessperson. For a while, as a municipal councillor and as a backbench MPP, I was able to combine business and political activity. Then, when I entered the Ontario cabinet, politics and government took over though I never severed completely my connection with the family company in Chatham. And, of course, for the last seven years I have concentrated on business.

I can't claim that my pattern would suit everyone, but it has provided me with great satisfaction and sustained, interesting activity. Also, I believe that my own exposure to both public and private sectors helped me do a better job in each. In terms of business–government contact you might say I have been one of those lobbied and one of those doing the lobbying. And certainly I have had my ups and downs in both sectors.

When I moved into the energy industry I really left active politics behind. From the other side of the fence, however, I continued to have a great deal to do with politicians and government officials. The natural gas industry is highly regulated and we are always in close contact with policy-makers and administrators. I found, too, that I was called on often to speak out on public issues, particularly on economic and business topics, and that I was asked to participate in the government-relations activities of industry and business organizations like the Business Council on National Issues (BCNI).

The fact that I became as involved as I did in BCNI certainly reflects at least in part the fact that there is still a serious shortage in the Canadian private sector of people who are knowledgeable and feel confident about dealing with government. I think that may be changing to some extent. Organizations like this give me hope that the change will be much more rapid in the next few years.

Business really doesn't have any choice. We have to understand government better and communicate more effectively with it. We also have to learn from it. One of the most important things we have to learn is how to be more sensitive to public expectations. As business people, our responsibilities go beyond the basic ones of providing goods, products, and services. Environmental protection, fair employment practices, general concern for the public interest far beyond the narrow confines of our own affairs — these are all important.

Governments, in developing their programs and their legislation, do analyse the impact on the public and the likely public reaction, including the impact on and reaction of business. When businesses are considering building a new plant — or perhaps, closing an old one — they have to look at the implications outside their own area of interest. Sometimes they have to do things that are not necessarily the most profitable, in the short term at least, in order to meet their public responsibilities.

I have cited in the past the example of my own company extending or expanding pipelines to serve small communities. Often, the financial return on these investments will be a long time in coming. Our capital might be more profitably used in some other way. We could probably avoid these projects for quite a long time. But we accept them as a responsibility, balancing them against another public interest consideration.

We generally can't make such investments if they would create a heavy cost burden for our other customers. Not every company has the same obligation a utility has to be prepared to show that virtually everything we do is in the public interest. In our case the requirement is more explicit and is formally enforced. But the attitude and the expectations exist, both in government and among the public.

You, as the next generation of business managers, have to sharpen your sensitivities, your understanding, and your government-relations skills. A company can't deal with so important a matter simply by appointing a vice president of public affairs and sending him off to wine and dine bureaucrats.

We are talking about a real corporate commitment, involving all the senior people and many not so senior. All of us in business management have a role, with the CEO in the lead, in communicating with government, in harmonizing our actions with the public interest, and in coming to terms with the objectives, the responsibilities, and the constraints of politicians and bureaucrats.

I won't talk at length about the techniques of dealing with government, but I do want to mention some basic principles. First, know your MP and your MPP. It's fundamental. And get to know him before you have a problem — it makes access easier and better when crises come. You won't be bothering him. He's anxious to know you.

If your company's operations are scattered, you and your colleagues collectively should know all your representatives. At Union Gas we get together over lunch or dinner once a year with all the MPs and MPPs from our region — that's over thirty at each level. We invite each party caucus group separately, and we have very open discussions that I believe are useful to both sides.

Don't be afraid of getting involved in the political process. A party label is not a badge of shame, even when another party is in power. Involvement will increase your understanding of the system. It won't get you any favours from government, but it won't impede your access to people in government either.

We have a corporate policy at Union that encourages employees to participate in politics, including standing for office. It hasn't created a rush to the hustings, but it underlines our commitment to public service and the public interest. I hope that in your corporate lives you will fight against the widespread view that a person who spends some years in politics or public service has opted out of the corporate ladder-climbing process. Politics and public service are important management-development courses, though many people in business don't see it that way. A period of such service is simply one of many alternative routes to the top.

A person who is interested and involved in politics has an extra dimension to his knowledge and his business capability. It should be recognized. Be sure to mention this interest in your résumé. When you are lobbying — that is, when you are advocating public policy action by government — be realistic. Take into account that a minister or a civil servant can't concentrate on your self-interest to the exclusion of everyone else's.

Every policy decision by government has a variety of effects on a range of people, and not all are beneficial. At the very least, if you have to urge a course that will hurt others, show that you are aware of the side effects and suggest some reasonable justification or offsetting action. I like to think that our best politicians would be ready to sacrifice their chances for re-election when a great principle is involved, but it would be foolish to think that they will do so over policy choices that are not fundamental.

If you push for action without giving thought to political consequences, someone will get hurt. In other words, if you've packed some rancid tuna, don't try to get a minister to approve it. And if you're a minister, don't do it. It all boils down, I suppose, to intelligence, understanding, and mutual respect. I am sure this group, when it moves into business, will enhance the supply of all three commodities.

Acknowledgements

My thanks, first of all, to friends and former staff from Treasury (and Municipal Affairs) to whom I sent drafts of various chapters: Peter Deane, Brian Donaldson, Milt Farrow, Ron Farrow, Eric Fleming, Bernie Jones, Tom Kierans, Phil Lind, Paul Little, Tom MacMillan, Ed Mahoney, Peter Regenstreif, Terry Russell, Don Stevenson, and Don Taylor. They corrected, commented, reminded me of things I had overlooked, and often disagreed with conclusions I had drawn from observations and reflections that I had made. Some I agreed with and made changes; others I "agreed to disagree."

Second, to Jordan Vanderveeken, who from 2009 to 2011 went through the scrapbooks and then photocopied same.

Third, to Deb Prosser, my secretary, who typed my handwritten manuscript, ultimately amounting to 1,200 pages, and then retyped them based on my initial revisions.

Fourth, to Joyce, my wife, who went over many of the drafts and made eminently sensible corrections.

Fifth, to Rod McQueen, who capably and thoughtfully "edited," reducing the 1,200 pages to the end result.

And finally, to editor and publisher Donald G. Bastian, who put it all together.

Author's Note on Personal References

I am a "saver" — too much so, I think — but this book is based on what was in my files and elsewhere, which made it possible to put together this story of my life. This volume is much shorter than earlier drafts. Anyone wishing to examine the full text may consult the draft which will be deposited in the Ontario archives.

SCRAPBOOKS

Mother's Scrapbook, 1935–1975, labelled FSMcK #1.
In 1999 I put together various clippings from pre-1964 and a tortoise-shelled scrapbook labeled WDMcK #2.

In August 1964 I was seeking the Progressive Conservative nomination. My mother started a scrapbook and this has been carried on ever since. I always had a scrapbook box behind my desk. After mother, my various offices at Queen's Park, then McKeough Supply did the "pasting." In all there are fifty-three, labelled WDMcK #3 to WDMcK #55.

CORRESPONDENCE

GGMcK 1956–1964 etc., FSMcK, etc., 1964–1989, two boxes.
Practically no correspondence seems to exist prior to 02/11/1956.
From 1954 to 1964 my father went to Florida each winter and I wrote him nearly every day. These files are from January to April or May

and from October or November to December. The major portion of each letter was about what was going on at McKeough Sons — sales, deposits, cheques, bum accounts, the monthly statements which I had prepared, as well as personal banking for my father and sister, but they contain a lot on what I was doing. Similarly, in 1960, my sister Ann had moved to Florida and in the files is correspondence to her from 1960 to 1964. Bob and Mary Heath moved to Montreal in 1963 and from then to 1964 some copies of my letters went to Mary Heath. Dad died in 1964 and from then on these are letters to mother in Florida up until 1969 and to Stewart and Jamie until 1989.

BLUE COPIES

There are fifteen file boxes of blues — copies of my letters — in the Ontario Archives. If a blue looks like the letter I was replying to was important, that letter can also be retrieved from the archives.

ARCHIVES DESCRIPTIVE DATABASE

RG 6-2: Correspondence of the Treasurer of Ontario

RG 6-32-3: Correspondence and subject files of the Minister and Deputy Minister of Finance

RG 19-115: Minister's Correspondence on Municipal Finance

RE 19-6: Office files of Darcy McKeough, Minister of Municipal Affairs

ONTARIO ARCHIVES

The scrapbooks, correspondence, blue copies, and speeches mentioned above have been deposited with the Ontario Archives. F2131 William Edward McKeough Family Fonds.

SPEECHES

Queen's Park — Municipal Affairs and Treasury did a great job of putting my speeches into binders and indexing them. They are in nineteen binders. There are five binders of speeches and remarks made since 1978. Speeches prior to 1967 have not survived, although a very few may be in the scrapbooks. (Note the gap from 14/07/1970 to 29/12/1971 — I can't believe I was silent!)

Bibliography

Aspinall-Oglander, Cecil Faber. *Roger Keyes: Being the Biography of Admiral of the Fleet Lord Keyes of Zeebrugge and Dover.* London: Hogarth Press, 1951.

Barnes, Sally, ed. *Bill: A Collection of Words and Pictures.* Toronto: Deneau, 1985.

Beattie, Kim. *Ridley: The Story of a School.* St. Catharines, Ontario: Ridley College, 1963. Two volumes.

Best, Patricia, and Ann Shortell. *The Brass Ring: Power, Influence and the Brascan Empire.* Toronto: Random House, 1988.

Chrétien, Jean. *Straight from the Heart.* Toronto: Key Porter, 1985.

Cronyn, Terence. *To the Glory of God: Ridley College Memorial Chapel.* St. Catharines, Ontario: Bonsecours Editions, 1981.

Dale, Stephen. *Lost in the Suburbs: A Political Travelogue.* Toronto: Stoddart, 1999.

Dutil, Patrice, ed. *The Guardian: Perspectives on the Ministry of Finance in Ontario.* Toronto: University of Toronto Press, 2011.

English, John. *Just Watch Me: The Life of Pierre Elliott Trudeau, 1968–2000.* Toronto: Knopf Canada, 2009.

Frisken, Frances. *The Public Metropolis: The Political Dynamics of Urban Expansion in the Toronto Region, 1924–2003.* Toronto: Canadian Scholars' Press, 2007.

Goodman, Eddie. *The Life of the Party: The Memoirs of Eddie Goodman.* Toronto: Key Porter, 1988.

Graham, Roger. *Old Man Ontario: Leslie Frost.* Toronto: University of Toronto Press, 1990.

Heine, William C. *Kooks & Dukes, Counts & No-Accounts: Why Newspapers Do What They Do.* Edmonton: Hurtig, 1986.

Hoy, Claire. *Bill Davis: A Biography.* Toronto: Methuen, 1985.

Ibbitson, John. *Promised Land: Inside the Mike Harris Revolution.* Scarborough, Ontario: Prentice Hall, 1997.

Macdonald, Donald C., ed. *Government and Politics of Ontario.* 2nd ed. Toronto: Van Nostrand Reinhold, 1980.

Macdonald, Donald C. *The Happy Warrior: Political Memories.* Toronto: Dundurn, 1998.

Macdonald, Donald S. with Rod McQueen, *Thumper: The Memoirs of Donald S. Macdonald.* Kingston and Montreal: McGill-Queen's University Press, 2014.

Manthorpe, Jonathan. *The Power and the Tories: Ontario Politics — 1943 to the Present.* Toronto: Macmillan, 1974.

McDougall, A. K. *John P. Robarts: His Life and Government.* Toronto: University of Toronto Press, 1986.

Miller, Win. *One Hundred and Sixty Years: From J. & W. McKeough to McKeough Supply Inc., The McKeoughs 1847–2007.* Chatham, Ontario: Chamberlain/Mercury Printing, 2007.

Mulroney, Brian. *Memoirs 1939–1993.* Toronto: McClelland & Stewart, 2007.

Oliver, Peter. *Unlikely Tory: The Life and Politics of Allan Grossman.* Toronto: Lester & Orpen Dennys, 1985.

Paikin, Steve. *Public Triumph, Private Tragedy: The Double Life of John P. Robarts.* Toronto: Viking, 2005.

Prince, Stephen. *The Blocking of Zeebrugge: Operation Z-O 1918.* Oxford: Osprey Publishing, 2010.

Roblin, Duff. *Speaking for Myself: Politics and Other Pursuits.* Winnipeg: Great Plains Publications, 1999.

Schmeelk, Richard J. *Mr. Canada: Adventures of an Investment*

Banker Inside and Outside Business. New York: Twin Dolphin Books, 2007.

Schull, Joseph. *Ontario Since 1867*. Toronto: McClelland & Stewart, 1978.

Shulman, Morton. *Member of the Legislature*. Toronto: Fitzhenry & Whiteside, 1979.

Speirs, Rosemary. *Out of the Blue: The Fall of the Tory Dynasty in Ontario*. Toronto: Macmillan, 1986.

Thorburn, Hugh G., ed. *Party Politics in Canada*. 6th ed. Scarborough, Ontario: Prentice-Hall, 1991.

Trudeau, Pierre. *Memoirs*. Toronto: McClelland & Stewart, 1993.

Walker, David. *Fun Along the Way: Memoirs of David Walker*. Toronto: Robertson Press, 1989.

White, Randall. *Ontario 1610–1985: A Political and Economic History*. Toronto: Dundurn, 1985.

Index of Names

Aird, John Black 185
Alexander, Lincoln 185
Allan, Duncan 108, 182, 221
Allan, James 37, 46, 68, 85, 101
Allin, Doug 117
Allison, Helen M. B. 20
Anderson, Bill 108, 150
Anderson, Hugh 205
Anderson, Louise 223
Angus, Belle 9
Anne, Princess 220
Apps, Syl 50
Armstrong, Jack 141
Ashburner, J. C. "Herf" 12
Ashe, George 108, 207
Aspinall, Philip 198
Atkins, Norman 98, 152, 158
Auld, James 45

Baillie, Jim 227
Bales, Dalton 56, 116, 120
Barford, Ralph 197, 208
Barlow, Doug 27
Barlow, June 27
Barnes, Sally 96, 103
Barnett, Henry "Barney" 199
Barnicke, Joe 85
Bassett, Douglas "Doug" 85, 97, 106, 197, 231
Bassett, Isabel 192
Bassett, Susan 106
Baxter, Jean 42

Baxter, Jim 25
Bayly, Terk 108
Beattie, Kim 14
Beckett, Dick 108
Beckett, Hollis 56
Beeston, Paul 229
Beith, Ian Hay 13
Bélanger, Marcel 183
Bell, Bob 64
Bell, Del 63
Bell, Elmer 155
Bellringer, Stephen 203
Bennett, Claude 108
Bennett, Jalynn 194, 197
Bennett, W. A. C. 182
Bernier, Luc 177
Best, Dunnery 209
Bieber, Owen 218
Birch, Margaret 101–02
Black, Conrad 176, 193, 195
Blumenauer, George 208
Boa, Fraser 18
Bourassa, Robert 182
Bousfield, John 73
Boyd, Helen "Betty Boop" 12
Boyer, Bob 128
Boyer, Pat 84
Boyle, William 222
Bradley, John 95
Brandt, Andy 231
Brannan, Carl 108

Bronfman, Edward 205, 207, 209
Bronfman, Peter 205, 207, 209
Brown, George 35
Brown, Ian 225–26
Brunelle, René 44, 49, 162
Bryden, Kenneth 40
Burgeajan, Ken 88
Burke, Edmund 32, 48
Burns, Robbie 82

Camp, Dalton 42–43, 98, 105–06
Campbell, Bill (Consumers Glass Co.)
    97, 195
Campeau, Robert 205
Carney, Pat 146
Carr, Jan 135
Carruthers, George 8, 145, 224
Carruthers, Sewell Ann (née McKeough)
    2, 5, 8, 17, 38, 116, 145, 224–25
Carter, Gerald Emmett 184
Carton, Gord 228, 231
Cass, Fred 38, 39
Cassidy, Michael 165
Channing, Carol 24
Chaplin, Jim 196
Charest, Jean 183
Child, Arthur 210
Chrétien, Jean 141, 145, 161–62, 167–68, 186,
    217, 222, 227
Churchill, Winston 148, 187
Clark, Joe 144, 158, 168, 177, 185, 228
Clarkson, Stuart 128
Clifford, Ted 86
Clinton, Bill 19
Closs, Moe 218
Cobourn, R. S. "Twink" 12
Coburn, Tom "Pro" 12–13
Cockwell, Jack 205, 211
Coolican, Denis 62
Couillard, Philippe 186
Crombie, David 80, 221
Cronyn, John 83, 115, 131, 170, 174, 200, 202,
    231
Crosbie, John 144, 218
Cross, James 50
Culver, David 112
Cumming, Lorne 53
Cunningham, Paul 131
Curley, Paul 89, 98, 200

Dafoe, John 40
Danforth, Harold 25–26, 28–29

Daniel, Bill 141
d'Aquino, Tom 145
Davies, Robertson 133
Davis, Bob 225
Davis, Kathy 178
Davis, William "Bill" Grenville 19, 49, 66,
    69, 78, 84–85, 87, 89, 90–92, 96, 98–103,
    106, 107, 113–14, 115, 117–18, 120, 123,
    126–27, 128, 129, 130–31, 133, 138–42, 143,
    145, 148, 150, 151, 152–53, 155, 162, 163,
    164, 169, 171–74, 175, 177, 178, 182–84,
    185, 193–94, 199–200, 201, 205, 207, 226,
    227, 228, 229–30, 231
Deane, Peter 54
DeGeer, Ross 98
de Grandpré, Jean 145
DeKoning, Larry 86
Demers, Gaston 40
Deutsch, J. J. 127
Diamond, Eff 73, 98
Diamond, Jack 70
Dick, Archibald Rendall 79, 104, 150,
    155–56, 182, 200
Dickie, Bill 138
Diefenbaker, John "Dief" 16, 21, 25–26, 28–29,
    30, 41, 42, 43, 44
Dillon, Richard "Dick" 128, 131, 141–42, 231
Dirksen, Everett 189
Dodge, David 227
Donato, Andy 46
Dowd, Eric 54
Drake, Charles 199
Drew, George 16–17, 25, 50, 100
Dunford, Robert 205
Dunne, Neil 54
Dymond, Matthew 30

Eagleson, Alan 38, 40, 85, 228, 231
Early, Don 231
Eaton, Edna 54, 108
Ebel, Greg 211
Eberlee, Tom 108
Edward, Duke of Kent 181
Elgie, Bob 103
Elizabeth II, Queen 42, 186
Elliott, Rick 225
Enders, Tom 168
Etherington, Bill 194
Evans, Arthur 128
Evans, Brian 165
Eves, Ernie 136
Eyton, Trevor 205, 215

Facal, Joseph 177
Farrill, Bryce 110, 118, 142
Farrow, Milt 80, 119
Flaherty, Jim 190
Fleck, Jim 150, 152
Fleming, Donald 44
Flood, Al 194
Foley, Kirk 170, 200
Forester, C. S. 9
Franklin, Edward 124, 130
Frisken, Frances 64–65
Frost, Leslie "Old Man Ontario"
    Miscampbell 27, 57, 58–59, 85, 100,
    101, 104
Frost, Gertrude Jane (née Carew) 35
Fullerton, Don 193–94
Fry, Christopher 18

Gagarin, Yuri 15
Gardiner, Frederick "Big Daddy" 57, 58–59
Garneau, Jean-François 183
Garneau, Raymond 183
Gathercole, George 115, 132
Gehry, Frank 70
George VI, King 17–18, 215
Getty, Don 127, 138, 182
Gielgud, John 24
Gillespie, Robert 135
Godfrey, Paul 157, 231
Goodman, Eddie 73, 84, 90, 119–20, 152, 158,
    159, 165, 175, 205, 209, 231
Gordon, A. St. Clair 106
Gordon, Walter 87
Grafstein, Jerry 18
Grant, John 135
Graybiel, Richard 47
Green, Stan 37
Greene, Joe 127
Greer, Harold 129
Greico, John 55
Griffith, H. V. 12
Grossman, Allan 54, 125
Grossman, Larry 78, 103, 207
Guinness, Alec 215
Gzowski, Peter 14, 24

Hamilton, Dick 15
Hamilton, John Russell "Hammy" 12, 15–16
Hamilton, William 29
Harder, Peter 198
Harding, Warren (Texas state treasurer) 111
Hargraft, Eve 41

Harper, Stephen 189, 228
Harrington, Conrad 214
Harris, Mike 66, 68, 135, 136, 189, 227
Harrison, Russ 193–94
Haslam, Robert 214
Hatfield, Richard 183
Hayhurst, Jim 88, 170, 200
Heath, Bob 24
Heath, Mary 24
Heath, Ted 134
Hedlin, Ralph 128
Hees, George 120
Henderson, Lorne 28, 102
Henderson, Maxwell 150
Henty, G. A. 9
Heubner, Louise 87–88
Hirsch, John 219–20
Hitler, Adolf 5
Hodgson, Lou 40
Honderich, Beland 47
Horsburgh, Russell 39
Horswill, Les 161
Hoy, Claire 99
Hudak, Tim 230
Hunkin, John 194
Hunter, Jean 54
Hurlbut, Robert 150
Hutchison, George 155

Inman, Mark 17–18
Irvine, Don 108
Ivey, Richard 199

Jackman, Hal 195–96, 208, 209
Jackson, Edward 2
Jackson, Ernie 33, 40, 43, 44, 46, 187, 231
Jacobs, Jane 78
James, Jesse 111
Jellicoe, Earl 214
Jellicoe, George 214
Johnson, Daniel 181
Johnstone, Bob 13

Kelly, Bill 98, 127, 152
Kelly, Fraser 124
Kennedy, Betty 150
Kennedy, Doug 102
Kennedy, Jacqueline "Jackie" Lee (née
    Bouvier) 24
Kennedy, John F. 16, 24
Kennedy, T. L. 100
Kerr, Brud 154

Kerr, Doug 154
Kerr, George 36, 89, 101
Keynes, John Maynard 113
Kierans, Eric 149
Kierans, Inta 176
Kierans, Tom 126, 141–42, 149–50, 152, 170, 176, 200, 231
Korthals, Robin 14

Lahn, Merv 208, 210
Lalonde, Marc 160
LaMarsh, Pat 42
Lamoureaux, Chuck 131
Lampel, Abe 21
Langford, Audrey 26
Langford, Jack 26
Laporte, Pierre 50
Laschinger, John 200
Latimer, Hugh 11, 31
Laughren, Floyd 110
Lawrence, Allan 38, 86, 87, 89, 90–91, 98, 100–01, 108
Lawrence, Bert 44, 86, 89, 90, 101, 108, 109, 116
Lawrence, Jack 15
Lawrence, Moira 101
Leech, James 205–06, 207–10
Lesage, Jean 50, 181
Lévesque, René 162–63, 168, 185
Lewis, Stephen 84, 122, 125, 130, 148, 151, 164, 165, 170–71
Libeskind, Daniel 70
Lind, Anne 176
Lind, Phil 85, 86, 90, 97, 98, 119–20, 143, 170, 176, 196, 200
Little, Paul 54, 118–20, 123, 128, 131, 200, 203
Livesey, Jack 97
Loiselle, Gilles 163
Lougheed, Peter 128, 137, 141–42, 144–45, 146, 182, 197
Lyons, "Coonie" 25

Macaulay, Hugh 152, 159
Macaulay, Robert "Bob" 128, 138
Macdonald, Donald C. 40, 41, 47, 49–50, 84, 128, 134, 135, 141–42, 163, 167, 175, 217
Macdonald, Flora 158
Macdonald, Ian 104, 105, 108, 118, 182
Macdonald, John A. 159, 181
Macdonald, John Sandfield 35
Macdonald, Ross 121–22
Macdonald, Ruth 134

MacKay, Elmer 220
Mackenzie, William Lyon 35
MacMillan, Pam 176
MacMillan, Tom 54, 161, 176, 200, 226
MacNaughton, Charles "Charlie" 45, 46, 49, 50, 59, 83, 84, 100–01, 111, 123, 124, 193
MacOdrum, Bruce 131
Magee, Brian 73, 85
Mahoney, Ed 85, 89, 97, 119
Maloney, Arthur 43
Mann, George 205, 206, 207–10
Manthorpe, Jonathan 86–87, 166
Marois, Pauline 186
Martin, Joe 85, 86, 97
Martin, Paul 214, 227
Martin, Paul Sr. 47
Matthews, Don 44
McAfee, Jerr 141
McAllum, Jim 73
McCague, George 108
McConnell, Rob 89
McCutcheon, M. T. "Mac" 29
McDougall, A. K. 188
McEwan, Ted 86
McFadden, David 152
McGee, D'Arcy 87
McGibbon, Pauline 185
McGregor, Bill 195, 203, 208, 213
McGregor, Stewart 195
McGuinty, Dalton 190
McIvor, Don 145–46
McKeough, Alice Maude 2
McKeough, Betsey Ann (née Stone) 2
McKeough, Charlotte 8
McKeough, Dorothy (née Lapp) 8, 128, 145, 200–01, 224
McKeough, Florence Sewell "F. S."(née Woodward) 2, 4–8, 9, 10, 11, 13–14, 16–17, 24, 42, 59, 78, 86, 110, 123, 212, 219, 224
McKeough, George Grant 1, 2, 3–8, 10, 11, 13, 16–17, 18, 21, 22, 26, 38, 124, 223, 224
McKeough, George Thomas 2, 26
McKeough, James "Jamie" Grant 13, 24, 86, 92, 158, 172, 192, 199, 208, 215, 223, 230
McKeough, Joanna (great-grandfather's stepmother) 2
McKeough, John (great-grandfather's brother) 2
McKeough, John "Frank" Franklin 2, 5
McKeough, Julia Rastall 192
McKeough, Kate Reagan 193

McKeough, Mabel Annie (née Stewart) 1, 3, 6, 42

McKeough, Margaret Joyce (née Walker) 3, 10, 24, 41–42, 44, 49, 51, 86, 91, 97, 109, 118, 134, 145, 156, 158, 159, 172, 176, 177, 178, 192, 202, 206, 208, 214, 215, 224

McKeough, Thomas (great-grandfather's father) 2

McKeough, Walker Stewart 13, 86, 158, 172, 192, 199, 208, 223

McKeough, William (great-grandfather) 2, 4, 26

McKeough, William "Will" Edward (grandfather) 2–3, 24, 26

McKeough, William Stewart 2, 3, 5

McKeough, Woodward Stewart 2, 8, 19, 20, 22, 26, 27, 51, 86, 97, 116, 118, 123, 145, 224–25

McLaughlin, Earle 229

McMurtry, Roy 102, 103, 162, 231

McNaughton, Monte 230

McRuer, J. C. 39

McTavish, Grant 224–25

Medland, Ted 110, 118

Meen, Arthur 108

Meighen, Max 196

Meighen, Michael 44

Meyboom, Peter 198

Miller, Ed "Laddie" 16

Miller, Frank 102, 162, 175, 177, 184, 206, 207, 208, 227

Mirvish, Ed 220

Mitchell, David 145

Monette, Richard 219

Moog, Gerhard 115

Morin, Claude 162

Mosher, Peter 153

Mulroney, Brian 146, 158–59, 185, 200, 217, 227

Munsinger, Gerda 43, 115, 120

Myers, Bill 85

Myers, Reg 32

Nader, Ralph 143

Nastich, Milan 111

Newkirk, Garnet "Cookie" 31–32, 34

Newman, Peter C. 181

Nielsen, Erik 197–98

Nixon, Harry 84

Nixon, Robert "Bob" 47, 84, 110, 122, 151, 227, 228

Norton, Keith 108

Nurse, Ivan 10

O'Connor, Larry 126

Olivier, Laurence 24

Packard, Jere 198

Paikin, Steve 229

Palmer, William "Bill" 45, 53, 108, 118

Parizeau, Jacques 162–63, 167–68, 176, 180, 184, 186

Parry, Frank 32

Parry, George 30, 31, 32, 34, 154

Parry, Myrtle 32

Parry, Rob 32

Parry, Verna 32

Pearson, Lester B. 26, 29, 42, 95

Pearson, Maryon 63

Peck, George 40

Pépin, Jean-Luc 94, 185

Perkins, Cy 39

Peterson, David 67, 110, 176, 184, 189, 217, 227

Peterson, Peter 218

Pethick, Jack 39

Pharand, Robert 90

Philip, Prince 42

Phillip, Kim 54

Phillips, Robin 219

Pittman, Walter 84

Plumptre, Beryl 63

Powis, Alf 195

Price, Bud 36

Price, Harry 65

Prichard, Rob 227

Prosser, Deb 223

Queen, Carmen 121

Queen Mother 215

Rae, Bob 185, 227

Randall, Stanley "Stan" 49, 77–78

Rattigan, Terence 23

Rattray, Keith 86

Raymont, Peter 153, 169

Redgrave, Vanessa 215

Regan, Gerry 228

Reilly, Len 36

Reisman, Simon 109

Reuter, Allan 124

Reynolds, Keith 83

Rice, Victor 195–96
Richardson, Nigel 70
Ridley, Nicholas 11
Riel, Louis 181
Ritchie, Ced 145, 193
Robarts, John 27–28, 30, 31, 32, 33, 35, 39, 44,
    45, 46, 48–50, 51, 52, 53, 57, 59, 60, 66,
    69, 70, 74, 75–77, 83, 84, 85, 88, 90, 92,
    94–96, 97, 100, 101, 104, 107, 110, 113,
    119, 123–24, 125, 131, 138, 172, 181, 183, 185,
    187–88, 193–94, 199, 227, 229–30, 231
Robarts, Norah 50, 94–95, 110
Robarts, Robin 199
Robarts, Timothy 95
Robb, Walter 36–37
Roblin, Duff 43–44, 85, 182, 230
Rogan, William 206
Rohmer, Richard 231
Romanow, Roy 228
Roosevelt, Franklin Delano 16
Roschkov, Vic 113
Rotenberg, David 89
Rowan, Malcolm 152
Rowe, Russell 159
Rowntree, Les 49
Rusk, James 160

Salomon, William 111
Samples, Mac (British consul-general) 156
Saxe, Dianne (née Shulman) 154–55
Schmeelk, Richard 111–12
Scrivener, Margaret 102
Seagram, Norman 222
Segal, Hugh 151, 227–28
Sellars, Bob 141
Sevigny, Pierre 43
Sewell, Jonathan III 181
Sharpe, Dick 197
Shaw, Neil 195, 214, 215, 216
Sheldon, Ruby 32
Shields, John 165
Shore, Marvin 165
Shoyama, Tom 109
Shulman, Morton "Morty" 154–55
Sickafuse, Katherine 95
Silvers, Phil 19
Simcoe, John Graves 53
Simonett, Jack 126
Sinclair, Gordon 121
Sinclair, Ian 176
Singer, Vernon 40

Smallwood, Joey 75
Smith, Adam (author) 177
Smith, Don (Ellis-Don) 115–16
Smith, Elizabeth Joyce "Bunty" 41
Smith, Jack 33
Smith, Jim 128, 131
Smith, Lancelot 56
Smith, Rick 63
Smith, Roger 218
Smith, Stuart 151, 157, 159–60, 165
Somerville, Ross "Sandy" 13
Sopha, Elmer 10, 40
Spooner, Wilf 46, 52
Stanfield, Robert 44, 121, 152, 158, 230
Stephenson, Bette 102
Stevenson, Don 182
Stewart, Charles Edward 3
Stewart, Ed 152, 183
Stewart, William "Bill" 33, 49, 202
St. Laurent, Louis 16, 26
Stone, Auntie Maude 25
Stone, Thomas 2
Stoute, Douglas 231
Sullivan, May 54
Sutherland, Hugh 65
Sutherland, Sylvia 135
Sutton, Joan 142, 201
Swanton, Tom 32, 33

Taft, Robert 16–17
Taft, William Howard 16
Taylor, Allyn 199
Taylor, F. Beatrice 18
Taylor, Jim 134
Temple, William "Bill" 25, 50, 215
Thatcher, Denis 155–56
Thatcher, Margaret "Iron Lady" 155–56
Thayer, Max 24
Thayer, Pam 24
Thompson, Grant 219
Thompson, John 97, 98, 170, 193, 200
Thompson, Win 219
Thomson, Roy 47
Timbrell, Dennis 102, 134, 140–42
Townshend, William 28
Tremonti, Anna Maria 152
Trotter, Sam 4
Trudeau, Margaret 182
Trudeau, Pierre 94, 144, 156, 162, 181–82,
    185, 227
Truman, Harry 24, 192

Turnbull, Brian 85
Turner, Geills 63, 109
Turner, John 63, 108–09, 121, 146, 155, 176, 197, 200, 217, 231

Verschuren, Annette 217
Victoria, Queen 35, 181

Waldon, David 208
Walker, David IV 41, 42–44, 134
Walker, David V 44
Walker, Richard "Dick" 85, 86, 97
Wardrope, George 52
Warren, Jake 134
Watkins, Mel 128
Watson, Andy 179, 208
Watson, Bill 85, 97–98, 200, 202
Watson, Jane 10
Waverman, Leonard 135
Webber, Murray 73
Webster, Norman 148, 159, 164, 170, 176
Weider, Jozo 109
Weir, Thomas 126
Welch, Robert "Bob" 40, 43, 44, 76, 84, 86, 87, 90–91, 101, 108, 162

Weldon, David 207
Wells, Tom 40, 44, 45, 101, 103, 162
Westcott, Clare 92, 152
White, Bob 218
White, John 49, 56, 65, 109–10, 131, 151, 166
Whiteacre, Bill 97
Whiteacre, Liz 97
Whittington, Dick 32, 33
Wilde, Oscar 13
Williams, Gwyn 89
Willson, Bruce 126
Wilson, Ben 131
Wilson, L. R. "Red" 196, 200, 214–16, 231
Windsor, Hugh 176
Winkler, Eric 150
Wintermeyer, John 34
Wishart, Arthur 39
Wolfe, James 180
Woodhouse, Kendal 54
Woodward, Arthur 4
Workman, Ken 62
Wriston, Walter 112

Zaritsky, John 116, 117, 120